بسم الله الرحمن الرحيم

D1453077

Marāqī 'l-Sa'ādāt

ASCENT TO FELICITY

In the name of Allāh, Most Gracious, Most Merciful.
All praise be to Allāh, Lord of the Worlds, and peace and blessings be upon His Messenger Muḥammad, Mercy to the Worlds.

Marāqī 'l-Saʿādāt

ASCENT TO FELICITY

A Manual on Islamic Creed and Ḥanafī Jurisprudence

ABŪ 'L-IKHLĀṢ AL-SHURUNBULĀLĪ
Author of *Nūr al-Īḍāḥ*

Translation, Notes and Appendices
FARAZ A. KHAN

White Thread
PRESS
LONDON • SANTA BARBARA

© Faraz A. Khan 2010
First Edition August 2010. Reprint October 2012

All rights reserved. Aside from fair use, meaning a few pages or less for non-profit educational purposes, review, or scholarly citation, no part of this publication may be reproduced, stored in a retrieval system, or transmitted in any form or by any means, electronic, mechanical, photocopying, recording, or otherwise, without the prior permission of the copyright owner.

ISBN 978-1-933764-09-2

Published by:
White Thread Press
London • Santa Barbara
www.whitethreadpress.com
info@whitethreadpress.com

Distributed in the UK by Azhar Academy Ltd. London
sales@azharacademy.com
Tel: +44 (208) 911 9797

Library of Congress Cataloging-in-Publication Data

Shurunbulali, Hasan ibn ʿAmmar, 1585 or 6–1659.
[*Maraqi al-saʿadat fi ʿilmay al-tawhid wa-al-ʿibadat.* English]
Maraqi 'l-saʿadat = Ascent to felicity : a manual on Islamic creed and Hanafi jurisprudence / Abu 'l-Ikhlas al-Shurunbulali, author of *Nur al-idah* ; translation, notes and appendices, Faraz A. Khan. — 1st ed.
p. cm.
Includes bibliographical references.
ISBN 978-1-933764-09-2 (softcover : alk. paper)
1. Islam–Customs and practices–Early works to 1800. 2. Islam–Doctrines–Early works to 1800. 3. Islamic law–Early works to 1800. 4. Hanafites–Early works to 1800. I. Khan, Faraz A. (Faraz Ahmed) II. Title.
BP174.S4713 2010
297.2–dc22
2010014339

British Library Cataloguing in Publication Data. A catalogue record for this book is also available from the British Library.

♾ Printed and bound in the United States of America on premium acid-free paper. The paper used in this book meets the minimum requirement of ANSI/NISO Z39.48-1992 (R 1997) (Permanence of Paper). The binding material has been chosen for strength and durability.

Book design and typography by ARM
Cover design by Faraz Qureshi

To

Shaykh Aḥmad al-Jammāl al-Ḥamawī,

who is a true inheritor of the Prophet ﷺ

and to my mother and father,

whom I can never thank enough

TRANSLITERATION KEY

ء (أإ)	’ (A slight catch in the breath. It is also used to indicate where the *hamza* has been dropped from the beginning of a word.)
ا	a, ā
ب	b
ت	t
ث	th (Should be pronounced as the *th* in *thin* or *thirst.*)
ج	j
ح	ḥ (Tensely breathed *h* sound.)
خ	kh (Pronounced like the *ch* in Scottish *loch* with the mouth hollowed to produce a full sound.)
د	d
ذ	dh (Should be pronounced as the *th* in *this* or *that.*)
ر	r
ز	z
س	s
ش	sh
ص	ṣ (A heavy *s* pronounced far back in the mouth with the mouth hollowed to produce a full sound.)
ض	ḍ (A heavy *d/dh* pronounced far back in the mouth with the mouth hollowed to produce a full sound.)
ط	ṭ (A heavy *t* pronounced far back in the mouth with the mouth hollowed to produce a full sound.)
ظ	ẓ (A heavy *dh* pronounced far back in the mouth with the mouth hollowed to produce a full sound.)
ع	ʿ, ʿa, ʿi, ʿu (Pronounced from the throat.)
غ	gh (Pronounced like a throaty French *r* with the mouth hollowed to produce a full sound.)
ف	f
ق	q (A guttural *q* sound with the mouth hollowed to produce a full sound.)
ك	k
ل	l
م	m
ن	n
و	w, ū, u.
ه	h
ي	y, ī, i
ﷺ	*Ṣalla ’Llāhu ʿalayhi wa sallam*—used following the mention of the Messenger Muḥammad, translated as, "May Allāh bless him and give him peace."
ﷷ	*ʿAlayhi ’l-sallam*—used following the mention of a prophet or messenger of Allāh, translated as, "May the peace of Allāh be upon him."
	Raḍiya ’Llāhu ʿanhu—used following the mention of a Companion of the Messenger ﷺ, translated as, "May Allāh be pleased with him."
	Raḍiya ’Llāhu ʿanhum—used following the mention of more than one Companion of the Messenger (and also after a female Companion in this work for lack of an appropriate glyph), translated as, "May Allāh be pleased with them."

Contents

And He taught you that which you knew not; and the favor of Allāh upon you has been immense indeed.

Qur'ān 4:113

Translator's Foreword

IN THE NAME OF ALLĀH, Most Merciful, Most Compassionate. All praise is for Allāh, the Creator and Sustainer of the universe, the Bestower of sincerity. May His peace, blessings, and mercy be upon the best of creation, His final Messenger, our beloved Master and Liegelord, Muḥammad ﷺ, the Imām of the people of *ikhlāṣ*; and upon his beloved family, venerable Companions, and all those who follow him ﷺ in excellence until the Day of Arising. *Amīn*. The eminent 7th-century Levantine scholar Imām Nawawī relates the following ḥadīth in his famous collection of Forty Ḥadīths (*Arbaʿīn*):

> Islam is built upon five: testifying that there is no deity except Allāh and that Muḥammad is the Messenger of Allāh, establishing the ritual prayer, almsgiving, making the pilgrimage to the House, and fasting in Ramaḍān (*Bukhārī, Muslim*).

These five components of the religion serve as its foundation and are hence known as its "pillars," since the "edifice" of Islam—or one's entire religious practice—is most centrally based on them. No matter how large a structure one constructs, or how elaborately one decorates that structure, the whole edifice is in peril if its foundation is not firmly established. This is spiritually no light matter. Therefore, an appropriate measure needs to be taken by the believer to ensure his foundation is established in the most perfect and firm fashion. He must learn how the five pillars are performed and diligently apply that knowledge in consistent practice. He then may turn to his Lord in hope of acceptance, in gratitude for the ability to perform them, and in repentance from his shortcomings therein. Aside from the very belief in one's heart, no other affair, whether worldly or religious, is of greater import. No tree stands tall or bears fruit unless its roots run deep, providing strength to withstand the forces of nature and ensuring it is adequately nourished; the foundation is of utmost concern.

The text before us, then, is an invaluable resource for this weighty agenda. It is entitled "Ascent to Felicity in the Sciences of Theology and Jurisprudence of Worship" (*Marāqī 'l-Saʿādāt fī ʿIlmayi 'l-Tawḥīd wa 'l-ʿIbādāt*). It is a concise yet comprehensive manual on these two sciences, the latter based on the Ḥanafī school of law. Theology is an extension of the first pillar, since the testification of faith forms the basis of the entire corpus of Islamic beliefs, while jurisprudence of worship deals with the remaining four pillars. The text additionally covers the legal rulings pertaining to slaughtering, ritual sacrifice and hunting, and therefore as a primer, is quite broad in its range of subjects. At the same time, it does not delve into extraneous juridical and creedal minutiae that would otherwise overwhelm the reader, but is rather a clear presentation of the most salient issues pertaining to these two sciences.

"Ascent to Felicity" (*Marāqī 'l-Saʿādāt*) is not only lucid in its presentation and relevant to this lofty aim, but also reliable in its content. Its author, Imām Ḥasan ibn ʿAmmār al-Shurunbulālī, is recognized as a leading jurist of the late Ḥanafī school. He is more well-known for his other text on worship, *Nūr al-Īḍāḥ*—a work which gained unprecedented acceptance across Muslim lands wherever Ḥanafī law was taught, forming an integral part of the curricula of seminaries in modern-day Turkey, India, Pakistan, Egypt, the Levant, and the Caucuses. He also authored two excellent commentaries on *Nūr al-Īḍāḥ*, the lengthier *Imdād al-Fattāḥ*, and its summarized version *Maraqī 'l-Falāḥ*, both of which also gained widespread approval. The *Imdād* specifically is referenced over seventy times, despite it covering only five chapters, in ʿAllāma Ibn ʿĀbidīn's magnum opus *Radd al-Muḥtār, the source* of legal verdict for the late Ḥanafī school throughout the Muslim world.

Not only is Ibn ʿĀbidīn's reliance on the *Imdād* a testament to its being a seminal legal work, of which this text is a summarized presentation, but also reflects Imām Shurunbulālī's aptitude as a jurist. Indeed, Ibn ʿĀbidīn specifically refers to Imām Shurunbulālī as *dhī 'l-taʾālīf al-shahīra*, or "one who authored the very well-known works [of jurisprudence]" as well as *faqīh al-nafs*, a title of utmost reverence and veneration from one jurist to another (*Radd al-Muḥtār* 1:3). Its meaning, as mentioned by Ibn ʿĀbidīn himself, is "one who is *innately* endowed with the utmost understanding [of jurisprudence]."[1] He gives this title to only one other jurist in his entire marginal gloss, namely, the 6th-century master Qāḍīkhān.

IMĀM SHURUNBULĀLĪ

Born in a village in Upper Egypt in 994/1586, his father took him to Cairo at the tender age of six. He memorized the Qur'ān and subsequently studied the Islamic sciences under numerous scholars, specifically Qur'ānic recitation under Shaykh Muḥammad al-Ḥamawī and Shaykh ʿAbd al-Raḥmān al-Masīrī, and jurisprudence under Imām ʿAbdullāh al-Naḥrīrī, ʿAllāma Muḥammad al-Maḥabbī, and Shaykh ʿAlī ibn Ghānim al-Maqdisī. He then went to Azhar University, which at that time was the sanctuary for advanced students. He pursued higher education there and surpassed his peers, for he was foremost in his knowledge of juridical passages and maxims. Word spread of his rank and skill, and he eventually became one of the most renowned juristconsults of the entire Muslim world. He assumed the post of professor at Azhar, whereby numerous aspiring students sat at his feet and benefited from his knowledge, many of whom themselves later developed into notable scholars of law. These included, from Egypt, ʿAllāma Aḥmad al-ʿAjmī, Sayyid Aḥmad al-Ḥamawī, Shaykh Shāhīn al-Armanāwī, and from the Levant, ʿAllāma Ismāʿīl al-Nāblūsī (father of the illustrious saint and jurist, Shaykh ʿAbd al-Ghanī al-Nāblūsī). Moreover, the high demands and taxing lifestyle of his roles as professor, jurisconsult (*muftī*) and jurist, did not in the least take away from his occupation as writer. He authored over sixty works, ranging from the aforementioned two commentaries, as well as his distinguished *Shurunbulāliyya*,[2] to numerous smaller treatises covering an array of specialized legal matters.

Upon visiting Cairo, one contemporary described him as follows: "[He is] the shining lantern of Azhar and its brilliant star . . . He gives life to eager minds . . . [and] possesses a beautiful character and magnificent eloquence . . .

1 In Arabic, *shadīd al-fahm bi 'l-ṭabʿ* (*Radd* 4:305, quoting *Al-Talwīḥ*).

2 This work is a marginal gloss (*ḥāshiya*) on *Durar al-Ḥukkām fī Sharḥ Ghurar al-Aḥkām*, spanning all chapters of law in the Ḥanafī school, and considered by some to be the most magnificent of his works (*ajalluhā*). It specifically became well-known during the Imām's life, as many scholars and students benefited from it, and as such is deemed the greatest indicator of his expertise and proficiency (*malaka*), as well as his profound depth (*tabaḥḥur*) of knowledge in jurisprudence (*Ṭarab al-Amāthil*, addendum to *Al-Fawā'id al-Bahiyya*, 466).

He is indeed the most extraordinary jurist of his age." His departure from this lowly abode took place on a Friday after the ʿaṣr prayer, the 21st of Ramaḍān, in the year 1069/1659. He was approximately 75 years old. May Allāh Most High envelop him with His infinite mercy. *Amīn*.[3]

When examining the Imām's life and career, one readily notes a unique success afforded to him by Allāh, as manifested in the extensive use of his written works by scholars and students in seminaries around the world. Historically, he is considered one of the finest scholars of the late Ḥanafī school with regard to his proficiency and expertise (*malaka*) in the field. Such an accomplishment can be attributed to a particular trait of the Imām, namely, sincerity (*ikhlāṣ*). He was a member of the Wafā'ī order, a branch of the Shādhilī path of Sufism, and had truly perfected his intention through his spiritual training and ethic. He not only possessed *ikhlāṣ*, but as indicated by his agnomen *Abū 'l-Ikhlāṣ*, he perfected it. He was "the father—or master—of sincerity." This, then, could serve as the greatest lesson to be learned from the Imām; the believer must earnestly strive to attain unto perfect *ikhlāṣ* in all his endeavors. As the esteemed Malikī jurist and saint Ibn ʿAṭā'illāh states in one of his famous aphorisms, "Actions are but erected forms; what gives them life is the presence of the secret of *ikhlāṣ* in them."[4]

A NOTE ON THE TRANSLATION, FOOTNOTES, AND APPENDICES

In translating this text, I used the edition published by Dār al-Kitāb al-Lubnānī, Beirut, edited by Muḥammad Riyāḍ al-Māliḥ, who did a wonderful service by using two different manuscripts, as well as one previously published version, for his edition. I did not, however, include any of his footnotes or appendices. With regard to the bracketed text he inserted in the original Arabic, only what I deemed relevant was retained. Moreover, there are several areas in the text that are either typos or mistakes in transcription. These were corrected based on a Turkish manuscript, as well as other legal works, and most are indicated in footnotes. Shaykh Husain Kadodia of South Africa was kind enough to

3 For the biographical information above, see Lakhnawī's *Ṭarab al-Amāthil*, addendum to his *Al-Fawā'id al-Bahiyya* (466–9), as well as Bashshār Bakrī ʿArrābī's biography of Shurunbulālī in *Imdād al-Fattāḥ* (Damascus: 2002) 13–14.

4 Aphorism no. 10 (See Tāj al-Dīn Aḥmad ibn ʿAṭā'illāh al-Sakandarī. *Al-Ḥikam al-ʿAṭā'iyya*. First Edition. Cairo: Dār al-Salām, 1427/2006).

check these issues in the Turkish manuscript, as I did not have direct access to it; I am deeply grateful to him for his assistance.

In rendering the work into the English language, I made the utmost attempt to stay close to the text while avoiding strict literalism. Liberty was taken at times to paraphrase, for the sake of clarity, fluidity and organization, which are of primary import for a manual on creed and law. Most of those instances are indicated in footnotes. In addition, the section headings within the chapters on jurisprudence correlate with the original Arabic text, while those in the chapter on creed were provided by myself, in an effort to present the chapter in a well-organized fashion.

Considering "Ascent to Felicity" (*Marāqī 'l-Saʿādāt*) is a primary text (*matn*), I attempted to supplement the text with relevant explanatory footnotes, hoping to provide a more complete picture of the issues discussed in it. For the sake of brevity and ease of mastery, a primary text presents only foundational juridical rulings. Other works within the school are therefore referenced for commentary (*sharḥ*) and discussion of related issues (*tafrīʿ*), so as to deepen the student's understanding of those rulings. For the annotation of this work, I relied on several authoritative works of theology and Ḥanafī jurisprudence. The sources used for the former are commentaries on the creed of Imām Ṭaḥāwī, by Imāms Maydānī and Ghaznawī; Imām Bājūrī's commentary on Laqqānī's *Jawharat al-Tawḥīd*; and the section on creed from ʿAlā' al-Dīn ʿĀbidīn's *Al-Hadiyya al-ʿAlā'iyya*. Those primarily used for the latter include Imām Shurunbulālī's *Imdād al-Fattāḥ* and *Marāqī 'l-Falāḥ*, as well as its marginal gloss by Imām Ṭaḥṭāwī; Imām Ḥaṣkafī's *Al-Durr al-Mukhtār*, with Ibn ʿĀbidīn's accompanying marginal gloss, *Radd al-Muḥtār*; and his son's *Al-Hadiyya al-ʿAlā'iyya*. The following works were less commonly used: Shaykh Zāda's *Majmaʿ al-Anhur*, Imām Mawṣilī's *Ikhtiyār*, Imām Zaylaʿī's *Tabyīn al-Ḥaqā'iq*, and its marginal gloss by Imām Shalabī. Several other works were sparingly referenced; a complete list is provided in the bibliography. It is the translator's sincere hope that the footnotes are clear in presentation and reliable in content, as they are the result of several years of sitting with and learning from scholars. Having said that, the reader is encouraged to study the present work—and any work on law or creed—with a qualified scholar to ensure correct understanding of the material. Moreover, the reader is requested to pardon the translator for any mistakes or shortcomings that might be in the work, despite the utmost effort taken to ensure accuracy, and to pray for all who had a part in transmitting the knowledge found in these pages.

As this is a translation, all supplications found in the main text are presented in English, while the original Arabic script is provided in an appendix. To facilitate the reader's learning of the supplications, a complete transliteration is also presented, followed by a translation. Additional relevant supplications related to the five pillars, such as those for ablution and various rites of the pilgrimage, are also included. Lastly—in the spirit of *Khitāmuhū misk* ("Its seal is pure musk") (Qur'ān 83:26)—a beautiful section on the etiquette of visiting the Beloved Messenger ﷺ in Madīna taken from Imām Mawṣilī's *Ikhtiyār* has been translated in the final appendix.

ACKNOWLEDGMENTS

It is rigorously authenticated that our Prophet ﷺ said, "Whoever does not thank people, has not thanked Allāh" (*Tirmidhī*, *Aḥmad*). Therefore, after thanking Allāh, I would like to extend sincere gratitude to the following people: to my parents and family, for all their love and support throughout my life; to my colleagues and co-students, whose dedication to the field only enhances my own; and to my teachers, who spend their days and nights transmitting sacred knowledge and thereby fulfilling an immense trust. It has been a tremendous honor to have simply met them, let alone to have sat at their feet as a student. Here, I would like to briefly mention those with whom I studied jurisprudence and who have encouraged me to impart that knowledge. Shaykh Aḥmad al-Jammāl is not only a Ḥanafī jurist (*faqīh*), but also a reflection of the Prophetic light in his character, words, and overall presence. Moreover, his sincerity to authentic tradition does not prevent him from being fully cognizant of the realities of our current times and circumstances when issuing legal verdicts. Dr. Ṣalāh Abū 'l-Ḥājj is an exceptional researcher of Ḥanafī law; his relentless work ethic and devotion to this knowledge reminds one of the great scholars of past whom we read about in biographical sources. I was honored to read *Marāqī 'l-Falāḥ* with him, which was very helpful in this translation and annotation. Dr. Ashraf Muneeb is a Ḥanafī scholar of immense knowledge, wisdom and spirituality, and is like a father for many of us in Amman. He first commissioned me to translate this text for Sunnipath's online course. He is a constant source of inspiration for us, and he patiently answers our questions related to both law as well as general advice. Shaykh Faraz Rabbani is a specialist of Ḥanafī law and was my first teacher of both creed and jurisprudence. I was honored to sit in his class on Imām Ṣāwī's commentary of Laqqānī's *Jawharat al-Tawḥīd* in theology, as well as his class on *Nur al-Īḍāḥ*, each of which was very in-depth and replete with references to major works of that science. Shaykh Faraz opened the doors of sacred knowledge for me, and I will only say that he is truly a gift to Muslims in the West, for which we should show much gratitude.

I would also like to express gratitude to the following teachers with whom I had the honor of studying either Ashʿarī or Māturīdī theology: Shaykh ʿAbdul Qādir al-ʿĀnī—a beautiful Iraqi scholar whose face radiated with light, and who recently departed this world, may Allāh have mercy on him; Shaykh Bilāl al-Najjār, a young, talented scholar whose mastery of primary texts in both theology and logic is an inspiration to all his students; and Shaykh Naeem Abdul Wali, who always challenges his student to contextualize theological discussions and to apply them to the modern public discourses of philosophy and science.

Lastly, I would like to thank a teacher from whom I benefited in both jurisprudence and creed, Muftī Abdur Rahman ibn Yusuf, who spent much time with me on the phone reviewing the present work, both the text and accompanying footnotes. He suggested key modifications, thereby ensuring that the material presented is fully accurate and reliable. It was an honor and pleasure working with him in publishing this text; White Thread Press truly exemplifies professionalism, diligence, and excellence in its efforts.

There are many other people from whom I benefited in my studies, and some whose general support was vital for me to work on this translation. I very much appreciate all of you, and your reward is with Allāh, whose bounty is far greater and more consequential than my inadequate words of gratitude.

May Allāh preserve our scholars and their families, and grant them well-being and expansive provisions. May He Most High have mercy on all of the eminent Imāms of our tradition. May He bestow His good pleasure on our master Imām Shurunbulālī for his efforts in preserving this religion so we may learn it today. And may He Most High send abundant salutations, peace, and blessings upon the leader of all Imāms; the most knowledgeable, pious, and beautiful of His creation; the fountainhead of jurisprudence, creed, and spirituality; the chosen Messenger and Seal of all Prophets; the Beloved of Allāh; our Liegelord Muḥammad ﷺ; and upon his family, Companions, and those who follow them in excellence until the Day of Arising. May Allāh make us worthy of being from his umma, ﷺ. *Āmīn. Wa ākhiru daʿwānā ani 'l-ḥamdu li 'Llāhi Rabbi 'l-Ālamīn.*

ABBREVIATIONS

Badāʾiʿ	Kāsānī's *Badāʾiʿ al-Ṣanāʾiʿ* on ʿAlāʾ al-Dīn al-Samarqandī's *Tuḥfat al-Fuqahāʾ*
Bājūrī	Bājūrī's *Tuḥfat al-Murīd* on Laqqānī's *Jawharat al-Tawḥīd*
Baḥr	Ibn Nujaym's *Al-Baḥr al-Rāʾiq* on Nasafī's *Kanz al-Daqāʾiq*
Birgivi	Birgivi's *Dhukhr al-Mutaʾahhilīn wa ʾl-Nisāʾ* treatise on menstruation
Bukhārī	*Ṣaḥīḥ al-Bukhārī*
Durr	Ḥaṣkafī's *Al-Durr al-Mukhtār* on Tumurtāshī's *Tanwīr al-Abṣār*
Fawāʾid	Lakhnawī's *Al-Fawāʾid al-Bahiyya*
Ghaznawī	Ghaznawī's commentary on Ṭaḥāwī's *ʿAqīda*
Hadiyya	ʿAlāʾ al-Dīn ʿĀbidīn's manual on Ḥanafī law (*Al-Hadiyya al-ʿAlāʾiyya*)
Hidāya	Marghinānī's commentary on his *Bidāyat al-Mubtadī*
Imdād	Shurunbulālī's *Imdād al-Fattāḥ* on his *Nūr al-Īḍāḥ*
ʿItr	Dr. Nūr al-Dīn ʿItr's *Al-Ḥajj wa ʾl-ʿUmra*
Kanz	Nasafī's *Kanz al-Daqāʾiq*
Maydānī	Maydānī's commentary on Ṭaḥāwī's *ʿAqīda*
Multaqā	Ḥalabī's *Multaqā ʾl-Abḥur*
Muslim	*Ṣaḥīḥ Muslim*
Nafaḥāt	Dr. Ṣalāh Abū ʾl-Ḥājj's *Nafaḥāt al-Sulūk* on Rāzī's *Tuḥfat al-Mulūk*
Radd	Ibn ʿĀbidīn Shāmī's *Radd al-Muḥtār* (*Ḥāshiya Ibn ʿĀbidīn*)
Shalabī	Shalabī's marginal gloss on Zaylaʿī's *Tabyīn al-Ḥaqāʾiq*
Tabyīn	Zaylaʿī's *Tabyīn al-Ḥaqāʾiq* on Nasafī's *Kanz al-Daqāʾiq*
Ṭaḥṭāwī	Ṭaḥṭāwī's *Ḥāshiya* (marginalia) on Shurunbulālī's *Marāqī ʾl-Falāḥ*
Tanwīr	Tumurtāshī's *Tanwīr al-Abṣār*

Introduction

IN THE NAME OF ALLĀH, the Most Merciful, the Most Gracious. All praise is for Allāh, Lord of all the worlds. May His blessings and peace be upon our Master Muḥammad, his family and Companions, all of them.

To proceed. The impoverished servant, Ḥasan al-Shurunbulālī, may Allāh constantly bless him with His everlasting grace, says:

This is a condensed primer whose purpose is to explicate the beliefs of the People of the Sunna and the Community (*Ahl al-Sunna wa 'l-Jamāʿa*), as well as the basis of valid worship, with regard to ritual prayer (*ṣalāt*), fasting (*ṣawm*), almsgiving (*zakāt*), and the greater pilgrimage (*ḥajj*). I have named it "Ascent to Felicity in the Sciences of Theology and Jurisprudence of Worship" (*Marāqī 'l-Saʿādāt fī ʿIlmayi 'l-Tawḥīd wa 'l-ʿIbādāt*). And Allāh [Most High] is the One who will provide success and ease in its completion, out of His pure generosity.

Islamic Creed

DIVINE ONENESS, ATTRIBUTES, AND REVELATION

Know that Allāh (may He be Glorified and Exalted) says in His Preserved Book, "And I have not created jinn and mankind except that they worship Me" (51:56). Hence, it is absolutely necessary for every legally responsible individual to know the reality of faith (*īmān*) and religious practice (*islām*), and his knowledge must be based on proofs. It is obligatory (*farḍ*) for him to learn that by which his worship will be sound and valid and to practice accordingly, while believing in those tenets of faith for which he has been made responsible in this life, in order to succeed [in both abodes] with the good pleasure of his Master (may He be glorified and exalted) and with His reward.

As for [sound] creed, it is for the heart to believe in, and the tongue to affirm, all that is known to have come from Allāh Most High. We declare that a person is of this creed by [his own] assertion, i.e., by his saying: I bear witness that there is no deity but Allāh;[1] and I bear witness that Muḥammad ﷺ is His servant and Messenger, the one sent with truth for all of humanity and jinn.

This amount of belief, along with its utterance [even] once in a lifetime, is sufficient for the believer's salvation from eternal punishment in the Fire, yet it is encouraged to repeat it constantly in order to attain unto higher degrees [in Paradise].

1 The first directive that is obligatory (*farḍ*) on every sane adult is to know—with firm conviction in the heart accompanied by affirmation of the tongue—that Allāh Most High *exists*, both preeternally and eternally, in an absolute manner, as opposed to the contingent existence of created things. That is, created things exist yet are bound by time, space, quantity, and quality, and this existence is contingent on the divine will. The existence of Allāh Most High, however, is not bound by anything, and is not contingent on any external factor. It is absolute, and it transcends time, space, quantity, and quality (see *Hadiyya* 364; *Bājūrī* 107, 134).

This statement of belief incorporates one's faith in Allāh, His angels, [His books,] His messengers, the Final Day, as well as predestination (*qadar*), both its good and its evil.

For verily we believe in our hearts, and affirm with our tongues, that Allāh Most High is One, without any partner;[2] that there is nothing like[3] Him; that nothing incapacitates Him; and that there is no deity other than Him.

He is preeternal, without beginning; eternal, without end.[4] He never perishes, nor ceases to exist. Nothing occurs except as He wills.[5]

Thoughts cannot reach Him, and minds cannot grasp Him. Creation cannot resemble Him.[6] He is Living (*Ḥayy*) and never dies. He is Self-Subsisting (*Qayyūm*)[7] and never sleeps. He is All-Hearing (*Samīᶜ*) and All-Seeing (*Baṣīr*).

---

2 For He has no partner in His essence (*dhāt*), meaning that His essence is not made up of composite parts, and that no other divine essence exists; nor in His attributes, meaning that each divine attribute is singular, and that nothing else shares any of His attributes; nor in His actions, meaning that nothing other that Him can be a cause *in reality* that creates an effect, but rather, everything that exists is created by Him alone, based on His knowledge, will, and power—may He be glorified and exalted. All of this, then, is the meaning of His attribute of "oneness" (*Maydānī* 47–8; *Bājūrī* 151–2).

3 The negation of any likeness or similarity of Allāh is based on the Qur'ānic verse, "There is indeed nothing like unto Him; and [yet] He is All-Hearing, All-Seeing" (42:11). This verse is unequivocal and hence serves as the basis by which all other texts of the Qur'ān and ḥadīth related to His attributes are understood (*Ghaznawī* 33).

4 That is, He Most High exists before creating time, and exists after annihilating time, for He is the Creator of time itself, and the Creator must exist before and after the existence of that which is created. Indeed, *change* is inconceivable with regard to Allāh Most High. Hence in reality, preeternity and eternity are one and the same with respect to Him—may He be glorified and exalted (*Hadiyya* 367).

5 His divine will (*irāda* or *mashī'a*) is His preeternal attribute of specification, i.e., whatever is specified by His will, comes into existence, and whatever exists was willed by Him Most High. This is evident in the well-known phrase of the early Muslims, "Whatever Allāh wills, exists; and whatever He does not will, does not exist" (*mā shā' Allāhu kān, wa mā lam yasha' lam yakun*) (*Maydānī* 54). The divine will also specifies the characteristics and traits of every existent thing, such as size, shape, location, and duration (*Bājūrī* 164).

6 These three phrases all express His divine attribute of "differing from creation," which entails that He Most High is neither a body, particle, accident, or quality; and hence does not possess related attributes, such as size or occupying space (*Bājūrī* 145). His attributes are not created, and His actions are neither an effect of a cause, nor acquired from an external source (*Maydānī* 55). One must be extremely cautious to not allow his mind to delve into the nature of Allāh's essence, for as mentioned above, it can never be grasped or perceived by thought or conception. On the contrary, attempting to do so will lead either to *nothing*, entailing utter disbelief, or to *something*, entailing likening Allāh to His creation. Rather, whatever occurs to one's mind is in contrast to Allāh (*Hadiyya* 365). Indeed, this inability to comprehend the Divine is our very comprehension of the Divine.

7 Allāh Most High is *Qayyūm*, meaning that (a) He is free from need of anything, whether a place or physical entity wherein to subsist (*maḥall*) or a specifier to cause existence (*mukhaṣṣiṣ*), and (b) all that exists is in need of Him, for He not only brings His creation into existence, but

He is an Interlocutor (*Mutakallim*) with preeternal speech that is an attribute of His essence, transcendent above any letters or sounds.

Physical directions cannot contain Him. He begets not, nor was He begotten. There is no equivalent to Him whatsoever.

His divine attributes are preeternal, and to Him belong the most beautiful Names.

Everything in the seven heavens and seven earths glorifies Him, "And there is not a thing except that it glorifies Him with praise" (17:44).

We praise Him for His continuous blessings, for He creates without need [for His creation]; sustains without difficulty; causes death without fear; and resurrects without hardship.

He was always preeternal, along with His attributes, before He created anything. He did not acquire any new attribute [after creating His creation] that did not exist before creation. So He was Lord without servant, Creator without creation, and the Giver of life and death before having given any life or death.

This is [true] because He is able to do all things, while everything is in utter need of Him. Every matter is easy for Him, and He is in need of nothing. Nothing is hidden from Him.

He existentiated creation, and apportioned out its lifespans and livelihoods. He knew all that mankind and jinn would do before creating the universe. He commanded them to obey Him, and prohibited them from disobeying Him.

All that exists runs its course based on His divine will (*mashī'a*) and power (*qudra*). He safeguards[8] and protects whomever He wills, out of His divine grace; and He diverts and forsakes[9] whomever He wills, out of His divine justice. So no one may object to His judgment, and no one may overrule His decision.

Good and evil are both predestined for His servants; their actions are His creation (*khalq*), yet their own acquisition (*kasb*).[10]

---

also continuously maintains its existence until its appointed term, as determined by His divine will (*Maydānī* 55–6).

8 In this context, "to be safeguarded" refers to a quality in the individual that propels him to avoid acts of disobedience, despite having the ability to do them (*Maydānī* 62).

9 "Forsaking" (*khidhlān*) is for Allāh Most High to cut off His divine aid and help from the servant (*Maydānī* 62). It is also defined as Allāh Most High creating sin, and an inclination toward it, in the servant. Its opposite is "enablement" (*tawfīq*), i.e., for Allāh Most High to create obedience, and an inclination toward it, in the servant (*Bājūrī* 239–41).

10 That is, there is no creator that exists other than Allāh Most High. He is the Creator of everything, which includes the actions of the servant, who has no ability to *create*. However, the servant does have the ability to *choose* his actions, as he has free will. Based on that choice then, Allāh *creates*

Allāh did not burden them with more than they can bear, yet they cannot bear more than what He has burdened them with. This, in turn, is the explanation of the well-known phrase: "There is no power nor might except through Allāh, the Sublime, the Great."

That is to say, no one has any strategy, strength, or movement away from disobeying Him except by His divine succor; and no one has the power or ability to uphold His obedience and to remain steadfast therein except by enablement (*tawfīq*) granted by Him.

All matters take place according to His divine knowledge, will, power, and decision. The divine will, then, has overcome all wills, and the divine decision has surmounted all strategies. He does whatever He wills, yet He never oppresses anyone whatsoever. He is transcendent above every evil or harm, exalted above every defect or blemish. "He is not asked about what He does, but they will be asked [about what they do]" (21:23).

He possesses everything, yet nothing incapacitates Him. Nothing can be independent, free from needing Him, for even a blink of an eye. Whoever then deems himself free from needing Allāh, for even a moment, has disbelieved.[11]

The ability (*istiṭāʿa*)[12] by which an action must occur—such as divine enablement to obey (*tawfīq*), which cannot be ascribed to any creature—occurs *with* that action. The ability that refers to health, capacity, readiness, and sound limbs, however, *precedes* the action.[13]

We believe in all of the above. We also believe that Muḥammad ﷺ is His

---

the action, if He Most High also wills for it to happen. Yet because the servant himself decided to do it, he is said to have *acquired* that action. Hence, the servant is judged by his "acquisition," while the act of "creating" belongs to Allāh alone (*Maydānī* 122; *Ghaznawī* 123; *Bājūrī* 247–51).

11 All of creation is in utter need of Allāh, who constantly maintains their existence, while true independence and freedom from need is a divine attribute, belonging only to Allāh. Hence, if the servant ascribes such an attribute to himself, he ascribes to himself a divine attribute and has in turn disbelieved (*Ghaznawī* 125).

12 There are some typos here in the Arabic published edition; the sentence has been translated correctly based on Imām Ṭaḥāwī's creed (see *Ghaznawī* 121–2).

13 Ability (*istiṭāʿa*) is of two types—real (*bāṭina*) and apparent (*ẓāhira*). Real ability is that which is concurrent with the servant's action. Allāh Most High creates it at the moment of the action, such that both exist simultaneously. If the act is one of obedience, the concurrent ability is termed "enablement" (*tawfīq*); if one of disobedience, then "forsaking" (*khidhlān*). In either case, the servant is not ascribed with real ability; rather, it is a creation of Allāh. Hence, at every moment of his existence, the servant is in utter need of Allāh and His will, aid, and enablement. Apparent ability, on the other hand, refers to the servant's own capacity to act, namely, "means" that he is endowed with, including health, well-being, and sound limbs, and it precedes the action. This is the ability that is perceived by creation, and hence the basis of the servant's accountability (*Ghaznawī* 121–2).

chosen servant, His selected Prophet, His Messenger that won His good pleasure. He is the seal of all prophets, the leader of the pious, the master of all messengers, and the beloved of the Lord of all the worlds.

Every claim to prophecy after him is heresy and utter disbelief.

He is the one sent with truth and guidance to all of jinn and all of mankind. Allāh manifested clear miracles to verify the prophecy of his message, such as the splitting of the moon, the walking of trees, the salutation of stones, and his informing of the unseen realm.

We believe that the Qur'ān is the speech of Allāh—speech without any modality.[14]

He sent it down to His Prophet ﷺ as a revelation. The believers confirm it as truth, and are certain that it is literally the speech of Allāh, not a speech that is created. No speech of man resembles it. Anyone that ascribes a human characteristic to Allāh Most High has disbelieved.

We believe that Allāh created all creatures as well as their actions. He measured out their livelihoods and lifespans. Everyone fully receives his own apportioned sustenance, whether lawful or unlawful, as it is inconceivable for one human to consume the sustenance of another, or vice versa.

Similarly, everyone completes his own appointed lifespan, in its entirety. Hence, one who is killed dies at the time of the end of his lifespan.[15]

DEATH, THE GRAVE, AND THE AFTERLIFE

Once the servant has completed his lifespan, Allāh commands the Angel of Death (to take his soul). When he is buried, Allāh returns life to the person

14 By negating any modality of divine speech, the author intends to affirm its preeternality, as well as maintain its transcendence above any aspects of human speech, such as letters, sounds, grammar, syntax, order, declension, initiation, silence, or any other quality associated with the finite. Rather, the speech of Allāh is a preeternal divine attribute of His essence. It is not created speech, and it bears no resemblance to speech that is created. However, the letters and words of the Qur'ān that are recited, as well as the resulting sounds, are created; yet those words indicate *some* of the meanings that are indicated by His preeternal divine attribute of speech. Because they indicate meanings also indicated by His preeternal divine attribute, it is not permissible for one to maintain that "the Qur'ān is created" (*Maydānī* 67–8; *Ghaznawī* 59–60; *Bājūrī* 176–9).

15 That is, the killer did not reduce his lifespan at all. Rather, the deceased completed it in its entirety. Regardless of the crime, the victim's life was to end at that moment, as one's predetermined lifespan cannot be shortened or lengthened. The killer is punished, however, due to the enormity that he chose to commit (*Bājūrī* 383–4).

such that he comprehends the questioning of the grave and is able to respond. Then two angels, Munkar and Nakīr, come to him and make him sit up. They then ask him: "What did you used to say regarding this man?"

If the servant was a believer, he responds: "He is the servant of Allāh and His Messenger. I bear witness that there is no deity except Allāh, and that Muḥammad is the Messenger of Allāh."

The two angels then say: "We surely knew that this is what you would say."

They then expand for him his grave the measure of seventy square cubits, and fill it with light for him. It is then said to him, "Sleep."

The servant will then say: "Shall I return to my family and inform them?"

The two angels will respond: "Sleep like a newly-wed bride who is not awakened except by the most beloved of family members."

The servant, then, remains in that state until Allāh resurrects him from that [comfortable] abode of his.

The hypocrite, on the other hand, responds to the questioning by saying: "I heard people saying something, so I said the same thing. I know not."

The two angels then say: "We surely knew you would say that."

It is then said to the earth: "Constrict upon him." It does so, such that his ribs are put out of place. He remains therein, being punished, until Allāh Most High resurrects him from that [horrible] abode of his.

This questioning occurs for every dead person, whether young or old. This includes those that disappear [and are not buried], like one in the body of a lion or one drowned in the sea. The prophets, however, are not questioned, according to the sounder position.

This questioning occurs after the soul is returned to the body, so that the deceased can answer Munkar and Nakīr's questions regarding his Lord, his religion, and his Prophet ﷺ. After the believer responds, it is said to him: "Look to your seat in the Fire. Allāh has replaced it for you with one in Paradise." So the believer sees both seats.

On the contrary, it is said to the disbeliever or hypocrite after his saying "I know not": "You do not know, and you never recited [the Qur'ān, in your life]." He is then struck with an iron hammer once, causing him to bellow a shout heard by all, other than men and jinn.

The punishment of the grave, then, is a reality for disbelievers, as well as some of the disobedient believers. And the bliss of the grave is a reality for whomsoever Allāh Most High wills.

There is benefit for deceased believers when the living supplicate [for them] and donate charity [on their behalf].[16]

The gathering of bodies and their revival on the Day of Judgment is a reality as well. The believer is given his book in the right hand, and the disbeliever in the left hand. The Scale, by which the measure of both good and bad deeds is known, is placed [for Judgment]. The Traverse is placed over the top of the Fire, and all creatures pass over it. Some cross at the speed of light; others like wind; others like fast steeds; others at a walking pace; and yet others like ants treading on earth—each individual crossing the Traverse based on his level [of faith and works]. This crossing is considered to be the fright of the Day of Judgment for the believer.

The intercession of the Chosen Prophet ﷺ, which is the greatest intercession[17] for the final ruling on that Day, as well as approaching his Watering Pool, are realities.

The speaking of body parts on that Day is also a reality.[18]

Paradise and Hell are realities, and both currently exist. Neither of the two, nor their inhabitants, will ever become extinct.

We affirm that Allāh Most High created both Paradise and Hell before creation, and then created inhabitants for each one. The people of Paradise enter it by His grace and generosity.[19] We affirm that He will endow them with the Beatific Vision of His essence, Exalted and Most High, without modality [i.e.,

---

16 According to *Ahl al-Sunna wa 'l-Jamāʿa*, a person may designate the reward of any voluntary good deed to another person, whether alive or deceased, without it decreasing from the performer's reward whatsoever. This applies to all types of worship, including ritual prayer (*ṣalāt*), fasting (*ṣawm*), pilgrimage (*ḥajj*), charity (*ṣadaqa*), recitation of Qur'ān or litanies, and the like. If the one for whom it is designated is deceased, the reward reaches him and provides some sort of benefit to him. Ṭabarānī relates in his *Awsaṭ*, on the authority of Ibn ʿUmar ﷺ, that the Prophet ﷺ said, "If one of you donates voluntary charity, then let him designate it for his parents, so that they both receive its reward, without decreasing his reward in the least bit" (*Marāqī 'l-Falāḥ, Ṭaḥṭāwī* 2:276–7). For obligatory acts of worship, see the section, "Being Absolved of the Obligation of Praying or Fasting" on p. 95 and its related footnotes.

17 His intercession ﷺ is for those of his nation that committed enormities (*Hadiyya* 398).

18 With regard to the events and states of the next life mentioned above, we wholeheartedly affirm them as realities, with full conviction and absolute certainty, since our knowledge of them is based on what is reported by definitive, unequivocal texts of the Qur'ān and narrations of our Prophet ﷺ. We have no doubts or misgivings in their being true and literal. However, our minds are unable to comprehend any aspect of them, and therefore we do not attempt to do so. For delving into their modalities might lead one to lose absolute certainty regarding them, which would entail disbelief (*Hadiyya* 400–01).

19 That is, not based on their good works, as the Prophet ﷺ informed us that even his entrance into Paradise is due only to being immersed in divine mercy (*Ghaznawī* 119–20). Nevertheless, the

indulging in the method of how this occurs] or corporealism [i.e., suggesting any resemblance between Him and creation].[20]

The people of the Fire enter it by His justice.[21] Some believers will enter it temporarily for certain sins, after which they are taken out, since no believer will remain in the Fire eternally.

SINS AND DISBELIEF

It is possible that Allāh Most High pardon those who are deserving of punishment due to sins, by His grace and through the intercession of His Prophet ﷺ, or the intercession of some elite of the faithful. However, this does not hold true for those deserving punishment due to disbelief, for pardoning them is not possible.[22]

We do not pronounce anyone who prays toward the *qibla* to be a disbeliever based on a sin he commits, unless he deems that sin to be legally permissible.

We believe in the possibility of evil deeds being erased by good ones, as He Most High has said, "Verily, good deeds cause evil ones to disappear" (11:114).

It is not possible for good deeds to be wiped out by the evil of sins, except by disbelief, as He Most High has said, "And whosoever rejects faith, indeed his works are obliterated, and he shall be among the losers in the Hereafter" (5:5).

We do not maintain that a sin committed by a believer will not harm him. We do hope for Paradise to be granted to all believers that perfect their actions, yet we do not guarantee Paradise for anyone except for those that Allāh Most

believer must fully strive to attain that mercy, since as the author later states, "Those deeds for which a person was created are facilitated for him" (see p. 31).

20 That is, because there is nothing whatsoever that is *like* Him Most High, the Beatific Vision granted to the believers in Paradise is one without any modality. His essence is not a physical body, and hence He Most High does not occupy space. There is no direction of gaze, nor distance between the one seeing and that which is seen. Rather, Allāh Most High will create in the believers the ability to see His essence, with their very eyes, in a way that cannot be understood by the intellect (*Maydānī* 68; *Ghaznawī* 62; *Bājūrī* 268–70).

21 That is, since He Most High commanded them to believe, based on their own free wills, and informed them of the punishment entailed in rejecting Him. Therefore, their punishment is out of His justice and divine wisdom (*Ghaznawī* 120).

22 That is, based on the divine decree, as Allāh Most High preeternally willed that those who would choose to disbelieve in Him would dwell in the Fire forever. Hence, even though it is logically possible that they be pardoned, in reality it is impossible since Allāh informed us of their punishment in the Qur'ān (*Bājūrī* 449–50).

High has honored with entrance, when explicitly mentioned in texts of the Qur'ān or ḥadīth.

We seek forgiveness for believers that commit sins, yet we fear for them. However, we do not cause them to despair. For indeed, both feeling secure from Allāh's wrath, as well as despair in His mercy, can take one out of the fold of Islam.[23] The way of truth, then, is between the two; it is the position of the people of the *qibla*.

A servant is not considered to have left his faith except by denying that which originally caused him to enter into it.[24]

The covenant that Allāh Most High took with Ādam ﷺ and his progeny is a reality.[25]

Allāh Most High preeternally knew the total number of inhabitants of Paradise and of Hell. Hence, no one can be added or subtracted from these numbers. The same holds true for the actions of creation. As such, those deeds for which a person was created are facilitated for him. The value of actions is determined by how one ends his life.

The one who has eternal felicity (*saʿīd*) is he for whom eternal felicity was decreed by Allāh, while the eternally damned (*shaqī*) is he for whom eternal damnation was decreed by Allāh.

PREDESTINATION AND TYPES OF KNOWLEDGE

The basis of predestination (*qadar*) is a secret of Allāh in His creation, to which no angel drawn near nor prophet-messenger has been exposed. To delve into this matter is a means of being forsaken [by the Divine], and a path toward being prevented [from steadfastness of faith]. So beware—take every precau-

---

23 Some scholars maintain that when disbelief is mentioned in some creedal statements, such as above, it is not to be understood literally, but rather as an exaggeration to divert believers from falling into the act being described. This interpretation is supported by the next statement: "A servant is not considered to have left his faith except by denying that which originally caused him to enter into it" (*Maydānī* 97).

24 That is, his very belief in Allāh's oneness, his submission to Him, and the resulting faith in all that is necessarily known of the religion (*Maydānī* 97).

25 As mentioned in the Qur'ān, "And when your Lord brought forth from the Children of Adam—from their loins—their descendants, and made them testify against themselves, [saying] 'Am I not your Lord?' They said, 'Indeed! We bear witness!' Lest you say on the Day of Resurrection, 'Verily, of this we were heedless'" (7:172).

tion not to dwell on this matter, whether in thought, reflection, or insinuations from the devil.[26] For indeed, Allāh Most High has veiled the knowledge of predestination from His creation and has prohibited them from seeking it, as He Most High has said, "He is not asked about what He does, but they will be asked [about what they do]" (21:23).

Hence if someone asks, "Why did He [Most High] do such and such?" then he has indeed rejected the command of the Qur'ān and has disbelieved.

This portion [of belief], then, is what is needed by one whose heart is illumined and who is among the saints of Allāh (Most High); it is indeed the level of those firmly rooted in knowledge. This is because knowledge is of two types: that which is accessible to creation, and that which is not. To deny knowledge that is accessible is disbelief, and to claim knowledge that is not accessible is also disbelief. Faith is not valid except by accepting knowledge that is accessible and by leaving the pursuit of knowledge that is not. And Allāh knows best.[27]

We affirm the existence of the Preserved Tablet, the Pen, and all that has been inscribed in it.

If all of creation were to unite in order to eliminate something whose existence had been inscribed in the Tablet based on Allāh's decree, they would not be able to prevent its existence. Likewise if they were to unite altogether in order to bring into existence that which was inscribed in the Tablet to not exist, they would prove incapable. The [ink of the] Pen has dried with regard to the existence of all that shall exist until the Day of Arising.

That which does not afflict the servant could never have afflicted him; and that which afflicts him would never have missed him.

The servant must know that Allāh's knowledge has preceded the existence of all that exists in His creation. So He decreed that which exists by His will, in

---

26 Because such thoughts are without doubt from the plotting and trickery of the devil. Hence, whenever they occur to one's mind, one should take refuge in the All-Merciful from the devil, and consign the matter of understanding predestination over to the One who knows it, in a state of belief, acceptance, and submission to the divine will (*Maydānī* 87).

27 Knowledge that is accessible to creation is that which is known by clear proofs, such as knowledge of Allāh's existence; knowledge of His oneness, power, and majesty; and knowledge of the Sacred Law, as revealed to the Prophet ﷺ. To deny such knowledge entails disbelief. Inaccessible knowledge refers to that which Allāh Most High has kept hidden from creation, which He alone knows. This includes the understanding of the divine decree and predestination, or knowledge of when the Day of Resurrection will occur. To claim or seek out such knowledge is also disbelief, as doing so entails a claim of partnership with the Divine in something He has preferred for Himself alone (*Ghaznawī* 80–81).

the most perfect manner, one that is rendered inevitable. None can overturn it, overrule it, remove it, change it, or affect it in any way. He Most High has said, "Indeed the command of Allāh is an absolute, divine decree" (33:38).

So woe to him who becomes a foe to Allāh's decree, who brings forth a diseased heart, and who is surely a transgressing fabricator.

The Throne and the Footstool are realities, as Allāh has made clear in His Book, yet He is free from need of the Throne or anything else. He encompasses all things in knowledge, and He has incapacitated His creation from encompassing anything. Therefore, that which He has explicitly mentioned in the Qur'ān is as He has said, while its meaning is that which He intended. We do not delve into such matters, neither interpreting them based on our opinions, nor falsely understanding them based on our vain desires. For indeed, no one is safe in his religion except he who submits to Allāh Most High and to His Messenger ﷺ, and who consigns unclear matters over to those who understand them. The foundation of one's entire religious practice will not be steadfast unless it is based on submission and surrender.

The Heavenly Ascent (*miʿrāj*) is a reality, as is the Night Journey (*isrā'*) from the Sacred Precinct (al-masjid al-ḥarām) [in Makka] to the Furthest Mosque (al-masjid al-aqṣā) [in Jerusalem]. The Prophet ﷺ was honored thereby, while awake, with his noble body.[28] He then ascended to the heavens, and finally to the summit where Allāh willed for him to reach; He honored him ﷺ with what He willed, and revealed to him ﷺ that which He revealed.

THE RANKS OF PROPHETS, COMPANIONS, AND SAINTS

We do not prefer any of the saints[29] over any of the prophets; rather, we affirm that a single prophet is better than all of Allāh's saints.

---

28 This statement serves to refute two other minority opinions that existed among the first generation of Muslims, namely (1) only his soul ﷺ was taken on the Night Journey and Heavenly Ascent, or (2) that his body ﷺ was taken as well, but while asleep. Rather, the correct position is that both his body and soul ﷺ were taken, and that he was awake throughout. The second generation of Muslims, as well as the entire community of believers since, reached consensus on this position (*Bājūrī* 332).

29 A saint is defined as one with experiential knowledge (*ʿārif*) of Allāh Most High and His divine attributes, based on what is possible for creation to know of Him. He remains steadfast in obedience and shuns acts of disobedience, meaning that he does not commit a sin without

The elite of the children of Ādam, i.e., the prophets, are better than all of the angels, while the pious among the masses of humanity are better than the masses of angels. However, the elite[30] of the angels are better than the masses of humanity.[31]

Every believer after his death is an actual believer—not simply in terms of legal judgment—just as he is in his sleep or inattentiveness. Similarly, prophets and messengers are actual prophets and messengers after their death. This is because that which actually possesses the attribute of prophethood or belief is the spirit (*rūḥ*), which does not change with death.

The miracles (*karāmāt*)[32] of saints are a reality; hence, we believe in that which has been transmitted regarding them in rigorously authenticated narrations.

It is possible for a saint to know that he is a saint, as well as for him to not know, as opposed to a prophet [who must know that he is a prophet].

It is permissible for a saint to manifest his miracle to one seeking guidance, in order to encourage the seeker, or to aid him in bearing the weightiness of acts of worship, but not out of pride or to impress others.

We love all of the Companions of the Messenger of Allāh ﷺ, yet we are not excessive in our love for any one of them.[33]

---

repenting from it thereafter, not that he does not commit sins at all, as he is not safeguarded from disobedience as prophets are (*Bājūrī* 364).

30 The elite of the angels are four: (1) Jibrīl (or Jibrā'īl), the Angel of Revelation; (2) Mīkā'īl, the Angel of wind, rain, and vegetation; (3) Isrāfīl, the Angel selected to blow the Trumpet; and (4) ʿIzrā'īl (or ʿAzrā'īl), the Angel of Death (*Hadiyya* 394, with marginalia of Shaykh Muḥammad Saʿīd al-Burhānī; Lane's Lexicon 1:2035).

31 The Māturīdī position on this matter, which is the stronger position, is that the order of rank in creation is as follows: our Liegelord Muḥammad ﷺ is the best of creation, without exception; followed by the other four Messengers of Firm Resolve, in this order—Ibrāhīm, Mūsā, ʿĪsā, and Nūḥ; followed by the rest of the messengers; followed by the prophets that are not also messengers, with their own relative ranks among each other; followed by Jibrīl, then Mīkā'īl, then the rest of the elite angels; followed by the righteous saints of the masses of humanity; followed by the masses of the angels, with their own relative ranks among each other (*Bājūrī* 306, 309).

32 The miracle of a saint differs from that of a prophet in that the latter is conjoined with a *challenge* (*taḥaddī*) to those that deny the message to replicate the miracle—which they are unable to do—as a confirmation by Allāh of the truth of the prophet in his claim to prophecy. The effect of the miracle, then, is as if Allāh says, "My servant is truthful in all that he conveys on My behalf" (*Bājūrī* 310–311). The miracle of a saint, however, poses no such challenge. In fact, because every saint is a follower of a prophet, the miracle that appears at the hand of the saint is no more than a miracle of that prophet, as Allāh honors a saint with such miracles only due to the blessing of his emulation of his prophet. It is, therefore, another proof of the truthfulness of that prophet (*Ghaznawī* 134).

33 That is, such that it would lead to disdain of others (*Ghaznawī* 127).

We do not disassociate ourselves from any of them [implying that they were guilty of a wrongdoing], and we do not speak of them except in a goodly manner.[34]

Whoever speaks well of the Companions of the Messenger of Allāh ﷺ; his wives, the mothers of the believers; and his children, has proven free from hypocrisy.

The righteous scholars of the early generations of Muslims, as well as those after them who follow their path—among the people of excellence and tradition, and those of jurisprudence and erudition—are not to be mentioned except in a beautiful manner. Whoever makes mention of them in an unbecoming manner has indeed deviated from the straight path.

We believe that Abū Bakr al-Ṣiddīq رضي الله عنه is the best of people after the prophets, followed by ʿUmar ibn al-Khaṭṭāb رضي الله عنه. Indeed, all of the Companions were in agreement regarding the caliphate of them both رضي الله عنهما; thus, whoever denies their caliphate has committed disbelief.

They are followed [in merit] by ʿUthmān, the Possessor of Two Lights[35] رضي الله عنه; and then Imām ʿAlī Ibn Abī Ṭālib رضي الله عنه, the Drawn Sword of Allāh, cousin of the Chosen Prophet ﷺ, and husband of Fāṭima al-Zahrāʾ, the Chaste (*batūl*). The entire community agreed to his worthiness of the Imamate, and such an agreement does not exist for other than him رضي الله عنه.[36]

So these four, then, are the rightly-guided caliphs and upright imāms.

The Messenger of Allāh ﷺ bore witness for ten of the Companions that they shall attain unto Paradise, and they are (1) Abū Bakr [al-Ṣiddīq]; (2) ʿUmar [ibn al-Khaṭṭāb]; (3) ʿUthmān [ibn ʿAffān]; (4) ʿAlī [ibn Abī Ṭālib]; (5) Ṭalḥa [ibn

---

34 Speaking ill of any of the Companions is impermissible. We remain silent regarding the conflicts that erupted among them, since those conflicts were based on earnest attempts at legal independent judgment (*ijtihād*) by them, and according to our religion, one who exercises legal independent judgment receives one reward if his judgment is incorrect and two rewards if correct. Thus, it is incumbent upon us to venerate the Companions, without exception, and to have full conviction in the moral integrity of them all (*Hadiyya* 405; *Bājūrī* 354).

35 He was given this title because he was blessed with the immense honor of marrying two daughters of the Messenger of Allāh ﷺ—Ruqayya, and then after her demise, Umm Kulthūm رضي الله عنها.

36 This statement must be understood in light of the entire discussion, as the author has already stated regarding the caliphate of Abū Bakr and ʿUmar, "Indeed, all of the Companions were in agreement regarding the caliphate of them both رضي الله عنهما; thus, whoever denies their caliphate has committed disbelief." Hence, his affirmation here that ʿAlī was the only one whose Imāmate found unanimous agreement is merely an acknowledgement of historical fact. It does not imply that the Imāmate of other Companions like Abū Bakr or ʿUmar did not deserve such unanimous acceptance. And Allāh knows best.

ʿUbaydillāh]; (6) Al-Zubayr [ibn al-ʿAwwām]; (7) Saʿd [ibn Abī Waqqāṣ]; (8) Saʿīd [ibn Zayd]; (9) ʿAbd al-Raḥmān Ibn ʿAwf; and (10) Abū ʿUbayda ʿĀmir ibn al-Jarrāḥ, who is the loyal trustee of this nation ﷺ.[37]

MATTERS OF FAITH

We deem communal unity to be a binding right, founded on submission to the head of state and obedience to him; we consider dissent and opposition to him to be disobedience.[38]

It is not permissible to establish two heads of state in one time period. We do not allow rebellion to our leaders, even if they are oppressive.

We deem congregational prayer behind any Muslim, whether righteous or corrupt, to be valid. We also perform the funeral prayer over every Muslim that dies, whether righteous or corrupt.

We believe that the religion of Allāh is one and the same, both in heaven and on earth; it is the religion of Islam. He Most High has said, "Indeed the only religion with Allāh is Islam" (3:19).

It is [a perfectly balanced religion, one that is] between extremism and laxity; between likening Allāh to His creation and denial of His divine attributes; between the negation of free will [compulsion (*jabr*)] and the assertion that the servant creates his own actions (*qadar*); and between feeling secure from Allāh's wrath and despairing in His mercy.

Actions are not a part of faith, as opposed to what the People of Ḥadīth have claimed.[39]

---

37 And their rank in merit is in the same order, followed by those Companions who fought at the Battle of Badr; and then those who fought at Uḥud; followed by those who took allegiance with the Messenger ﷺ at Ḥudaybiyya, for which they attained unto Allāh's good pleasure; followed by the rest of the Companions ﷺ (*Hadiyya* 404; *Bājūrī* 340–50).

38 Since obedience to the ruler is effectively obedience to Allāh and His Messenger ﷺ, as the Qur'ān says, "And obey Allāh, His Messenger, and the people of authority among you" (4:59). Hence, the ruler must be obeyed, unless he commands the citizenry to disobedience. Political dissent, on the other hand, entails rebellion, sowing corruption on the earth, and inciting tribulation among Muslims. This ruling holds true even if the ruler is oppressive, as mentioned next in the text. Finally, we do not make supplication against our rulers; rather, our way is to ask Allāh to rectify them and grant them safety, well-being and success, in both their religious and worldly affairs (*Ghaznawī* 108).

39 The essence of faith is conviction in the heart (*taṣdīq*), of everything that the Prophet ﷺ brought in his message. It entails both submission (*idhʿān*) and acceptance (*qabūl*), as many disbelievers *knew* the veracity of his message ﷺ yet did not submit to it and accept it in their hearts, and

Faith itself does not increase or decrease; thus, the increase of faith mentioned [in the Qur'ān and ḥadīth texts] refers to an increase in its fruits and the illumination of its light [that dawns on the believer].[40]

It is not permissible to describe Allāh Most High as having the ability to oppress, to be foolish, or to lie because that which is inherently inconceivable does not fall under the realm of the divine attribute of power (*qudra*).

It is not possible for Him to break His divine promise, yet there is disagreement with regard to His divine threat. Some of our scholars[41] maintain that it is possible for Him to not execute His divine threat [of punishment], out of His divine generosity, as that is becoming of His majesty. Yet this is not possible with regard to His divine promise [of reward], as that would be baseness, which is inconceivable for His Exalted Majesty.

It is not obligatory on Allāh Most High to do that which is good or best for the servant.[42]

It is not possible, according to us, for Him to place on the servant a burden greater that he can bear.

---

hence were not *believers*. Internal conviction (*taṣdīq*) is the condition of the validity of faith. Its expression on the tongue, specifically with the phrase "There is no deity but Allāh, and Muḥammad is His Messenger ﷺ," is a condition for being considered Muslim in this life, along with its accompanying legal rights and rulings. The condition for the perfection of faith is its manifestation on one's limbs through spiritual works; hence, actions are not part of faith itself, yet are essential for its perfection (*Bājūrī* 111, 116–9).

40 This is the position of some scholars, including Imām Abū Ḥanīfa. It is based on the definition of faith as firm conviction in the heart based on certainty, which does not have any disparity or levels. The other position, which is deemed stronger and is held by the majority of scholars, is that faith itself does increase or decrease, based on spiritual works. One of the central proofs of this position is the obvious disparity of faith between prophets or saints versus laymen or corrupt believers (*Bājūrī* 128–31). As the author of the *Hadiyya* states, faith does not increase or decrease with respect to its *quantity* but does with respect to its *quality*; and no one has any doubt about this (404).

41 Ahl al-Sunna wa 'l-Jamāʿa is in agreement that the divine threat against disbelievers will be executed and that the divine promise of reward for righteous believers will not be broken. However, there is disagreement regarding the divine threat against corrupt believers. The opinion of some Māturīdīs is that it is not possible for Allāh to break His threat, while the position of the Ashʿarīs and other Māturīdīs is that He could choose to not execute His threat, as that is not deemed treachery or deceit but rather a manifestation of His magnificent generosity and compassion (*Bājūrī* 242–3; *Minaḥ al-Rawḍ al-Azhar* 366–367).

42 Nothing is *obligatory* on Allāh Most High, as He does whatever He wills with His creation. As for any Qur'ānic verses or ḥadīth texts that appear to indicate obligation on Him Most High—such as, "And there is no creature in the earth except that *upon* Allāh is its sustenance," (11:6)—they are understood as referring to His divine promise, out of His infinite bounty (*Bājūrī* 257).

The faith of a blind follower is valid, due to his conviction, even though he might be sinful for not basing his faith on any logical proof.[43]

If one repents from an enormity, his repentance is valid and accepted, even if he is persisting in another enormity; hence, he will not be punished for the one from which he repented.

One's repentance from enormities does not absolve him from having to repent from minor sins; it is possible, then, for him to be punished for those minor sins.[44]

THE DIVINE NAMES

The Divine Names are only those that have been revealed; hence, one cannot ascribe a name to Allāh (Glorified and Exalted) unless it has come to us through revelation and the Sacred Law (*sharīʿa*).

It is permissible to refer to the Truth [i.e., Allāh] (may He be Glorified) with the terms "thing" (*shay'*)[45] or "existent" (*mawjūd*), whether in Arabic or another language (*fārisiyya*). Similarly, one may use "self" (*nafs*)[46] to refer to Allāh. He Most High is a "thing," yet like no other thing.

As for the terms *nūr* (light), *wajh* (face), *yad* (hand), *ʿayn* (eye), *janb* (side), and the like, they may not be used to refer to Allāh Most High in a language other than Arabic without being interpreted [nonliterally], because they are from the Vague and Unclear Terms (*mutashābihāt*)[47] [used in the Qur'ān and ḥadīth], as opposed to the first two terms [i.e., "thing" and "existent"].

43 The blind follower in faith spoken about here is one who has conviction, yet without any deduction or proof, but rather only by believing someone else without knowing that person's proof. His faith is valid, yet he is sinful for not basing it on *some* level of logical proof, if he is able to do so; otherwise if unable, he is not sinful (*Bājūrī* 92–4).

44 Yet as mentioned in authentic ḥadīths, minor sins can be effaced by various acts of obedience, such as ablution (*wuḍū'*), the ritual prayer (*ṣalāt*), the Friday prayer (*jumuʿa*), fasting (*ṣawm*), and an accepted pilgrimage (*ḥajj mabrūr*), as well as by simply avoiding enormities (*Bājūrī* 417–19). The author is emphasizing, however, that one cannot simply rely on such effacement, but rather should repent from minor sins as well, as he could be taken to account for them.

45 This is because, according to Muslim theologians, a "thing" is defined as "that which exists" (*Bājūrī* 461), and there is no doubt that Allāh Most High exists.

46 What is meant by "self," when referring to Allāh Most High, is His essence (*dhāt*) (*Bājūrī* 148).

47 With regard to such terms, there were historically two central approaches among scholars. The early generations in general believed in them as Allāh and His Messenger ﷺ intended, without feeling the need to understand the realities of their meanings. They consigned that understanding

Some words may be used to refer to Allāh Most High when used in compound constructions, but not otherwise, such as: "Raiser of degrees," "Fulfiller of needs," "Destroyer of legions," "Remover of worries," and "Fierce in punishment." This is because, with regard to the Names of Allāh Most High, we do not exceed the limits set up by the Sacred Law, whose texts do not mention these names other than in compound constructions.

It is not permissible to refer to Him as "the veiled" (*maḥjūb*). Some scholars, however, did permit the use of "The One who veils Himself" (*muḥtajib*). This is because the first name suggests being overcome by another, as opposed to the second name. And Allāh knows best.

Some terms are such that neither they nor their opposites may be used to refer to Allāh Most High, such as "the still," "the awake," or "the intelligent," since the Sacred Law does not mention them or their opposites.[48]

Likewise, one may not use the terms "the one who enters" or "the absent" to refer to Him; it is permissible, however, to say "He (Most Glorified) is hidden from creation."

The events that unfold at the end of time, as reported to us by the Prophet ﷺ, are realities. These include the emergence of the Anti-Christ (*dajjāl*); the Beast of the Earth (*dābbat al-arḍ*); Gog and Magog (*ya'jūj wa ma'jūj*); the descent of ʿĪsā عليه السلام; and the rising of the sun from the West.

We do not give credence to any diviner or soothsayer, nor one who claims anything in opposition to the Book, Sunna, or scholarly consensus.

This, then, is our religion and belief, both outward and inward. We are absolved, in front of Allāh Glorified and Exalted, of anyone who opposes what we have mentioned and clarified above. We ask Allāh Most High to make us steadfast in faith, and to end our lives upon it. We ask him to safeguard us from whims contrary to the aforementioned, and from vile opinions, such as of those who liken Allāh to His creation (anthropomorphists—*mushabbiha*);

over to Allāh Most High and, while negating their literal meanings, did not attempt to interpret them. Later scholars, however, encountered many innovations and deviant sects that made it incumbent upon them to interpret those texts in a manner befitting the majesty of Allāh, so as to safeguard the community from falling into disbelief by likening Allāh to His creation. For example, they maintained that "His hand" refers to "His power," and "His descent" refers to the "descent of His mercy," etc. The latter approach provides more understanding and is more useful in refutation, and is hence a stronger position (for later times), while the former is deemed safer and therefore, according to some, more ideal for the believer (*Hadiyya* 401–2; *Bājūrī* 215).

48 Their opposites being "the moving," "the one asleep," or "the unintelligent," as Allāh Most High is well exalted and transcendent above such terms.

who deny any of His attributes (*muʿaṭṭila*); who allege that the servant creates his own actions (*qadariyya*); who deny the free will of servants (*jabriyya*); or others who contravene what is agreed upon by the community and who side with deviation. We absolve ourselves from them, and they are, according to us, misguided.

We believe in the noble angelic scribes, as well as the appointed guardian-angels[49]—while we consign their number over to the Lord of all the worlds—just as we believe in the prophets and messengers. May Allāh's blessings and peace be upon them all, forever into eternity, as many blessings as the number of all that ever existed and all that exists, in this life, the next life, and the Day of Judgment. All praises are for Allāh, the One who guided us to this, and we would not have been guided had Allāh not guided us. We ask Allāh for pardon and well-being, in our religious and worldly affairs, for us and our parents, children, teachers, and brethren in Allāh. And Allāh knows best.

49 There is a small typo here in the Arabic published edition, which has the word "and" between "appointed" and "guardian." However, they are understood to be the same category, as confirmed in the manuscript, where the term is used without the "and."

Purification (Ṭahāra)

Purification[50] is valid with the following types of water: rain water, well water, spring water, river water, sea water [even if salty], and water from melted snow or hail.[51] Such water may be used for purification as long as it remains "purifying," namely, to remain with its natural characteristics, with nothing having mixed with it such as to "condition" it and thereby remove its "purifying" quality. This ruling applies whether the water is flowing or in a large cistern, namely, one with a surface area of at least ten by ten cubits with a depth such that its floor is not exposed by scooping water out [with both hands].

ABLUTION (*WUḌŪ'*)

The obligatory integrals (*farḍ*, pl. *furūḍ/farā'iḍ*)[52] of *wuḍū'* are four, namely:

1. Washing the face, whose lengthwise demarcation is from the top

---

50 Legally, purification refers to the removal of filth from one's body, garments, and place of prayer; as well as the removal of one's state of ritual impurity, thereby rendering the person in a state of ritual purity (*Ṭaḥṭāwī* 1:42; *Imdād* 31).

51 The above list of types of water is not restrictive; rather, it only serves to provide examples of water in nature that may be used for *wuḍū'* and *ghusl*, namely, unconditioned water. This is in contrast to water that is conditioned, meaning that it may not be referred to as simply "water," but rather needs a further description that conditions it in order to be accurately identified, such as rose water. That is, rose water cannot be called "water" without the description "rose" that conditions it, while spring water or river water may be accurately identified by the term "water" alone, and hence is unconditioned (*Marāqī 'l-Falāḥ* 1:46; *Badā'i'* 1:93–4).

52 An obligatory integral (*farḍ*) is that which an action is composed of and that which must be performed for the action to be complete and valid. If any one integral is omitted, the entire action is deemed invalid, and the person would have incurred sin if it were intentionally omitted. A mandatory requisite (*wājib*) is that which must also be performed; however, its omission does not entail invalidity, but does entail sin if intentional (*Ṭaḥṭāwī* 1:92).

of the forehead to the bottom of the chin for someone without a thick beard,[53] or [for one with a thick beard] to the bottom of the beard [that lies on the face, as opposed to the hair that hangs below the chin].[54] Its demarcation in width is from one earlobe to the other, even for someone with a beard;

2. Washing the two arms, up to and including the elbows;
3. Wiping[55] a fourth of the head;[56]
4. Washing the two feet, up to and including the ankles.

Among the emphasized *sunnas*[57] of *wuḍū'* are the following:

1. The intention (*niyya*),
2. Using the toothstick (*siwāk*),
3. Mentioning the Name of Allāh (*tasmiya*),[58]
4. Washing the hands up to and including the wrists in the beginning of *wuḍū'*,[59]

---

53 The legal definition of washing is causing water to flow over the area such that it drips, with a minimum of two drops (*Marāqī 'l-Falāḥ* 1:92; *Imdād* 60; *Durr, Radd* 1:65).

54 Regarding the obligatory integral of washing the face, it is sufficient to wash the exterior of a thick beard, "thick" meaning that beneath which the skin cannot be seen. For a thin beard, however, water must reach the underlying skin itself (which occurs naturally when running water over the face since that skin appears from beneath the thin beard) (*Marāqī 'l-Falāḥ* 1:99; *Imdād* 64).

55 The legal definition of wiping is *placing* the wet hand onto the limb, or more specifically, wetness *touching* an area (*Marāqī 'l-Falāḥ, Ṭaḥṭāwī* 1:96; *Radd* 1:67; *Badā'i'* 1:65).

56 The demarcation of the head is that above the ears. Hence, one may not wipe over hair that hangs below the ears, *even* if tied up above the head; rather, the hair that is wiped must grow out from above the ears (*Marāqī 'l-Falāḥ, Ṭaḥṭāwī* 1:96; *Durr, Radd* 1:67; *Badā'i'* 1:71).

57 An emphasized (*mu'akkada*) *sunna* is defined as that which the Messenger of Allāh ﷺ, or his rightly guided successors after him, performed regularly and consistently without omission except once or twice, such as the call to prayer and its commencement (*adhān* and *iqāma*), praying in congregation (*jamā'a*), and rinsing the mouth and nose in *wuḍū'*. Leaving out a *sunna* once without a valid excuse is mildly disliked (*makrūh tanzīhan*) and entails "doing wrong" (*isā'a*). If one persistently leaves a *sunna* without an excuse, then it could be sinful depending on the level of its emphasis, as some *sunna* acts are more emphasized than others. However, the sin is deemed less severe than that incurred by omitting a mandatory requisite (*wājib*), and *a fortiori* an obligatory integral (*farḍ*) (*Marāqī 'l-Falāḥ, Ṭaḥṭāwī* 1:101, 116; *Radd* 1:70–1).

58 That is, to say *Bismillāhi 'r-Raḥmāni 'r-Raḥīm* ("In the Name of Allāh, Most Merciful, Most Compassionate"), or to say *Bismillāhi 'l-'Aẓīmi wa 'l-ḥamdu li 'Llāhi 'alā dīni 'l-islām* ("In the Name of Allāh, the Great. Praise be to Allāh for the religion of Islam") (*Durr, Radd* 1:74).

59 The intention and the mentioning of the Name of Allāh are also to be done at the onset of *wuḍū'*, while the toothstick is to be used before or while rinsing the mouth (*Marāqī 'l-Falāḥ* 1:104–6, 113; *Fatḥ Bāb al-'Ināya* 1:35; *Durr* 1:72; *Imdād* 68). Using the toothstick is deemed a *sunna* of the *wuḍū'* itself, not the prayer, such that its merit is attained for every prayer performed with a *wuḍū'*

5. Maintaining the correct order of limbs, as Allāh Most High has listed in His Book,[60]
6. Continuity,[61]
7. Washing [those limbs that are washed] three complete times,[62]
8. Rinsing the [entire] mouth [three times],
9. Rinsing the [soft part of the] nose [three times],
10. Running one's wet fingers through the beard,[63]
11. Running one's wet fingers in between the fingers and toes,[64]
12. Wiping the entire head [once, and the ears with the same water],
13. Rubbing[65] [the limbs when washing them],
14. Starting with the right limb [when washing the arms and feet],
15. Starting with the tips of the fingers and toes [when washing the arms and feet],
16. Starting with the front of the head [when wiping it],
17. Wiping the back of the neck,[66] but not the throat.

Among the etiquette (*ādāb*)[67] of *wuḍū'* are the following:

---

in which the person used it. If one does not have a toothstick or cannot use it for health reasons, then its merit is attained by using one's finger and thumb instead (*Marāqī 'l-Falāḥ* 1:106; *Imdād* 68).

60 Namely, face, arms, head, and feet (see Qur'ān 5:6). Performing *wuḍū'* in this order is not an obligation, yet (as with any emphasized *sunna*) one would have done wrong (*isā'a*) by leaving this *sunna* (*Imdād* 73).

61 That is, to continue washing the limbs of *wuḍū'* without pausing, such that each successive limb is washed before the previous one dries. Some defined it as not engaging in another act, unrelated to *wuḍū'*, while performing *wuḍū'* (*Marāqī 'l-Falāḥ*, *Ṭaḥṭāwī* 1:113; *Imdād* 72; *Tabyīn* 1:6; *Majmaᶜ al-Anhur* 1:16).

62 That is, the *sunna* is to *completely* wash each limb three times, irrespective of whether one does so with three scoops of water. For example, if one washes the arm three times yet the entire arm does not get wet except by the third wash, then those three acts of washing are deemed *one* complete wash, and two more remain to fulfill the *sunna*. Hence, to *completely* wash the limb more or less than three times is contrary to the *sunna* (*Marāqī 'l-Falāḥ*, *Ṭaḥṭāwī* 1:110–1; *Radd* 1:80).

63 This is to be done after having washed the face three times (*Imdād* 70, *Radd* 1:79).

64 Placing the hand or foot under running water, such that the skin between the fingers and toes becomes wet, is sufficient in fulfilling this *sunna* (*Marāqī 'l-Falāḥ* 1:110; *Imdād* 71).

65 The legal definition of rubbing is to run one's hand or the like over the washed limb (*Imdād* 72; *Radd* 1:83).

66 After wiping the head, one wipes the back of the neck with the back of one's fingers without taking new water; this is recommended (*mandūb*), not an emphasized *sunna* (*Durr*, *Radd* 1:84).

67 An etiquette (*adab*) is that which the Prophet ﷺ did once or twice without establishing it as a normative practice (*sunna*). One is rewarded for doing it, yet there is no blame or sin for omitting it. It is synonymous with recommended act (*mustaḥabb* or *mandūb*), supererogatory act

1. Facing the *qibla* [direction of the Kaʿba in Makka],
2. Avoiding the water used in *wuḍū'* [from getting on one's body or clothes],
3. Making supplication (*duʿā'*) with those words that have been narrated [p. 185],
4. Mentioning the Name of Allāh when washing each limb,
5. Performing *wuḍū'* by oneself,[68]
6. Rushing to perform *wuḍū'* before the prayer time comes in, unless one has a chronic excuse [see p. 59],
7. Reciting the two testifications of faith after *wuḍū'* [p. 187],
8. Drinking from the leftover water afterwards.

Among the things disliked (*makrūhāt*)[69] in *wuḍū'* are the following:

1. Wasting water (*isrāf*),[70]
2. Using too little water when washing,[71]
3. Striking or slapping the face with water when washing it,[72]

(*taṭawwuʿ*), and voluntary act (*nafl*). Its omission is not deemed mildly disliked unless a specific prohibition exists (*Marāqī 'l-Falāḥ*, *Ṭaḥṭāwī* 1:116; *Radd* 1:84, 439).

68 This etiquette is conjoined with the next one in the Arabic published edition as well as in the manuscript, yet is actually a separate etiquette, as listed by the author himself in *Nūr al-Īḍāḥ* (see *Imdād* 75–6) and by Imām Tumurtāshī in his *Tanwīr al-Abṣār* (1:85–6).

69 There are two types of disliked actions: prohibitively disliked (*makrūh taḥrīman*) and mildly disliked (*makrūh tanzīhan*). The first type refers to an act that is mandatory (*wājib*) to abstain from, making it sinful to do without an excuse. The second type refers to an act that is better to avoid, yet no sin is incurred for doing it, even without an excuse (*Marāqī 'l-Falāḥ*, *Ṭaḥṭāwī* 1:123; *Durr*, *Radd* 1:89). Between the two is "to do wrong" (*isā'a*)—that is, to do something worse than mildly disliked, yet less severe than prohibitively disliked, and hence not sinful per se. It is often associated with omitting an emphasized *sunna* once, without an excuse; *habitual* omission of an emphasized *sunna* without an excuse, however, would entail sin, albeit less severe than omission of something mandatory (*wājib*), or *a fortiori* obligatory (*farḍ*) (*Radd* 1:318–19, 381).

70 Wasting is defined as using more water than what is legally deemed necessary. This includes completely washing a limb more than three times, while believing it to be from the *sunna* (*Ṭaḥṭāwī* 1:123; *Radd* 1:89).

71 That is, it is also disliked to use less water than what is established by the *sunna*, whereby washing resembles wiping. If one does so to the extent that the drops of water are not clearly apparent on the limb, then the washing might not even be valid, since the definition of washing is the flowing of water over a limb such that it drips with at least two drops (*Marāqī 'l-Falāḥ*, *Ṭaḥṭāwī* 1:92, 124; *Radd* 1:65, 89).

72 This is deemed mildly disliked (*makrūh tanzīhan*), as it entails leaving an etiquette of *wuḍū'*, namely, to avoid getting used water on one's clothes. Slapping one's face is also unbecoming to the demeanor and self-respect of a Muslim, which is also related to etiquette (*adab*) (*Durr*, *Radd* 1:89).

4. Speaking during *wuḍū'*, other than making supplication,
5. Having someone else assist[73] one in *wuḍū'* without a valid excuse.

The legal reason for performing *wuḍū'* is the desire to do that which is not permissible except in a state of *wuḍū'*, such as the ritual prayer (*ṣalāt*) or touching a copy of the Qur'ān; or the legal reason could also be the divine command being directed to someone due to the near expiration of the prayer time.

The conditions of being legally responsible to perform it are the following:[74]

1. Islam,
2. Puberty,
3. Sanity,
4. Termination of menstruation, postnatal bleeding, or the state of ritual impurity,
5. Access to and ability to use sufficient purifying water,
6. Ability to perform the prayer (*ṣalāt*),
7. The divine command being directed to the person due to the near expiration of the prayer time.

The conditions of the validity of *wuḍū'* are the following:

1. That purifying water completely encompass the skin [of those limbs that must be washed; i.e., the obligatory integrals];
2. The removal of anything that blocks water from reaching the surface of the skin;[75]
3. The ending of any state that contradicts it [*wuḍū'*] while washing

---

73 It is not disliked whatsoever to seek assistance in bringing or pouring the water for one's *wuḍū'*. Rather, it is disliked for one without a valid excuse to have someone else assist in the actual washing or wiping of the limbs (*Radd* 1:86).

74 That is, one is not obligated to perform *wuḍū'* unless all of these conditions are fulfilled.

75 That is, for both washing and wiping, a necessary condition of validity is the absence of any solid barrier on the surface of the limb that would prevent the wetness from reaching the limb itself, such as paint (or nail polish). Otherwise, the integral would not be fulfilled and the *wuḍū'* (or *ghusl*) would be deemed invalid. An exception, however, would be for one whose profession entails dealing with such a substance, such as a painter, who would be excused for small amounts on his nails. Furthermore in general, the dirt underneath one's nails is not deemed a barrier (*Marāqī 'l-Falāḥ* 1:99–100; *Majmaʿ al-Anhur* 1:21).

[i.e., while performing *wuḍū'*], such as the appearance of urine at the tip of the penis.[76]

Its legal ruling (*ḥukm*) is the permissibility of that which was impermissible before it, such as performing the prayer and touching a copy of the Qur'ān.

Its integrals (*rukn*, pl. *arkān*) are its aforementioned four obligatory elements.

The categories of *wuḍū'* are three: obligatory, mandatory, and recommended.

1. Obligatory (*farḍ*), namely, when a person is in a state of minor ritual impurity and intends on doing [any of the following:]

   (1) The ritual prayer,
   (2) The prostration of recital,
   (3) Touching a verse of the Qur'ān [unless with a nonattached barrier];[77]

2. Mandatory (*wājib*), namely, when a person is in a state of minor ritual impurity and intends on performing circumambulation (*ṭawāf*) around the Kaʿba or touching a book of Qur'ānic exegesis (*tafsīr*);[78]

---

76 The phrase used here in the Arabic published edition is a bit confusing, as perhaps a mistake was made during transcription, but the meaning given in the translation is accurate based on the manuscript, as well as the author's other works *Marāqī 'l-Falāḥ* (1:97) and *Imdād al-Fattāḥ* (63).

77 This prohibition also extends to any writing of a complete Qur'ānic verse, whether in a book, on a coin, or elsewhere. He may not touch *any* part of a copy (*muṣḥaf*) of the Qur'ān (including pages, margins, cover, binding, etc.), yet with other religious books like of jurisprudence or ḥadīth, the prohibition applies only to touching the Qur'ānic verse itself. This prohibition also applies to Qur'ānic translation (and transliteration) in other languages, not just Arabic. The prohibition of touching also extends to the other revealed books, namely the Gospel, Torah, and Psalms, despite their having been tampered with and hence abrogated (*Marāqī 'l-Falāḥ*, *Ṭaḥṭāwī* 1:205–6; *Durr*, *Radd* 1:118–9, 195). For the prohibition related to touching, to do so with a barrier attached to the book, or with one's sleeve (or any part of one's garment being worn), is deemed prohibitively disliked (*makrūh taḥrīman*) (*Marāqī 'l-Falāḥ*, *Ṭaḥṭāwī* 1:206), yet with a nonattached barrier is permissible.

For a person in *major* ritual impurity, the following things are prohibited: ritual prayer (*ṣalāt*), recitation of a verse of Qur'ān, touching it (as applied above) unless with a nonattached barrier, entering a mosque, and *ṭawāf* (*Marāqī 'l-Falāḥ* 1:211).

For the prohibitions related to a woman in menstruation or postnatal bleeding, see the related section on p. 56.

78 Some scholars of the Ḥanafī school deemed it permissible for a person in a state of minor ritual impurity to touch a book of Qur'ānic exegesis *only* if most of its content is not actual Qur'ānic script, which is the opinion that Ibn ʿĀbidīn inclines toward. Others maintained that even if most is Qur'ānic script, one may still touch the rest of the book that is not Qur'ānic script, which is a weaker opinion. In any case, there is agreement that someone in that state may not touch the actual Qur'ānic script in any book, exegetical or otherwise (*Ṭaḥṭāwī* 1:206; *Radd* 1:119).

3. Recommended (*mandūb*), namely, when a person is in a state of minor ritual impurity, in the following cases:

    (1) Before touching a book of jurisprudence (*fiqh*) or the like [out of veneration],[79]
    (2) To renew one's *wuḍū'* for another prayer,
    (3) To avoid disagreement of scholars of other schools of thought, such as after having touched a woman [or one's genitalia],
    (4) Before sleeping,
    (5) After waking up from sleep,
    (6) After every sin,
    (7) After laughing out loud outside of the prayer (*ṣalāt*).

Wuḍū' is nullified by any one of the following things:

1. Anything that exits[80] from the two openings[81] [namely the penis or vagina, and the anus],
2. Filth that *flows*[82] from other than the two openings, such as blood[83] [or pus],

79 It is recommended to perform *wuḍū'* before touching books of jurisprudence, theology, or ḥadīth (i.e., religious texts), if one is in a state of minor ritual impurity, yet a dispensation exists for those that deal with such books on a regular basis (*Marāqī 'l-Falāḥ* 1:127, 206; *Hadiyya* 32).

80 With respect to the two openings, the appearance of filth at the tip or edge of the opening is considered "exit" and therefore nullifies *wuḍū'* (*Marāqī 'l-Falāḥ* 1:131–2; *Badā'iʿ* 1:121; *Tabyīn* 1:7; *Ikhtiyār* 1:18). Hence, a man must ensure that no wetness or filth remains at the tip of the opening before commencing *wuḍū'*.

81 According to Imām Abū Ḥanīfa, women's clear vaginal discharge is not impure (*najis*) and hence, its exit does not nullify *wuḍū'*, as legally it resembles sweat (*Radd* 1:112, 208, 233). If colored though, its exit nullifies *wuḍū'*, as that entails the flowing of filth.

82 As opposed to the two openings, "exit" from the rest of the body does not occur by mere appearance at the skin surface. Rather, the filth must "flow" beyond the point of exit, that is, move to a place that normally must be cleaned, before *wuḍū'* is nullified. This ruling applies even if the filth does not exit on its own but is squeezed out (*Hadiyya* 26; *Durr*, *Radd* 1:92–3). However, if the fluid simply rises and appears at the surface of the skin without actually moving out, such as blood surfacing at an abrasion, then *wuḍū'* is not nullified. As a result, that fluid is not impure, for an internal fluid is only rendered impure if it exits in a manner that nullifies *wuḍū'*. Hence, if such blood (that surfaced without moving) is dabbed with a cloth or affects one's garment, neither of the two would be rendered impure (*Hidāya* 1:17; *Marāqī 'l-Falāḥ* 1:140; *Radd* 1:92, 95; *Fatḥ al-Qadīr* 1:41).

83 This also includes bleeding in one's mouth, which nullifies *wuḍū'* if the color of one's saliva becomes red or pink, as opposed to yellow. In addition, the blood that exits from one's body due to

3. Vomiting a mouthful[84] or more,
4. Sleeping in a position such that the buttocks are not firmly planted onto the ground, such as while lying down or leaning one one's side,[85]
5. Loss of consciousness,
6. Insanity,
7. Drunkenness,
8. Laughing out loud, by an adult, while performing the prayer (*ṣalāt*),
9. Contact between an erect penis and vagina.[86]

THE PURIFICATORY BATH (*GHUSL*)

The following three actions are obligatory integrals of the *ghusl*:

1. Rinsing the [entire] mouth [once],
2. Rinsing the nose [i.e., up to the bone, once],
3. Washing whatever is possible, without undue difficulty or hardship, of the entire body [once].[87]

Among the emphasized *sunnas* of the *ghusl* are the following, in this order:

---

a mosquito bite is not enough to be deemed "flowing," and hence does not nullify *wuḍū'* (*Hadiyya* 27; *Durr, Radd* 1:94).

84 The criteria of a mouthful is that one's mouth cannot withhold the vomit without strain. This ruling applies to any type of vomit, but not to phlegm, no matter how much comes out (*Hadiyya* 26; *Ikhtiyār* 1:18; *Hidāya* 1:17; *Tabyīn* 1:9).

85 As opposed to sleeping in a position with one's buttocks firmly planted onto the ground (or any firm surface), whereby *wuḍū'* is not nullified. This ruling applies even if he were leaning onto something to the extent that, if it were removed, he would fall down (*Hadiyya* 27; *Badā'iʿ* 1:135; *Tabyīn* 1:10; *Durr, Radd* 1:95–6).

86 That is, without a thick cloth or the like acting as a barrier, "thick" meaning that which prevents feeling body heat from the other organ (*Marāqī 'l-Falāḥ, Ṭaḥṭāwī* 1:139). Also, according to the Ḥanafī school, direct skin contact with someone of the opposite gender, or direct skin contact with the penis or vagina, does not nullify *wuḍū'* (*Hadiyya* 28).

87 Hence, it is obligatory (*farḍ*) for water to reach the following parts of the body: the immediate inner part of the ears; the skin beneath one's beard, moustache and eyebrows, (for all) regardless of thickness; all of one's hair including the roots, although the roots alone are sufficient for a woman's braided hair; the inside of one's navel; the underskin of a woman's clitoral hood; and the external orifice of the genitals (*Badā'iʿ* 1:142; *Majmaʿ al-Anhur* 1:21; *Durr* 1:103–4).

1. Intention (*niyya*),[88]
2. Washing the hands until the wrists,
3. Washing one's private parts [front and rear],
4. Washing off any filth from the body,
5. Performing *wuḍū'* first, followed by pouring water over the entire body, starting with the head [for a total of three times].[89]

The *ghusl* is of three types:

1. Obligatory (*farḍ*), namely, when any one of the following things occur:

    (1) The emission of sperm/sexual fluid (*manī*)[90] that leaves its normal place inside the body *with pleasure* [even if it exits without pleasure], for any reason, such as a wet dream or by looking [at someone or something with lust];
    (2) The disappearance of the head of the penis into the vagina, or the anus, of a living human being whose body is desirable [even if without emission of sexual fluid];
    (3) The ending of menstruation or postnatal bleeding;

2. Mandatory (*wājib*), namely, for someone who becomes Muslim while in a state of major ritual impurity, although the sounder opinion is that the bath is obligatory (*farḍ*) on him, not mandatory (*wājib*);
3. Recommended (*nafl*), for any one of the following reasons:

    (1) The Friday prayer (*jumuʿa*),
    (2) The two ʿĪd prayers,
    (3) Entering into the state of pilgrim sanctity (*iḥrām*),

---

88 That is, at the onset, along with mentioning the Name of Allāh (*basmala*), which is done before revealing one's nakedness (*ʿawra*—see p. 74) (*Hadiyya* 28).

89 If, however, one is immersed under flowing water or rain, and remains therein for the length of time it would take to wash the body three times, then he would have fulfilled the *sunna* of washing the entire body three separate times (*Marāqī 'l-Falāḥ* 1:156).

90 For males, *manī* refers to sperm; it is defined as a thick, white fluid that exits in spurts as lustful discharge (orgasm), followed by a listlessness of the sexual organ. For females, *manī* refers to sexual fluid; it is thin and yellow, and also comes with an orgasm (*Marāqī 'l-Falāḥ* 1:144).

(4) The Day of ʿArafa,[91]
(5) Entering Makka,
(6) Entering Madīna, the Illuminated City,
(7) Visiting the Prophet ﷺ.

The *ghusl* is not necessary after any of the following:

- □ The exit of *madhy* or *wady*;[92]
- □ Waking up after having a wet dream yet finding no wetness, even for a woman;
- □ The insertion of a finger or the like into the vagina;
- □ Intercourse with an animal, without the emission of sperm.

DRY ABLUTION (*TAYAMMUM*)

Tayammum is permissible when there is a valid excuse, such as [the following:]

- □ Being roughly one Hāshimite legal mile (*mīl sharʿī*) [1.16 mi (1.86 km)][93] away from water,[94]
- □ Extreme cold,[95]
- □ Sickness,[96]

---

91 That is, for those on the pilgrimage (*ḥajj*), to be performed after midday (*zawāl*). Also for the first four cases above, *ghusl* is actually an emphasized *sunna*, not merely recommended (*Marāqī ʾl-Falāḥ* 1:160–1).

92 *Madhy*, or presexual fluid, is defined as a thin, clear fluid that exits when one is aroused, yet not as sperm (*manī*) does, and its exit is not followed by a listlessness of the sexual organ. *Wady* is a thick, murky white fluid that often exits the penis after urination, or could precede it. By scholarly consensus, there is no need to perform *ghusl* after the exit of either *madhy* or *wady*, yet *wuḍūʾ* would be required (*Marāqī ʾl-Falāḥ* 1:150; *Durr*, *Radd* 1:111).

93 This distance is estimated to be about a half-hour walk (*Ṭaḥṭāwī* 1:169). Reasonable likelihood of this distance is sufficient for *tayammum* to be permissible (*Marāqī ʾl-Falāḥ* 1:169; *Radd* 1:155). For the modern equivalent used in the text above, see Bashshār Bakrī ʿArrābī's note on the *Lubāb*, p. 34, n. 7.

94 Whether on a journey or within a city, even one's city of residence (*Marāqī ʾl-Falāḥ*, *Ṭaḥṭāwī* 1:169; *Hadiyya* 34; *Durr* 1:155).

95 Such that the person fears, with reasonable likelihood, illness or loss of (or damage to) a limb by using the water, and does not have access to any means of heating the water (*Marāqī ʾl-Falāḥ*, *Ṭaḥṭāwī* 1:170–1; *Hadiyya* 34; *Durr* 1:156).

96 That is, if a person is ill and fears that the sickness will worsen or become prolonged by performing *wuḍūʾ* or *ghusl*, whether due to the water itself or the movement entailed, then he may

- □ Wounds on most of the body,[97]
- □ Fear of thirst,[98]
- □ Fear of an enemy or a wild beast [around the water],[99]
- □ Lack of apparatus [to take water out of the well],
- □ Fear of missing the funeral prayer (*janāza*) or the ʿĪd prayer, even if building upon one's prayer [if one's *wuḍū'* is nullified during the prayer], as opposed to the Friday prayer or a normal prescribed prayer.[100]

If one forgets that he has water in his caravan [and therefore performs *tayammum* due to lack of water], he does not have to make up those prayers [upon remembering the water in the caravan]. And Allāh knows best.

Tayammum may be performed with any pure substance of the earth,[101] such

---

perform *tayammum* instead. His fear, however, must be based on reasonable likelihood, whether by (1) a clear and obvious sign, (2) past experience, or (3) a medical opinion from a skilled, Muslim physician who is not openly corrupt (*fāsiq*) (*Durr, Radd* 1:156; *Hadiyya* 34).

97 See last paragraph of this section with its accompanying note.

98 Whether for oneself, one's travel partner, or one's animal; at present or in the future (*Marāqī 'l-Falāḥ* 1:171; *Durr* 1:157).

99 If the fear arose from a threat, or if there was actual prevention from using the water, then the prayer would have to be repeated afterwards, although the *tayammum* was still permissible. If one feared the presence of an enemy or animal without threat or prevention, the prayer would not have to be repeated (*Marāqī 'l-Falāḥ, Ṭaḥṭāwī* 1:171; *Durr, Radd* 1:156–7).

100 That is, if one fears that by performing *wuḍū'*, or even *ghusl*, he will miss the entire funeral or ʿĪd prayer, then he may instead perform *tayammum* to ensure catching the prayer, as those two prayers have no replacements. This ruling holds even if he is in the midst of the prayer when his *wuḍū'* is nullified, in which case he could perform *tayammum* and then continue the prayer from where he left off. This ruling does not apply if he himself broke his *wuḍū'*, in which case he would have to restart the prayer as a latecomer after renewing *wuḍū'*. The ruling also does not apply to the Friday prayer or to any of the five daily prescribed prayers, since each has a replacement—ẓuhr for the Friday prayer, and the make-up prayer (*qaḍā'*) for the normal prescribed prayer. For the latter however, if one has reasonable surety or certainty that the prayer time will expire before performing *wuḍū'* or *ghusl*, then out of precaution he may perform *tayammum* and pray (although it does not fulfill his obligation). He would then perform it again (which is obligatory to do so) as a make-up prayer (*qaḍā'*), after having performed the proper *wuḍū'* or *ghusl* (*Marāqī 'l-Falāḥ, Ṭaḥṭāwī* 1:172–4; *Durr, Radd* 1:161, 164).

101 As long as the substance of the earth is not malleable, which excludes metals; nor can burn into ashes, which excludes plantlife or wood (*Marāqī 'l-Falāḥ* 1:175; *Hadiyya* 34–5). If one has access to neither water nor such a substance, or is unable to use either one, then out of reverence for the sacred time, it is mandatory (*wājib*) to perform an "imitation prayer." That is, one must go through its motions including bowing (*rukūʿ*) and prostrating (*sujūd*), yet without its intention and—whether in a state of major or minor ritual impurity—without recitation of Qur'ān. The prayer, of course, would later have to be made up (*Durr, Radd* 1:168).

as dirt, sand, antimony (*kuḥl*), limestone, stones, or dust, even the dust on clothes.[102]

Hence when a Muslim intends[103] to remove the state of ritual impurity, strikes the earth once and wipes his face completely with dirt [or whatever substance he is using], strikes it a second time[104] and wipes his arms [up to and including the elbows] completely with dirt, he becomes pure, even if he were in a state of major ritual impurity (*junub*). He may then perform as many prayers as he wishes [even spanning multiple prayer times], both obligatory (*farḍ*) and voluntary (*nafl*), until either his *wuḍū'* is nullified, or his excuse for performing *tayammum* ends.

If one has wounds on his body, yet his uninjured limbs are more than his injured limbs, he must wash the uninjured limbs and wipe the wounded ones, as long as wiping them does not hurt him. Otherwise, he may leave those limbs [neither washing nor wiping them].[105]

One may not, however, wash some limbs and perform *tayammum* as well.

WIPING FOOTGEAR (*KHUFFS*)

Both men and women may wipe[106] *khuffs*, whether travelling or while in residence.

The *khuffs* must cover both ankles, even if made out of dense wool (*jūkh*).[107]

---

102 That is, provided the dust is visible on the hands after rubbing the garment (*Durr, Radd* 1:160).

103 Unlike with *wuḍū'* or *ghusl*, the intention is an obligatory condition (*farḍ*) for the validity of *tayammum*. Moreover, in order to perform a ritual prayer (*ṣalāt*) with *tayammum*, its intention must be specifically for "leaving the state of impurity" or for "the permissibility of performing a ritual prayer" (*Marāqī 'l-Falāḥ* 1:167; *Badā'iʿ* 1:178).

104 "Strike" in this context means "to place." Both "strikes" are a condition for a valid *tayammum* (*Marāqī 'l-Falāḥ, Ṭaḥṭāwī* 1:177).

105 For *wuḍū'*, "most" of the limbs is based on the number of limbs, while for *ghusl*, it is based on total body surface area. For either type of purification, if half or more of the limbs to be washed are injured, one may perform *tayammum*. If less than half are injured, one may not perform *tayammum* but instead must wash the uninjured limbs, and wipe the injured limbs with a wet hand or, if that entails harm, with a wet cloth. If that too would cause harm, then one may leave the injured limbs altogether and just wash the uninjured ones. Finally, one does not have to wash the uninjured limbs if doing so would cause water to reach the injured limbs (thereby causing damage); rather, he may perform *tayammum* (*Marāqī 'l-Falāḥ, Ṭaḥṭāwī* 1:182–3; *Hadiyya* 37).

106 For both *khuffs* as well as casts, bandages, dressings and the like, what is meant by "wiping" is its legal definition, namely, wetness *touching* an area.

107 That is, even if the *khuffs* are not made out of leather, it is still valid to wipe them if they

In order to be able to wipe *khuffs*, one must have completed *wuḍū'* before its nullification. However, it is not a condition to complete *wuḍū'* before wearing the *khuffs*. That is, if one were to wash his two feet, wear the *khuffs*, and then complete his *wuḍū'*, it would be valid to wipe the *khuffs* afterwards.

If one is resident [i.e., not on a journey], he may wipe [*khuffs*] for one complete day and night [24 hours]. A traveller, however, may wipe [them] for three complete days and nights [72 hours].

This time period [during which one may wipe *khuffs*] begins from the time *wuḍū'* is nullified, after having worn them in a state of ritual purity.

The minimum required area that must be wiped is an amount equivalent to the surface area of the person's three smallest fingers; this much of the *top* of each one of the pair must be wiped.[108]

Each *khuff* must be free from holes[109] that [if combined] are equivalent to the surface area of the person's three smallest toes. Hence, if the holes of one of a pair are less than that area, it is still valid to wipe it, even if each one is such. [That is] the holes of both *khuffs* are not combined [when estimating; rather, each one of the pair is considered separately].

The *sunna* method of wiping the *khuffs* is to begin at the toes, with one's fingers spread apart, and to wipe [once] toward the shin.

---

fulfill the following conditions:

- They are made from thick material, such as wool, or broadcloth;
- Due to their thickness, they remain on the foot without having to be tied (with the exception of a zipper or the like that is attached to the *khuff*);
- They are not see-through;
- They completely cover the foot, up to and including the ankles (which must be covered from the sides, yet there is no harm if they can be seen from above);
- One can walk a distance of at least (approximately) 3.48 mi (5.6 km) (*farsakh*) without their tearing (aside from small holes that are excused—see text above);
- Water does not seep through them when wiping (see *Imdād* 126; *Marāqī 'l-Falāḥ*, *Ṭaḥṭāwī* 1:186–7; *Ḥalabī Kabīr* 120–3; *Hadiyya* 39; *Tabyīn* 1:52; *Lubāb* 42; *Durr* 1:179. For calculation of *farsakh*, see Bashshār Bakrī ʿArrābī's note on the *Lubāb*, p. 34, n. 8).

108 It is not valid to wipe any other part of the *khuff*, such as its bottom, sides, heel, or leg portion (i.e., above the ankles). Only the top of the *khuff* is given consideration. Also, even if the minimum obligatory (*farḍ*) area (mentioned above) of the top of the *khuff* becomes wet from purifying water, such as by rain or a wet cloth, it is valid (*Marāqī 'l-Falāḥ* 1:190–1; *Hadiyya* 40; *Badā'iʿ* 1:87).

109 This also includes wear and tear of the *khuff* to the extent that one could not walk at least (approximately) 3.48 mi (5.6 km) (*farsakh*) with such deterioration (*Hadiyya* 41). It does not include, however, the normal lines of stitching of the *khuff*; that is, any hole through which a large sewing needle cannot fit is not given any consideration (*Marāqī 'l-Falāḥ* 1:189).

The following things invalidate the wiping of *khuffs*:[110]

- ☐ Anything that nullifies *wuḍū'*,
- ☐ Taking [even] one of the pair off,
- ☐ The expiration of the time period, unless [based on reasonable likelihood,] one fears harm to his feet due to extreme cold,
- ☐ Most of one foot leaving a *khuff*.[111]

It is not valid to wipe a turban, cap, face veil, or gloves.

WIPING CASTS

If one has a broken or wounded limb, he may wipe[112] its cast, bandage, or dressing for as long as the excuse remains, even if it were placed on the limb while the person was in a state of major or minor ritual impurity.

It is not a condition to wipe the entire cast,[113] although it is according to a weaker opinion.

It is also not necessary to wash the exposed skin in between the wrapping of a dressing placed over skin where a venesection [or the like] was performed.[114]

---

110 Additionally, if water reaches most of one foot (or most of both feet) despite wearing *khuffs*, then one may no longer wipe them (and rather must completely wash both feet) (*Hadiyya* 41; *Radd* 1:184–5).

111 The *khuff* has two main portions: (1) the foot portion, which is the part that is normally below the ankles, and (2) the leg portion, which is the part that is normally above the ankles.

If one is not intentionally removing the *khuff* but rather the foot comes out on its own (by for example walking), then as long as *most* of the *foot* remains in the foot portion of the *khuff*, one may continue wiping. Once most of the foot reaches the leg portion of the *khuff*, it is as if the entire foot has been taken out, and so one may no longer wipe the *khuff*. If, however, one *purposely* removes the *khuff*, then once most of the *heel* of the foot reaches the leg portion of the *khuff*, one may no longer wipe them (*Hadiyya* 41; *Durr*, *Radd* 1:184).

112 For either *wuḍū'* or *ghusl*, one must wash the injured or wounded limb if able to, even if by using warm water. Otherwise if unable to wash it, he must wipe it directly. If he cannot wipe the limb itself, it becomes mandatory (*wājib*) to wipe the cast or bandage placed on it. If wiping the cast or bandage harms him, then he may leave it altogether (*Marāqī 'l-Falāḥ*, *Ṭaḥṭāwī* 1:195–6; *Durr* 1:186). What is meant by "wiping" in this section is its legal definition, namely, wetness *touching* an area.

113 Rather, one must wipe *most* of the cast or dressing (*Marāqī 'l-Falāḥ* 1:196; *Durr* 1:187; *Hadiyya* 42).

114 Rather, one may wipe the exposed skin while wiping the dressing. This exemption from washing the exposed skin applies only if taking off the dressing would harm him, since if he were to wash the exposed skin, the entire dressing might become wet whereby wetness could reach the

If the cast or bandage falls off, and the limb had not yet healed, then neither the [previous] wiping nor the ritual prayer [if he were praying] is invalidated.

If a new cast or bandage is placed on the wounded limb [to replace the older one], it is not necessary to wipe it if the original one had previously been wiped, yet it is recommended to do so.

Like *khuffs*, [wiping] the cast does not require an intention.[115]

MENSTRUATION (*ḤAYḌ*), POSTNATAL BLEEDING (*NIFĀS*), AND DYSFUNCTIONAL UTERINE BLEEDING (*ISTIḤĀḌA*)

Menstruation [i.e., menstrual blood (*ḥayḍ*)] is defined as blood that exits from the uterus[116] of a woman free from disease[117] or pregnancy, after the age of adolescence.[118] Its minimum duration is three days [72 complete hours], while its maximum is ten days [240 complete hours];[119] its average is between the two, i.e., five days.

---

wound and cause damage to it. If, however, he is able to undo the dressing, he must do so, wash the uninjured skin, and directly wipe the wound. Yet if wiping the wound would harm him, then he may leave it alone and, after washing the uninjured skin, re-wrap the dressing and wipe the dressing over the wound (*Marāqī 'l-Falāḥ*, *Ṭaḥṭāwī* 1:196; *Radd* 1:187).

115 As opposed to wiping *khuffs*, wiping a cast (or bandage/dressing) has the legal ruling of "washing," and is hence not deemed a "replacement." Some key rulings that differ as a result include the following: there is no time limit for wiping a cast; it is not a condition that the cast be worn while the person is in a state of ritual purity (minor or major); a cast may be worn on one leg only, while the other foot is still washed; wiping a cast is not nullified by its removal or coming off (i.e., *before* healing of the limb); the cast may be replaced with another, without having to re-wipe the new one if the person were in a state of ritual purity, although doing so is better; if it is removed or comes off *after* healing of the limb, washing the area alone suffices if the person were in a state of ritual purity (as opposed to the entire limb as with the *khuff*); if one wears another cast over the first cast, wiping the second one (i.e., the outer one) suffices; water seeping underneath the cast such that the limb gets washed does not nullify the wiping; the cast does not have to completely cover any particular area, nor prevent water from seeping through, nor remain on the limb by itself without additional fastening; multiple holes in a cast, regardless of how big, do not nullify the wiping; and lastly, the cast may be worn over any limb of the body (*Hadiyya* 42; *Durr*, *Radd* 1:186–8).

116 And actually comes out of the vagina (*Birgivi* 67).

117 That is, a disease that would cause blood to exit (*Marāqī 'l-Falāḥ* 1:200).

118 That is, puberty. Legally, the minimum age of puberty for girls is nine lunar years (about eight years and nine months on the solar calendar) (*Hadiyya* 43; *Marāqī 'l-Falāḥ* 1:200; *Badā'i'* 1:157). Additionally, menstrual blood does not normally come after menopause, which legally occurs at fifty-five lunar years (*Marāqī 'l-Falāḥ* 1:200). However, some women do have a later, or earlier, menopause.

119 It is not a condition, however, that the bleeding during the ten days be continuous; rather, any break within the possible days of menstruation is deemed menstruation in retrospect (*Marāqī 'l-Falāḥ* 1:201).

If the bleeding is for less than three days, or more than ten days, then it [the excess blood] is not menstruation;[120] rather, it is dysfunctional uterine bleeding (*istiḥāḍa*).[121]

During the period of menstruation [i.e., its maximum ten complete days], *any* color that is seen, as well as intermittent breaks from bleeding [again, within the possible ten complete days], is considered menstrual blood, [thus] preventing her from praying or fasting.[122] The fasts must be made up [if during Ramaḍān], as opposed to the prayers.

The following things are also unlawful during menstruation:[123]

- ☐ Sexual intercourse,
- ☐ *Ṭawāf*,[124]
- ☐ Entering a mosque [even if only to pass through],
- ☐ Being touched from [right below] the navel to [right below] the knee,[125]
- ☐ Reciting the Qur'ān,[126]
- ☐ Touching a copy of the Qur'ān, unless with a [nonattached] barrier.[127]

---

120 In the Ḥanafī school, it is imperative that a woman record her menstrual habit and lochial habit, as well as any other blood she sees, in order to correctly apply related legal rulings.

121 Another related scenario is if the bleeding exceeds her normal menstrual habit and continues beyond ten complete days (240 hours), in which case the bleeding that occurred after her habit is in retrospect deemed dysfunctional uterine bleeding. If, however, the bleeding does not exceed ten complete days, then all of it is deemed menstruation, and its entire duration is considered her new menstrual habit (*Hadiyya* 43; *Badā'iʿ* 1:158).

122 However, every time the blood completely stops within the ten days—meaning there is no color at all—she must resume her obligatory worship of praying and, if Ramaḍān, fasting.

123 As well as during postnatal bleeding (*Marāqī 'l-Falāḥ* 1:204–5).

124 The *ṭawāf* itself would be valid, yet she would have incurred sin, as performing *ṭawāf* in that state is prohibitively disliked (*makrūh taḥrīman*). She would therefore have to perform expiation (see related section in chapter on *Ḥajj*, p. 162) (*Marāqī 'l-Falāḥ* 1:207; *Durr, Radd* 1:194).

125 That is, without a cloth or the like acting as a barrier, even if there is no pleasure. If her husband touches her in that area with a barrier, then there is no harm, even if they both experience pleasure. They may also kiss and lie down together, and they should not purposely sleep in separate beds, as that resembles the behavior of the Jews (*Ṭaḥṭāwī* 1:208; *Hadiyya* 44; *Durr, Radd* 1:194).

126 That is, even a part of a verse, if with the "intention" of recitation. She is, however, allowed to recite Qur'ānic verses of praise, supplication, or protection, such as Sūrat al-Fātiḥa or the last three *sūras*, with the intention of praise, supplication, or protection, not with the intention of recitation (*Marāqī 'l-Falāḥ, Ṭaḥṭāwī* 1:204–5; *Hadiyya* 44; *Durr, Radd* 1:195). Lastly, the prohibition applies to recitation of Qur'ān, by moving one's lips and uttering words, not to mentally "reading" the Qur'ān, which is permissible for a woman in menstruation.

127 See related note on p. 46.

If her period ends within ten days [but after the duration of her regular habit], she may not have intercourse except after one of three things:

1. Performing a *ghusl*;
2. Performing *tayammum* [if there is a valid excuse (see p. 50)], as well as praying [*ṣalāt*] with it [that *tayammum*], even if a voluntary prayer;
3. Missing an obligatory prayer, which occurs if her period ends with enough time to at least perform the *ghusl* and say the *taḥrīma* before the prayer time expires; if that occurs, it is permissible to have intercourse with her afterwards [even if she did not perform the *ghusl*]. If, however, the time between the ending of her period and the expiration of the prayer time is very slight, such that she would not have enough time to take the *ghusl* [coupled with the *taḥrīma*], then she is not considered to have missed an obligatory prayer [and intercourse would remain impermissible].

If her period goes past ten days, it is permissible[128] to have intercourse with her as soon as it passes the tenth day [240 complete hours], due to the certainty [that the menstruation is complete and] that the extra bleeding is dysfunctional uterine bleeding.

The minimum duration of *ṭuhr*[129] is fifteen [complete] days [360 complete hours], yet it has no maximum duration, except when establishing a standard menstrual habit in a situation of continuous bleeding.[130]

Postnatal bleeding (or lochia) (*nifās*), is defined as blood [that exits] after delivery, or after most of the baby has exited,[131] even after miscarriage of a fetus

---

128 It is still recommended (*mustaḥabb*), however, to not have intercourse with her until she performs *ghusl*, so as to avoid scholarly disagreement. The same ruling applies to a woman who completes forty days of postnatal bleeding (*Marāqī 'l-Falāḥ* 1:209).

129 *Ṭuhr* refers to the interval of purity between two menstrual cycles, or between a lochial cycle and a menstrual cycle.

130 That is, the only situation when there is a maximum duration of *ṭuhr* is when a standard menstrual habit needs to be established, which occurs if a girl begins puberty with continuous bleeding. In such a case, she is given a menstrual habit of ten days, and a *ṭuhr* duration of the rest of the lunar month, namely, either nineteen or twenty days depending on the month (*Hadiyya* 44).

131 Hence, once most of the baby has exited—"most" referring to the chest if it comes out head first, or the navel if feet first—then the blood seen afterwards is postnatal bleeding, whereby she is absolved from praying (and fasting, both of which become prohibited for her). Before that, however, any blood seen is deemed dysfunctional uterine bleeding, and so she must still perform the prayer. She should perform *wuḍū'* if able to; otherwise, she may perform *tayammum*. If she is

whose body had [some sort of] physical development.[132] Postnatal bleeding has no minimum duration, while its maximum duration is forty days [960 complete hours]. It is from the first of twins.[133] Its ruling [i.e., of postnatal bleeding] is like that of menstruation.

The following cases are considered to be dysfunctional uterine bleeding:

- ☐ Any bleeding of a pregnant woman, even [bleeding] during delivery before most of the baby has exited;
- ☐ Bleeding [after delivery] for more than forty days [i.e., the excess blood is dysfunctional uterine bleeding];
- ☐ If she bleeds past her normal habit, of either menstruation or postnatal bleeding, and the bleeding exceeds the maximum duration [of either one; in that case, the bleeding after the duration of her habit is considered dysfunctional uterine bleeding];
- ☐ Any bleeding of a girl that has not yet reached adolescence.

Dysfunctional uterine bleeding (*istiḥāḍa*) is like a continuous nosebleed [in its legal ruling];[134] it does not prevent [the permissibility of] fasting, praying, sexual intercourse, or *ṭawāf.*

If such bleeding continues for the duration of an entire prayer time, then the woman must perform *wuḍū'* at the beginning of each prayer time, just like someone with chronic urinary incontinence, constant diarrhea, constant gas release, or continuous bleeding [from any part of the body].[135]

---

unable to bow and prostrate, she may pray with head movements (see "Prayer of the Sick Person," p. 94). *Despite being in labor,* however, she may not delay the prayer past its time, and if she does then she would have disobeyed her Lord (*Durr, Radd* 1:199; *Hadiyya* 45). As the author of *Munyat al-Muṣallī* states (as quoted by Ibn ʿĀbidīn), "So reflect on this situation; do you find any excuse for one [i.e., a healthy-able person] who delays the prayer past its time? O what painful punishment awaits the one who abandons the prayer!" (*Radd* 1:199).

132 Such as a hand, foot, finger, nail, or even hair. If no physical development appears on the fetus, it is not deemed a baby. In that case, the blood that exits afterwards is deemed menstrual blood *if* it lasts three full days (72 hours) and was preceded by a complete *ṭuhr* (i.e., of at least fifteen days) since her last menstrual period; otherwise, it is deemed dysfunctional uterine bleeding (*Hadiyya* 45; *Durr, Radd* 1:201).

133 That is, if a woman delivers twins, then the blood that exits after the first baby is considered postnatal bleeding, which prevents her from praying and fasting. Legally, twins are two babies from the same womb, separated by less than half a year (i.e., six lunar months) (*Durr, Radd* 1:200).

134 However, dysfunctional uterine bleeding does not have to be continuous; it can be, and most often is, intermittent.

135 That is, she takes the legal ruling of someone with a chronic problem, excused from having

There are three conditions for people with chronic excuses: the condition of establishing the excuse, the condition of its continuity, and the condition of its termination.

1. The condition of establishing the excuse, as stated above, is for the excuse to continue for the duration of an entire prayer time, such that the person is unable to perform *wuḍū'* and the prayer without the occurrence of the excuse. Afterwards, the person is considered chronically excused; therefore, he may pray any amount of obligatory or voluntary prayers, after having performed *wuḍū'* with it [the excuse], despite the occurrence of that excuse [after the *wuḍū'*]. The *wuḍū'* [performed in such a state] is invalidated only by the expiration of the prayer time.[136]
2. The condition of continuity of the excuse is its occurrence in every prayer time afterwards, even if only once [within each prayer time].
3. The condition of its termination [whereby one is no longer excused] is for a prayer time to elapse without a single occurrence of the excuse.

TYPES OF FILTH AND PURIFICATION FROM THEM

Filth (*najāsa*) is of two types: heavy (*mughallaẓa*) and light (*mukhaffafa*).[137]

Heavy filth includes [the following:]

- ☐ Spilled blood,[138]
- ☐ Feces,[139]

---

to make *wuḍū'* after each occurrence of that problem, based on the criteria mentioned next in the text above.

136 Or by any other nullifier of *wuḍū'* for which the person is not excused (*Marāqī 'l-Falāḥ* 1:213).

137 This distinction is only with respect to the amount of filth that is excused for the ritual prayer (*ṣalāt*). Aside from that, both types are equivalent in rendering liquids impure by admixture and in the method of purifying substances rendered impure by them (*Marāqī 'l-Falāḥ* 1:217).

138 That is, from all animals (including humans, i.e., if it flows). The following, however, are cases in which the blood is not impure: that which remains in the meat and blood vessels of an animal slaughtered according to Sacred Law (*dhabḥ*); blood in the liver, spleen, and heart; blood that does not nullify one's *wuḍū'* (i.e., by surfacing without flowing); blood or any fluid of bugs, mosquitos, or roaches; and blood of fish (*Marāqī 'l-Falāḥ*, *Ṭaḥṭāwī* 1:219). However, all parts of an animal with flowing blood that is not slaughtered according to Sacred Law, including its meat and hide, are impure (*Marāqī 'l-Falāḥ* 1:219).

139 This includes the feces of any land animal, predatory or otherwise. The urine of animals

- Wine (*khamr*),[140]
- Sperm or sexual fluid (*manī*).[141]

Light filth includes the following:

- Urine of animals whose meat is permissible to eat,[142]
- Urine of horses,
- Droppings of birds whose meat is not permissible to eat.[143]

A place with discernible filth[144] on it is purified by the removal of the body of filth [even if washed only once], except for that which is difficult to remove.[145]

A place with indiscernible filth on it is purified by washing and squeezing the area three times.[146] If the area cannot be squeezed, then [it is purified by washing it three times, waiting between each wash] until the water stops dripping.[147]

---

whose meat is impermissible to eat, as well as the saliva of predatory land animals and dogs, are also deemed heavy filth (*Marāqī 'l-Falāḥ* 1:220).

140 This also includes all intoxicating drinks (*Hadiyya* 47; *Radd* 1:213).

141 Anything whose exit from the human body necessitates *wuḍū'* or *ghusl* is deemed heavy filth, including blood (or pus) that *flows*; urine; feces; sperm or sexual fluid (*manī*); presexual fluid (*madhy*); white, murky fluid that accompanies urination in men (*wady*); the blood from menstruation (*ḥayḍ*), postnatal bleeding (*nifās*), or dysfunctional uterine bleeding (*istiḥāḍa*); and a mouthful (or more) of vomit (*Marāqī 'l-Falāḥ* 1:220–1; *Badā'iʿ* 1:193). If *wuḍū'* is not nullified thereby, such as blood that surfaces but doesn't flow, or vomit that is less than a mouthful, then the fluid is not impure (*Ṭaḥṭāwī* 1:220; *Badā'iʿ* 1:195).

142 Such as deer, sheep, goats, and cows (*Marāqī 'l-Falāḥ* 1:221).

143 That is, predatory birds, such as eagles, falcons, and hawks. Droppings of nonpredatory birds that do not fly, such as chickens, duck, and geese, are heavy filth. Droppings of nonpredatory birds that fly, such as pigeons and sparrows, are pure (*Marāqī 'l-Falāḥ* 1:69, 220–2).

144 Discernible filth refers to that which can be seen after having dried, such as blood. That which cannot be seen after drying, such as urine, is termed indiscernible filth (*Marāqī 'l-Falāḥ*, *Ṭaḥṭāwī* 1:226; *Durr*, *Radd* 1:218–9).

145 Difficulty is defined as having to use other than water, such as soap, to remove any remaining trace of the filth, i.e., color or smell. Hence, once the body of filth is removed with water, one is not obligated to use soap or to heat the water to remove any remaining color that cold water alone cannot remove. Also, once the body is removed with water, any remaining smell is excused even if it is not difficult to remove (*Marāqī 'l-Falāḥ*, *Ṭaḥṭāwī* 1:226; *Hadiyya* 50; *Durr*, *Radd* 1:219; *Tabyīn* 1:75).

146 Placing the affected area under flowing water such that water strikes the area, leaves it, and is replaced with other water for a total of three times (based on reasonable likelihood), takes the place of washing and squeezing three times (*Marāqī 'l-Falāḥ*, *Ṭaḥṭāwī* 1:229; *Durr*, *Radd* 1:222). If one does wash and squeeze, each squeeze should be with one's full strength, until the area stops dripping. If, however, the cloth or fabric is delicate, then after each of the three washes one may simply let it dry so as not to ruin the item (*Marāqī 'l-Falāḥ*, *Ṭaḥṭāwī* 1:228; *Durr*, *Radd* 1:221; *Hadiyya* 51).

147 For that which by its nature cannot be squeezed, such as pottery or carpets, one lets it dry

The amount of heavy filth that is excused [for the sake of the prayer] is the size of a *dirham* (silver coin).[148] The amount of light filth that is excused is less than a fourth of one's [entire] garment [or one's entire body].[149]

Light spray of urine is excused if [the size of] each dot is [no larger than] the head of a [pin-sized] needle.[150]

[The following situations are examples of filth not transferring from one area to another:][151]

- □ The moisture[152] that appears on a dry, pure garment, after being wrapped in a damp, impure garment[153] that would not drip if squeezed, is not deemed impure.
- □ A wet [clean] foot that steps on impure ground, without any trace[154] of filth appearing on the foot, is not deemed impure.
- □ A damp, pure garment that is placed on impure ground, without any trace of filth appearing on the garment, is not deemed impure.
- □ The body of one who sleeps in a [dry] impure garment, which be-

after each wash, for a total of three times. "Drying" in this context means for it to no longer drip, or as Ibn ᶜĀbidīn mentions, to become such that one's hand would not get wet from touching it; complete drying is not a condition. Furthermore, one may expedite the process by soaking the water up with a pure cloth (or vacuum suction) after each wash (*Durr*, *Radd* 1:221).

148 That is, the surface area of the inner concave circle of the palm. The way to determine its size is to place water on the hand with the palm extended; the water which remains on the palm indicates the approximate area (about 3–5 cm in diameter) (*Marāqī 'l-Falāḥ* 1:222; *Durr*, *Radd* 1:211; *Hadiyya* 48). Although excused, to pray with that amount of filth is disliked (*makrūh tanzīhan*), and entails doing wrong (*isā'a*), yet is not sinful. Praying with filth less than that amount is disliked yet does not entail doing wrong (*Radd* 1:210–11).

149 There are two positions on this matter: the amount excused is (1) one-fourth or less of one's entire body or garment (as inserted in brackets above), or (2) one-fourth or less of the limb affected, such as the hand, foot, etc.; or of the segment of the garment affected, such as the sleeve, front panel of shirt, etc. Ibn ᶜĀbidīn inclines toward the latter position (*Radd* 1:213–4), yet both are sound and followable, as each is given precedence by various Ḥanafī imāms (*Durr* 1:213–4; *Marāqī 'l-Falāḥ*, *Ṭaḥṭāwī* 1:223; *Hadiyya* 49).

150 The legal reasoning is that such spray is difficult to avoid (*Hidāya* 1:38).

151 Another case is if filth falls into pure water causing some water to splash on one's garment or body—if a trace of the filth appears, the filth transferred; otherwise, it did not (*Marāqī 'l-Falāḥ*, *Ṭaḥṭāwī* 1:224). In addition, if wind passes over filth and then over a clean garment, the garment is not rendered impure unless a trace of the filth appears on it (*Hadiyya* 49).

152 That is, moisure that has no trace of filth, and that would not drip if the garment were wrung (*Hadiyya* 49).

153 That is, a garment affected with filth that then became wet with water (or any pure liquid), as opposed to a garment damp from urine (or any impure liquid), since the moisture that would then appear on the originally dry, pure garment would be the urine itself and hence impure (*Hadiyya* 49).

154 A trace of filth is either its color, smell, or taste (*Marāqī 'l-Falāḥ* 1:225; *Imdād* 37).

> comes wet from [his] sweat, without any trace of filth appearing on his body, is not deemed impure.

An area [whether body, garment or otherwise] with filth on it may be cleaned by water, even if used (*mustaʿmal*),[155] as well as any liquid that [by its nature] removes[156] [filth], such as rosewater or vinegar.

Complete chemical transformation (*istiḥāla*) is a means of purification [of filth itself], such as feces turning into salt or ashes.[157]

A leather sock (*khuff*) or the like [such as a sandal] may be purified by [scraping or] rubbing [the affected area] on the ground or with dirt, *if* the filth on it had a solid body.[158] Washing in that case is not necessary.

A sword or the like[159] may be purified by wiping [its surface].[160]

The ground [of natural earth][161] may be purified by drying,[162] as long as no

155 The legal definition of "used" water (*mā' mustaʿmal*) is that which is used (a) on the body for any act of worship, such as washing one's hands before or after a meal with the intention of fulfilling the *sunna*, or (b) on the body, fulfilling an obligatory integral (*farḍ*) of *wuḍū'* or *ghusl*, even if unintentionally, such as a person in a state of ritual impurity washing his hands without an intention of *wuḍū'* or *ghusl*. In any case, "used" water is pure and may be used to remove filth, but is not *purifying* for the purposes of *wuḍū'* or *ghusl* (*Hadiyya* 14–5). Water used on other than the body, such as pots, clothes, or food, is not legally deemed "used" (*mustaʿmal*), and hence remains pure *and purifying* (for *wuḍū'* or *ghusl*) as long as there was no filth on the object (*Radd* 1:133).

156 A liquid that removes (filth) by its nature is one that is readily squeezed out of a cloth (that is soaked in that liquid) when wrung, such as rose water or vinegar, as opposed to milk, oil, or the like (*Tanwīr, Durr, Radd* 1:205).

157 Or like grape juice, which is pure, transforming into wine, which is impure, and then transforming into vinegar, which is pure (*Radd* 1:218).

158 Filth with a solid body refers to that which remains and can be seen on the outer surface of the *khuff* after drying, such as dung or blood. If the filth does not have a solid body, such as urine or wine, then the affected area must be washed, as the leather would have absorbed the filth. However, if one immediately rubs the liquid filth in dirt such that it *acquires* a solid body (i.e., after the leather sock becomes affected with the filth yet before its absorption), then the area may be purified by rubbing or scraping as described above (*Hadiyya* 51; *Kanz, Tabyīn* 1:70–1; *Hidāya* 1:36; *Durr, Radd* 1:206).

159 That is, any smooth surface without cracks or pores, such as a mirror; fingernail or toenail; bone; glass; china or porcelain; smooth, polished wood, silver, copper, etc., without engraving; or smooth tile surface (excluding the grout in between tiles due to their rough texture). The basis of this ruling is that such surfaces do not absorb the filth, while that which remains on the surface is removed by wiping (*Hadiyya* 51; *Hidāya* 1:37).

160 That is, wiping with a dry cloth—without any need for water or a liquid—such that no trace of filth remains, regardless of whether the filth is solid or liquid, with or without a solid body (*Marāqī 'l-Falāḥ* 1:231; *Hadiyya* 51; *Tabyīn* 1:72).

161 That is, as opposed to a rug on the ground. Rather, this issue deals with the earth as well as anything connected to the earth with stability such as trees, plants, or walls of a building (*Hadiyya* 52; *Marāqī 'l-Falāḥ, Ṭaḥṭāwī* 1:231; *Durr, Radd* 1:206–7).

162 Drying here does not refer to becoming completely dry, but rather *for the moisture to disap-*

trace of the filth remains visible, for the sake of praying [on that earth], but [its dirt may] not [be used] for *tayammum* [as the dirt is rendered pure, but not purifying].

A garment or one's body with dried sperm on it may be purified by scraping off the sperm.[163]

The hide of [any] dead animal is purified by actual tanning, [carried out by chemical agents] such as sant tree pods (*qaraẓ*) or pomegranate seeds; as well as by natural tanning, through the use of dirt, the sun, wind, or the like.

Thereafter [once the hide has been purified], one may pray on it or perform *wuḍū'* from [water inside] it [like from a water sack made from the hide]. An exception [however] is the skin of pigs and humans.[164]

Hides of animals whose meat may not be eaten may also be purified by slaughtering according to the Sacred Law (*dhakāt sharʿiyya*), as opposed to the meat [which remains impure].[165]

Anything [i.e., any body part] that does not have flowing blood in it is not rendered impure upon death [of the creature], such as [the following:]

- Hair,
- Cut feathers [as opposed to plucked ones, the ends of which are impure],
- The horn,
- The claw,
- Bone, as long as there is no fat on it.

A deer's pouch of musk, like the musk itself, is pure and may be eaten; the same ruling applies to civet (*zabād*).

---

pear; once this occurs—by any means, even if by wind or the passage of time—the area is rendered pure (for the prayer as mentioned above) (*Radd* 1:207).

163 That is, by scraping it off with one's hand such that it breaks apart (*Radd* 1:207).

164 The pig is impure in essence (*najis al-ʿayn*), meaning every physical part of its body, without exception, is impure. Hence, tanning does not purify its hide. Human skin is pure, yet it is forbidden to use and derive benefit from any part of the human body, out of reverence to it (*Hidāya* 1:23; *Durr* 1:136). The hides of all other animals, including dogs, elephants, and predatory animals, are purified by tanning (*Durr* 136–7).

165 The general rule is that any hide that may be purified by tanning may be purified by slaughtering according to the Sacred Law. For an animal whose meat is permissible to eat, the meat is also rendered pure by such slaughtering; if its meat is impermissible, the meat remains filthy (*Durr*, *Radd* 1:137).

WELLS

A small well of water is rendered impure if filth falls into it, such as urine, blood, or chicken droppings, even if a small amount without any trace of it appearing in the water.

The same ruling applies for a large amount of dung of camels, donkeys, or cattle, as opposed to a small amount [which is excused], namely, that which is not considered large by the one who sees it [in the well].

The following things also do not render the well impure:

- Pigeon or sparrow droppings;
- Dead creatures that have no blood[166] in them, such as [large] mosquitoes,[167] flies, wasps and scorpions;
- [Dead] sea creatures;[168]
- A creature that falls in [the well] yet comes out alive, as long as there was no filth on its body, including humans, camels, cattle, donkeys, predatory birds, and predatory land animals [i.e., anything but pig].

If an animal dies in a well,[169] then there are three categories [with regard to the legal ruling of how much water to remove, based on the creature's size, namely:]

1. Small, like a mouse, in which case it is mandatory (*wājib*) to remove 20 buckets [of water];
2. Medium, like a pigeon, in which case it is mandatory (*wājib*) to remove 40 buckets;
3. Large, in which case it is mandatory (*wājib*) to remove all of the water. The same ruling applies if the animal was small [or medium], yet its carcass became bloated or fragmented into pieces. If

166 That is, flowing blood (*Radd* 1:123, 148).

167 Mosquito blood is not impure, even if it was taken from another source, since it is not considered to have "flowed" (*Radd* 1:123; *Hadiyya* 13).

168 That is, creatures that are born in water and reside therein, such as fish, crabs, frogs, etc. Creatures that are born on land yet reside in water, such as duck and geese, do render wells (or any small body of water) impure upon their death (*Hadiyya* 13).

169 Or if a dead carcass is cast into the well (*Hadiyya* 16).

it is not possible to remove all of the water, then it is mandatory (*wājib*) to remove 200 buckets.

If the saliva of the animal touches the water, then all the water must be removed if the saliva was impure or doubtful. If it was pure yet disliked, then it is [merely] recommended (*mustaḥabb*) to remove the water [see next section for detail].

TYPES OF SALIVA

Saliva is of four types [with regard to the ruling of water that is mixed with it]:

1. Pure and purifying, and not disliked [to use for purification or to drink]: This is the saliva of a human being whose mouth was clean, even if in a state of major ritual impurity or a non-Muslim; the saliva of horses; and that of animals whose meat is permissible to eat.
2. Impure: This water may not be used for purification in any case, nor may it be drunk except by one in dire need, just as he may eat meat of an animal not ritually slaughtered. This category includes the saliva of dogs, pigs, and [predatory land animals such as] lions, wolves, hyenas, apes, and the like.
3. Disliked[170] if other [pure] water is available: This includes the saliva of housecats, released chickens,[171] predatory birds such as hawks or falcons, and creatures that roam around houses like mice and snakes. If no other water is available, it is not disliked to use this water for purification.
4. Saliva in which there is doubt regarding its *purifying* nature: This is the saliva of mules and donkeys. If no other water is available, one makes *wuḍū'* with this water, followed by *tayammum*, and then prays.

---

170 That is, mildly disliked (*makrūh tanzīhan*) (*Durr* 1:150).

171 That is, not enclosed in an area and fed, but rather released such that they roam around, as their beaks might touch filth. Enclosed chickens that are fed pure feed, however, do not roam around in filth (other than their own, which they avoid), and hence the use of water mixed with their saliva is not disliked (*Radd* 1:149).

CLEANING AFTER RELIEVING ONESELF (*ISTINJĀ'*)

[After urination] a man must ensure that no drops of urine remain in the urethra (*istibrā'*), until no trace of wetness [even] appears at the tip of the organ, since its appearance [there] prevents the validity of *wuḍū'*.[172]

If the filth [that exits the body] does not move beyond the exit hole itself, then it is *sunna*[173] to clean that area (*istinjā'*), by using a stone that removes [the filth], or the like.[174] One should wipe forwards and backwards until the area is clean. It is ideal to wash the area afterwards,[175] until one feels convinced that the filth is removed. Moreover, one should continue washing until the bad smell is gone. Finally, it is not permissible to expose one's nakedness [to others,[176] even to perform *istinjā'*].

If the filth moves beyond the exit hole, yet the amount that moved is less than what is excused,[177] the prayer [performed with it] is still valid. If, however, that amount is more [than what is excused], it is obligatory (*farḍ*) to remove it [with water or a liquid that removes], just as it is obligatory (*farḍ*) to perform the *ghusl* if one is in a state of major ritual impurity.

It is disliked to clean oneself (*istinjā'*) with a bone, dried dung, food, or

---

172 Ensuring that no drops of urine remain in the urethra (*istibrā'*) can be performed in many ways, such as by walking, clearing one's throat, lying on one's side, or gently squeezing the organ (without harming oneself), depending on whatever the person feels comfortable doing (*Durr* 1:230, *Marāqī 'l-Falāḥ* 1:74). One may not clean oneself (*istinjā'*) beforehand. The aim of *istibrā'* is to be *certain* that no trace of wetness remains at the surface of exit, which would otherwise prevent the validity of one's *wuḍū'*. Therefore, *istibrā'* is obligatory (*farḍ*), yet only for men, due to the nature of their organ. Women need only remain still for a moment after urination, and then may clean themselves (*istinjā'*) (*Radd* 1:230).

173 Cleaning oneself (*istinjā'*) is an emphasized *sunna* (*mu'akkada*), for both men and women, after using the lavatory. To do so after only passing gas is a reprehensible innovation (*bid'a*), since the gas itself is not impure (*Marāqī 'l-Falāḥ* 1:75).

174 One may use a stone that removes the filth (as opposed to a smooth stone) or the like, namely, anything that is pure and that removes, without causing harm, and without being an item of value or a respectable item (*Marāqī 'l-Falāḥ* 1:76). It is recommended, but not an emphasized *sunna*, that one wipe three times, or if more is needed, an odd number of times (*Durr*, *Radd* 1:225). One may use toilet paper, despite it having value, as it is specifically manufactured for cleaning oneself (*istinjā'*).

175 The optimal method is to both wipe (with toilet paper or the like) *and* to wash with water; followed in merit by only washing; followed in merit by only wiping, yet the emphasized *sunna* is fulfilled by any of these methods (*Radd* 1:226).

176 That is, anyone with whom the person may not have sexual intercourse (*Radd* 1:225).

177 That is, the surface area of the inner concave circle of the palm (see related note, p. 61).

anything of value like silk or cotton. It is also disliked to use one's right hand for cleaning oneself.[178]

One should enter the lavatory with the left foot, and seek refuge from Allāh beforehand. [While relieving oneself] one should sit neither facing the *qibla*, nor with one's back toward it.[179] Likewise, one should not face the sun or the moon.[180] One should not speak without necessity.

[After finishing] one should exit with the right foot, and then say: "Praise be to Allāh, Who removed harm from my body and granted me well-being" [p. 188].

After the servant purifies his garments, body, and prayer area, and commences the prayer (*ṣalāt*) or the like; accompanied with the truly beneficial purification [i.e., of the heart] from the likes of rancor and hatred, and from everything besides Allāh; intending to carry out His divine command; bearing in mind the greatness of His majesty and honor; with full hope that He will accept that which He has enjoined on him [of worship]; *then* it is hoped for him [the servant] to be granted Eternal Joy due to the [divine] acceptance of his devotion.

---

178 To use any of those things, or to use one's right hand, is prohibitively disliked (*makrūh taḥrīman*) (*Durr, Radd* 1:226–7).

179 Facing the direction of the *qibla* while relieving oneself, or turning one's back toward it, is prohibitively disliked (*makrūh taḥrīman*), even within a building. To face its direction, or turn one's back toward it, while cleaning oneself (*istinjā'*) is not sinful, yet entails poor etiquette since one's nakedness is revealed (*Marāqī 'l-Falāḥ, Ṭaḥṭāwī* 1:85–6; *Durr, Radd* 1:228).

180 To face the body (disc) of the sun or moon while relieving oneself is deemed mildly disliked (*makrūh tanzīhan*), unless one is inside a building in which case there is no harm (*Radd* 1:228).

The Ritual Prayer (Ṣalāt)

PRAYER TIMES

The times of the prescribed prayers are five:

1. The time of fajr (*ṣubḥ*) is from the entrance of true dawn[181] until [right before] sunrise.[182]
2. The time of ẓuhr is from [immediately after] midday (*zawāl*)[183] until [the time] when the shadow of any object is twice its own length, or [according to a second opinion] equivalent to its own length, excluding the amount of shadow at midday.[184] Imām Ṭaḥāwī preferred the second opinion, which is that of the two companions [Abū Yūsuf and Muḥammad].

---

181 "True dawn" refers to the horizontal white light that spreads across the horizon, as opposed to "false dawn," which is the vertical light that appears earlier and is followed by darkness (hence its name). The difference between the two, as well as the difference between the disappearance of the red and white twilight after sunset, is said to be 3 degrees (normally 12 minutes) (*Durr*, *Radd* 1:239–41). However, other factors could affect the time difference, such as location and latitude. Also, with respect to modern tables of prayer timings, the 18-degree time for fajr is more precautionary and should therefore be used, especially for fasting.

182 That is, at the start of sunrise, when the top of the disc first emerges above the horizon, the time of fajr is expired (*Hadiyya* 54; *Majmaʿ al-Anhur* 1:69).

183 The most accurate method of determining midday is to dig a straight stick into even ground (i.e., at a 90-degree angle) and note its shadow. If it continues to shorten, it is not yet midday. Once it ceases to shorten, it is midday and, hence, it is disliked to perform prayer at this time (see p. 71). After that, once the shadow begins to lengthen, the time of ẓuhr has entered (*Majmaʿ al-Anhur* 1:69; *Tabyīn* 1:80).

184 That is, the length of the still shadow at midday, that has ceased to shorten and not yet begun to lengthen, is excluded when determining the end of ẓuhr and beginning of ʿaṣr (*Tabyīn* 1:80).

3. The time of ʿaṣr is from that point [on which there is disagreement] until [right before] sunset.[185]
4. The time of maghrib is from that point [sunset] until the disappearance of the red twilight, according to the position given for legal verdict (*fatwā*).[186]
5. The time of ʿishāʾ and witr is from that point until [right before] fajr. One may not pray witr before ʿishāʾ due to the condition of praying them in the correct order.[187]

The following times are recommended (*mustaḥabb*):[188]

- □ For fajr, when light begins to appear (*isfār*);[189]
- □ For ẓuhr in the summer, when the weather becomes cooler;
- □ For ʿaṣr, to delay it until *before* the sun changes;[190]

185 That is, when the disc of the sun is completely below the horizon, the time of ʿaṣr has expired and the time of maghrib begins (*Majmaʿ al-Anhur* 1:70).

186 This is the opinion of the two companions (Abū Yūsuf and Muḥammad) and, as stated in many classical Ḥanafī works including this text, the position of legal verdict (*fatwā*) for the Ḥanafī school. The opinion of Imām Abū Ḥanīfa, however, is that the end of maghrib (and hence the beginning of ʿishāʾ) occurs later, namely, with the disappearance of the white twilight after sunset. This opinion is also a reliable position in the school, as it is given precedence in the *Ikhtiyār* (1:57), *Fatḥ al-Qadīr* (1:196–7), *Kanz*, *Tabyīn* (1:80–1), and other works. Ibn ʿĀbidīn seems to support this opinion in terms of its legal strength. At the end of his discussion, however, he affirms the opinion of the two companions, citing the numerous works that explicitly state it as the position of legal verdict. His main reasoning is that the practice of most Muslim lands in his time corresponded with it (*Radd* 1:241).

187 If, however, one does so out of forgetfulness, or prays them in order yet later realizes that ʿishāʾ alone was invalid, then he does not have to repeat the witr prayer since such excuses are deemed acceptable (*Majmaʿ al-Anhur*, *Al-Durr al-Muntaqā* 1:70; *Durr*, *Radd* 1:241).

188 That is, it is recommended for men to pray at these times, unless doing so would entail missing the congregation, as that takes precedence (*Ṭaḥṭāwī* 1:255). For women, it is recommended to pray fajr while it is still dark, and the remaining prayers after the men's congregation has finished (*Marāqī 'l-Falāḥ* 1:254; *Durr* 1:245). Some Ḥanafī scholars, however, maintained that for women, it is recommended to pray all five prayers at the beginning of their times since they do not pray in congregation (*Radd* 1:166, 245).

189 That is, it is recommended for the men to delay fajr until a time before sunrise such that, if one realized that his prayer was invalid, he would have enough time to perform *ghusl* (if needed) and repeat the prayer at the same pace with which he performed it the first time, and still finish before sunrise (*Hadiyya* 54; *Radd* 1:245). The recommended delay is to both start and end the prayer once light has appeared (*Majmaʿ al-Anhur* 1:71).

190 That is, such that one can look at its disc without harm. To delay the prayer to this point is deemed prohibitively disliked (*makrūh taḥrīman*), even for a sick person or a traveller (*Marāqī 'l-Falāḥ* 1:256, 260). The recommended delay is to before this time, as it allows one to pray extra

- ☐ For ẓuhr in the winter and for maghrib [always], to pray as soon as the time enters;
- ☐ In cloudy weather, to pray ᶜaṣr and ᶜishāʾ as soon as the time enters; while for the other prayers, to delay them somewhat.[191]

There are three times of the day in which any prayer that was obligatory *before*[192] these times is rendered invalid if performed *in* these times:

- ☐ At sunrise,[193]
- ☐ At midday,[194]
- ☐ At sunset, except for ᶜaṣr of that day.[195]

It is disliked to pray voluntary prayers in the following times:

- ☐ The three times mentioned above;

---

voluntary prayers beforehand, since it is disliked to do so after having prayed ᶜaṣr (*Majmaᶜ al-Anhur* 1:71; *Tabyīn* 1:83).

191 Namely, to somewhat delay fajr, ẓuhr, and maghrib, so as to ensure that the time has truly entered (*Durar* 1:53; *Majmaᶜ al-Anhur* 1:71; *Tabyīn* 1:85).

192 That is, one cannot perform make-up prayers during these three times, nor a prostration of recital for a verse recited before these times, all of which would be invalid and sinful. If, however, something becomes obligatory (or mandatory) *within* one of these three times, its performance *within* that time would be valid. For example, if a funeral procession arrived for its prayer (*janāza*) within such a time, the prayer is performed therein, and that would not be disliked at all. If a verse of prostration were recited within such a time, the prostration could be performed therein, as it would be valid yet mildly disliked (*makrūh tanzīhan*). It would be better to delay the prostration until after that time. If a person on *ḥajj* or *ᶜumra* initiated a *ṭawāf* within such a time, then the mandatory (*wājib*) two *rakᶜas* to be performed upon completion would be *valid* therein, yet prohibitively disliked (*makrūh taḥrīman*) and hence sinful. Therefore, one must wait until the time ends before performing that prayer. Finally, it would be prohibitively disliked (*makrūh taḥrīman*) to perform any *voluntary* prayer in one of these three times, even one with a specific cause such as the two *rakᶜas* of greeting the mosque (*Hadiyya* 55).

193 That is, until the sun is approximately one or two spears length (a spear is about 12 hand-spans, or 3 m) above the horizon (*Marāqī ʾl-Falāḥ* 1:260; *Hadiyya* 55; *Radd* 1:558). This is roughly 15–20 minutes after sunrise.

194 That is, when the shadow stops shortening, yet before it starts lengthening. Hence, if one performs an obligatory or mandatory prayer during this time, such that any part of the prayer (before completion of the last integral—see p. 77) falls in this short span of time, the prayer itself is rendered invalid (*Ṭaḥṭāwī* 1:260). This is roughly 7–10 minutes before ẓuhr.

195 That is, at the dimming of the sun during the last portion of the day before sunset, such that one can look at it without any harm to the eye (*Marāqī ʾl-Falāḥ*, *Ṭaḥṭāwī* 1:260). An exception is ᶜaṣr of that day, which remains valid even during that time and hence obligatory to pray, *despite the sin entailed in delaying it to this time* (*Al-Durr al-Muntaqā* 1:73; *Hadiyya* 55). This is roughly 15–20 minutes before sunset, although it depends on certain factors such as latitude and time of the year.

- ☐ During a religious sermon (*khuṭba*);[196]
- ☐ Before the obligatory prayer of fajr,[197] except for the two *rakʿas* of *sunna*;
- ☐ After the obligatory prayer of fajr is performed, without exception [until after the disliked time of sunrise];
- ☐ After the ʿaṣr prayer is performed, until sunset.[198]

It is not valid to combine any two obligatory prayers in one prayer time, except at ʿArafāt and Muzdalifa; that is, the pilgrim on *ḥajj* may combine ẓuhr and ʿaṣr [in the time of ẓuhr on the Day of ʿArafa], and must delay maghrib until [the time of] ʿishā' at Muzdalifa.

THE CALL TO PRAYER (*ADHĀN*) AND ITS COMMENCEMENT (*IQĀMA*)

The *adhān* and *iqāma* are emphasized *sunnas*[199] for the five daily prayers[200] and the Friday prayer, yet not for any other prayer.

196 That is, specifically once the imām appears or stands up for it, until after the prayer itself is completed. Another time in which it is disliked to perform voluntary prayers is after sunset, before the performance of the obligatory (*farḍ*) prayer of maghrib, so as not to delay the prayer much, as that is deemed mildly disliked (*makrūh tanzīhan*) (*Hadiyya* 56; *Ṭaḥṭāwī* 1:264–5). Also, it is prohibitively disliked (*makrūh taḥrīman*) to delay the maghrib prayer until the time when "the stars are numerous in appearance" (perhaps 40 minutes or so after sunset, although this depends on certain factors such as latitude and time of the year), as it is to delay the ʿishā' prayer until half of the night has passed. "Night" refers to the period from sunset until true dawn (*Marāqī 'l-Falāḥ*, *Ṭaḥṭāwī* 1:257–8).

197 That is, after the time of fajr enters (true dawn), yet before the actual performance of the obligatory fajr prayer.

198 For the time periods of (a) between true dawn and sunrise, and (b) between the performance of ʿaṣr and the dimming of the sun before sunset, make-up prayers can be performed therein, but not voluntary prayers, nor the mandatory (*wājib*) two *rakʿas* to be performed upon completion of *ṭawāf*. It would be prohibitively disliked (*makrūh taḥrīman*) to do them in these times. Rather, one must wait until (a) after the post-sunrise time period in which prayers are also disliked, and (b) after sunset (maghrib) (*Hadiyya* 55).

199 Yet with regard to incurring sin if omitted, they are at the level of mandatory (*wājib*), as they are among the sacred symbols (*shaʿā'ir*) of Islam. However, this applies only to men, as it is deemed prohibitively disliked (*makrūh taḥrīman*) for women to perform either the *adhān* or *iqāma*, since it is disliked for them to pray in their own congregation (without men) (*Hadiyya* 56–7; *Durr* 1:257; *Majmaʿ al-Anhur, Al-Durr al-Muntaqā* 1:76).

200 That is, whether prayed on time (*adā'*) or late (*qaḍā'*), on a journey or while residing, even if he is praying *alone*. For a traveller, the *iqāma* alone fulfills the *sunna*, while the *adhān* beforehand

When one hears the *adhān* performed according to the *sunna*, he should respond[201] to the one performing it, and then make *duʿā'* for the Prophet ﷺ to be granted the Station of Mediation (*wasīla*) [p. 190].

The phrase *Allāhu akbar* is said four times at the beginning, while the remaining phrases are said twice. The same applies to the *iqāma*.

Hence, the person calling the *adhān* says the following [p. 189]:

"Allāh is the greatest" (four times).

"I testify that there is no deity except Allāh" (twice).

"I testify that Muḥammad is the Messenger of Allāh" (twice).

"Come to the prayer" (twice).

"Come to success" (twice).

In the *adhān* for fajr, he adds: "Prayer is better than sleep" (twice).

In the *iqāma*, he adds: "The prayer has commenced" (twice).

Both additions [for fajr and for the *iqāma*] are said after the phrase "Come to success."

"Allāh is the greatest" (twice).

"There is no deity except Allāh" (once).

The person calling the *adhān* should pause shortly between each set of phrases, while he should hasten in the *iqāma*. Between the two, he should sit [for a short amount of time], except for maghrib.

It is disliked for someone in a state of major ritual impurity to perform either

---

is recommended (*mandūb*). For a man praying alone in his house, the *adhān* and *iqāma* of the neighborhood mosque fulfill the *sunna*, although it is still recommended for him to perform both (*Hadiyya* 57; *Majmaʿ al-Anhur* 1:75; *Marāqī 'l-Falāḥ* 1:273; *Durr, Radd* 1:257, 264–5).

201 The *sunna* method of performing the *adhān* is as follows: in Arabic, by a man, in the prayer time, and free from grammatical mistakes or exaggerated melodious intonation. If performed accordingly, then one should respond to it by repeating each set of its phrases. One also adds *Lā ḥawla wa lā quwwata illā bi 'Llāh* ("There is no power nor might except through Allāh") after *Ḥayya ʿala 'ṣ-ṣalāh* and after *Ḥayya ʿala 'l-falāḥ*. Also, after *Aṣ-ṣalātu khayrum mina 'n-nawm*, one does not repeat it but says instead *Ṣadaqta wa bararta wa bi 'l-ḥaqqi naṭaqta* ("You are right and did well; with the truth did you speak") or *Mā shā Allāhu kān* [*wa mā lam yasha' lam yakun*] ("Whatever Allāh wills, exists [and whatever He does not will, does not exist]") (*Hadiyya* 59). Verbally responding to the *adhān* is considered mandatory (*wājib*) by some, recommended (*mandūb*) by others, who instead deem it mandatory to respond with one's feet (i.e., to pray in congregation) (*Ṭaḥṭāwī* 1:283; *Durr, Radd* 1:265). Some cases where one does not respond verbally are if one is praying, delivering a sermon (*khuṭba*) or listening to one, teaching a lesson or studying in one, eating, having intercourse, or relieving oneself (*Marāqī 'l-Falāḥ* 1:284). If it is performed contrary to the *sunna*, then it is disliked and hence one neither listens to it nor responds with repetition. This includes an *adhān* with mistakes or exaggerated melodious intonation, as opposed to mere beautification of the voice, which is permissible (*Majmaʿ al-Anhur* 1:76; *Kanz, Tabyīn* 1:90–1). Also, if it is performed before the prayer time, it does not fulfill the *sunna* and hence must be repeated afterwards (*Durr, Radd* 1:258).

the *adhān* or the *iqāma*, or for someone in a state of minor ritual impurity to perform the *iqāma*.[202]

Neither of the two may be recited except in Arabic, even if it is known that it is the *adhān*, according to the sounder position (*aṣaḥḥ*).

It is recommended that the person calling the *adhān* be a righteous person; be one who knows both the *sunna* of how to perform the *adhān* as well as the prayer timings; be in a state of ritual purity; face the *qibla*; place his index finger in each ear;[203] and turn [only] his face toward the right when saying "Come to the prayer," and the left when saying "Come to success."

CONDITIONS (*SHARĀ'IṬ*) OF THE PRAYER

It is not valid to begin the prayer without having fulfilled its conditions,[204] which are, namely:

1. Being in a state of ritual purity, from both minor and major ritual impurity;
2. Being free from any physical filth, on one's garments, body, and place of prayer,[205] except for that which is excused [see above, p. 61];
3. Covering one's nakedness (*ʿawra*), which for the man is the area right below the navel until right below the knees; and for the woman the entire body except for the face, hands and feet. The [nakedness of the] slave girl is the same as that of the man, except for the abdomen and the back [which are part of her nakedness];

---

202 It is not disliked for him to perform the *adhān*, although doing so in a state of ritual purity is recommended. If *adhān* is performed by someone in a state of *major* ritual impurity, it is disliked (as mentioned above) and hence should be repeated. The same applies if performed by a child that has not reached the age of discernment. The *iqāma* is not repeated, regardless of who performs it, unless an unrelated action separates it from the prayer. This includes excessive eating or speech, as the *sunna* is to commence the prayer with the end of the *iqāma* without a break (*Majmaʿ al-Anhur*, *Al-Durr al-Muntaqā* 1:78; *Durar* 1:56; *Radd* 1:258, 268).

203 Or place his hands over the ears, or even one hand over one ear (*Majmaʿ al-Anhur* 1:77; *Durar* 1:55; *Radd* 1:260).

204 Both conditions and integrals (see next section) are obligatory (*farḍ*). Hence, if any one of the conditions or integrals is omitted, the prayer itself is rendered invalid (*Hadiyya* 60).

205 That is, the place of both feet, both knees, both hands, and the forehead. If, however, one's garment falls onto filth elsewhere during the prayer and there is no transfer, the prayer is valid (see discussion on transfer of filth, p. 61) (*Hadiyya* 60; *Radd* 1:270).

4. Facing the *qibla* [i.e., the Kaʿba] itself, for one in Makka who can see the Kaʿba; or facing the direction (*jiha*)[206] of the *qibla* for others;
5. The entrance of the prayer time;[207]
6. The intention, the place of which is in the heart;[208]
7. The *taḥrīma* [opening *Allāhu akbar* of the prayer], the place of which is the tongue; hence, it must be *uttered* such that one can hear himself. Additionally, it must coincide with the intention in the heart, without a separation like talking, eating, or [any] action that contradicts the actions of the prayer.[209] Likewise, everything uttered in the prayer, which excludes the intention, takes the same ruling, so one should give it due consideration.[210]

Some of the above conditions are overlooked if there is a valid excuse, such as lack of water to remove excess filth; lack of a garment to cover oneself; fear of an enemy, preventing one from facing the *qibla*, in which case one prays in

---

206 That is, within 45 degrees on each side when facing the Kaʿba (*Majmaʿ al-Anhur* 1:83).

207 Another condition is conviction, or reasonable surety, that the prayer time has entered (*Hadiyya* 61). Hence, if one is not at least reasonably sure that the time has entered but prays anyway, then the prayer is invalid, *even* if it were prayed within the time.

208 The intention is a firm determination of the heart to do something. The minimum valid intention for the prayer is such that if the person were asked regarding it, he would be able to respond immediately, without having to think or reflect. When making the intention for an obligatory (*farḍ*) or mandatory (*wājib*) prayer, one must also specify which prayer is about to be performed, such as *ʿaṣr* for example. This is not a condition for emphasized *sunna*, *tarāwīḥ*, or general voluntary (*nafl*) prayers, as the intention of prayer alone suffices. Finally, the follower in a congregation must also intend praying behind the imām, yet without having to specify the imām (*Marāqī 'l-Falāḥ* 1:306–9; *Majmaʿ al-Anhur* 1:85–6; *Tabyīn* 1:99; *Durr*, *Radd* 1:278–282).

209 That is, if one makes the intention to pray yet engages in an unrelated action—such as eating or speaking—before the prayer, without renewing the intention, then the prayer is invalid. If, however, there is no separation between the intention and the *taḥrīma*, or the separation is by something related to the prayer—such as *dhikr*, *wuḍū'*, or walking to the mosque—then the prayer is valid. Also, the intention cannot be made after the *taḥrīma*. Finally, the *taḥrīma* must be done in the standing position, even if the back is bent, as long as the hands could not touch the knees if extended (i.e., not in the bowing position) (*Hadiyya* 61–2; *Marāqī 'l-Falāḥ* 1:301–2; *Tabyīn* 1:99; *Durr*, *Radd* 1:279).

210 That is, everything recited in the ritual prayer must be *uttered* such that the person can hear himself (assuming a quiet environment), or—based on another opinion—minimally that one's lips and tongue move. Otherwise, if one simply *thought* of the recitation, litanies and supplications without *uttering* them, they are given no consideration, so the prayer itself is rendered invalid (*Marāqī 'l-Falāḥ* 1:303–4). An exception to this ruling with respect to recitation of Qur'ān is the follower in congregational prayer, as it is sinful for him to recite Qur'ān behind the imām. The follower does recite all litanies and supplications of the prayer though.

whatever direction he feels secure; or general inability to face the *qibla*, due to sickness or the like, in which case one prays in whatever direction he is able.

If one does not know the direction of the *qibla*,[211] he should make a reasonable educated guess (*taḥarrī*) and pray in that direction.[212]

If one has many containers of water, with more than half of them containing purifying water, and has doubt as to which one[s] of them contains purifying water, he should also make an educated guess and then use the water of that container.

If one has multiple garments and at least one of them is pure, he should make an educated guess and pray in that garment.[213]

INTEGRALS (*ARKĀN*) OF THE PRAYER

1. The *taḥrīma* according to Imām Muḥammad, while according to the other two Imāms, it is a condition (*sharṭ*) [as mentioned above];
2. Standing[214] if one is physically able,[215] except for voluntary prayers;[216]

211 That is, and there is no one from that locality to inform him, nor any mosque or prayer niche (*miḥrāb*) there aligned toward the *qibla* (*Imdād* 251).

212 In which case the prayer is valid even if he later comes to know that he was incorrect. If he finds out during the prayer, he must immediately turn accordingly, and then continue in the prayer without having to restart (*Imdād* 252–3; *Multaqā* 1:84).

213 For these two cases, however (as opposed to the earlier case of the *qibla*), if he later comes to know that he was incorrect, he must repeat the prayer (*Marāqī 'l-Falāḥ* 1:64).

214 Standing is defined as a position in which if one were to extend his arms toward his knees, they would not reach them (*Marāqī 'l-Falāḥ* 1:310; *Durr* 1:298). According to the majority, one's feet should ideally be spaced the width of about four outspread fingers apart. This is considered an emphasized *sunna* according to *Imdād* (267). Incidentally, the narration of "foot-to-foot" describing the members of congregational prayer is an expression meaning that they would stand side-by-side, not a literal depiction of their feet (*Radd* 1:299).

215 That is, if one is physically able to stand and perform prostration (*sujūd*), then standing is an integral and hence obligatory (*farḍ*). If he is unable to stand, or if standing is very difficult, then he may pray sitting yet with normal bowing (*rukūʿ*) and prostration (*sujūd*). If he is able to stand yet not able to perform prostration, then he must pray with head movements (see related section, p. 94). It is recommended that he do so while sitting, although he may do so while standing as well (*Durr*, *Radd* 1:299).

216 Hence, voluntary prayers may be prayed sitting, yet doing so without an excuse entails half the reward. An exception is the two-*rakʿa sunna* of fajr, which must be performed standing due to it being the strongest of emphasized *sunnas* (*Hadiyya* 62; *Durr* 1:299).

3. Recitation of Qur'ān, even if only one verse,[217] in any two *rakʿas* of the obligatory prayer and in all *rakʿas* of witr and voluntary prayers, unless one is a follower in a congregation, since there is no recitation of Qur'ān for him;[218]
4. Bowing (*rukūʿ*);[219]
5. Prostration (*sujūd*), namely, with one's forehead, both hands, both knees, and bottom of the toes of both feet;[220]
6. The final sitting, for [at least] the length of *tashahhud*.[221]

It is obligatory (*farḍ*) for the one praying to end the prayer by his own action. It is mandatory (*wājib*) that this action be saying the word *as-salām* [twice] for every prayer, as we shall mention below.

---

217 That consists of at least two words, such as *Thumma naẓar* ("Then he looked" Qur'ān 74:21), in order to fulfill the obligatory (*farḍ*) integral (*Marāqī 'l-Falāḥ* 1:311). Also, the recitation must be done in the standing position and, as mentioned earlier, *uttered* such that the person would be able to hear himself if it were a quiet environment (see related note, p 75) (*Hadiyya* 62–3).

218 If the follower recites Qur'ān, even the Fātiḥa, it is deemed prohibitively disliked (*makrūh taḥrīman*). Rather, he listens attentively if the imām recites aloud, or remains silent if the imām recites silently (*Marāqī 'l-Falāḥ* 1:314; *Tanwīr*, *Durr* 1:366; *Hadiyya* 63).

219 Bowing (*rukūʿ*) is defined as bending the back to the extent that if one were to extend his arms toward his knees, they would reach them (*Ṭaḥṭāwī* 1:315; *Durr* 1:300; *Hadiyya* 63).

220 It is obligatory (*farḍ*) to place the following limbs on the ground: a part of the forehead, one hand, one knee, and a part of one toe of either foot. This fulfills a minimum valid prostration (*sajda*). The prostration is not valid unless the place bears the weight of the head. Also, the place of the forehead cannot be elevated above the place of the feet by more than 25 cm. Both prostrations of each *rakʿa* are obligatory (*Radd* 1:300; *Marāqī 'l-Falāḥ*, *Ṭaḥṭāwī* 1:316–7; *Hadiyya* 63). It is mandatory (*wājib*) to place most of the forehead, the hard part (bone) of the nose, both hands, both knees, and the toes of both feet on the ground. It is an emphasized *sunna* to place the bottom of the toes on the ground such that they face the *qibla* (*Radd* 1:320, 335–6, 339; *Marāqī 'l-Falāḥ*, *Ṭaḥṭāwī* 1:316–9; *Hadiyya* 66).

221 That is, the shortest time it takes one to recite the *tashahhud* completely (from *At-Taḥiyyātu li 'Llāhi* until *ʿabduhū wa rasūluh*—see p. 191), as fast as possible yet with proper articulation of its words. Also, the final sitting must be performed *after* all other integrals for the prayer to be valid. For example, if one realizes after the final sitting that a prostration was omitted earlier, he would prostrate and then *repeat* the final sitting (and then perform the forgetfulness prostration). Otherwise if he does not repeat the final sitting, the prayer would be rendered invalid (*Marāqī 'l-Falāḥ* 1:456; *Durr*, *Radd* 1:301; *Hadiyya* 64).

MANDATORY REQUISITES (*WĀJIBĀT*) OF THE PRAYER

Among them[222] are the following:[223]

1. To say the words *Allāhu akbar* specifically [as opposed to other phrases of remembrance] to begin every prayer [i.e., for the *taḥrīma*];
2. To recite the Fātiḥa[224] as well as a *sūra* or three verses[225] after it, in any two *rakʿas* of the obligatory prayer and in all *rakʿas* of the voluntary prayer;
3. To do the above recitation specifically in the first two *rakʿas* of the obligatory prayer;
4. To perform prostration with [most of] the forehead and [the hard part of] the nose;
5. To perform the second prostration before moving on to other parts of the prayer;
6. To be still for at least a moment[226] in every integral of the prayer;[227]
7. The first sitting;[228]

---

222 If a mandatory requisite is omitted, the prayer is still valid yet deficient. If it were omitted on purpose, it is sinful and hence mandatory (*wājib*) to repeat the prayer, just as it is if one does something prohibitively disliked (*makrūh taḥrīman*) during the prayer. If omitted by accident, then one must perform the forgetfulness prostration at the end of the prayer (see related section, p. 106) (*Hadiyya* 65; *Durr* 1:306–7).

223 It is also mandatory (*wājib*) to rise from the first sitting as soon as one has recited the *tashahhud*. If one forgets and instead remains sitting until he recites *Allāhumma ṣalli ʿalā Muḥammad*, he has missed this requisite. If he recites less before recalling and standing, then it is excused (*Durr, Radd* 1:313; *Hadiyya* 66). Another mandatory requisite is to perform each obligatory (*farḍ*) and mandatory (*wājib*) element of the prayer in its proper place. If, for example, one finished the recitation and then accidentally remained standing while thinking—not engaged in any sort of remembrance, but rather silent for the length of time it takes to say *Subḥāna 'Llāh* three times in a measured pace—then he missed this requisite by delaying bowing, and would therefore need to perform a forgetfulness prostration (*Durr* 1:315).

224 That is, the entire Fātiḥa, as each verse is mandatory. An exception is if one fears the time expiring for fajr, because sunrise actually nullifies the prayer. In that case, he simply recites one verse to fulfill the obligation and complete the prayer on time (*Hadiyya* 65; *Durr, Radd* 1:307).

225 That is, three short verses, the shortest being *Thumma naẓar, Thumma ʿabasa wa basar, Thumma adbara wa 'stakbar* (Qur'ān 74:21–3), or one long verse of equivalent length or more, such as Āyat al-Kursī (2:255) or the like (*Durr, Radd* 1:308).

226 That is, for enough time to say *Subḥāna 'Llāh* once (*Hadiyya* 66; *Durr* 1:312).

227 That is, in bowing (*rukūʿ*) and prostration (*sujūd*), as well as in the standing after bowing (*qawma*) and in the sitting between prostrations (*jalsa*) (*Hadiyya* 66; *Radd* 1:312).

228 That is, the sitting after the first two *rakʿas* in a three or four-*rakʿa* prayer, for the length

8. To recite the entire[229] *tashahhud* in both sittings;
9. To say the word *as-salām*;[230]
10. To recite the *qunūt*[231] in the witr prayer [see p. 192];
11. To recite the [six] extra *takbīrs*[232] in the two ʿĪd prayers;
12. For the imām, to recite Qur'ān out loud in [the first two *rakʿas* of] the loud obligatory prayers;[233]
13. For both the imām and the one praying alone, to recite Qur'ān silently in the other *rakʿas* of the obligatory prayers.[234]

EMPHASIZED *SUNNAS* OF THE PRAYER

Among them[235] are the following:

---

of time to recite the *tashahhud* therein. The sitting after the forgetfulness prostration is also a mandatory (*wājib*) requisite (*Hadiyya* 66).

229 Hence, omitting a part of it takes the same ruling as omitting all of it, namely, requiring a forgetfulness prostration if by accident, or being sinful if on purpose (*Durr*, *Radd* 1:313).

230 That is, *twice* when ending the prayer, each one being mandatory. Adding *ʿalaykum wa raḥmatu 'Llāh* is a *sunna* (*Hadiyya* 67; *Durr*, *Radd* 1:314).

231 Any supplication (*duʿā'*) fulfills this requisite (see related note, p. 97) (*Hadiyya* 67; *Durr* 1:315).

232 That is, three in the first *rakʿa* and three in the second, each one being mandatory (*Durr*, *Radd* 1:315). This is the optimal method according to the Ḥanafī school, yet to do seven in the first *rakʿa* and five in the second is also valid, for which one must follow the imām in prayer (*Marāqī 'l-Falāḥ* 2:155–6).

233 Namely, both *rakʿas* of fajr, the first two *rakʿas* of maghrib and ʿishā', both *rakʿas* of the Friday prayer and two ʿĪd prayers, and the *tarāwīḥ* and congregational witr in Ramaḍān. For these *rakʿas*, a man praying alone has the choice of reciting aloud or silently, even if making up the prayer. Women do not recite aloud for any prayer (*Mukhtār* 1:76; *Hadiyya* 67; *Radd* 1:315).

234 Namely, all *rakʿas* of ẓuhr and ʿaṣr, the third *rakʿa* of maghrib, and the third and fourth *rakʿas* of ʿishā' (*Hadiyya* 67; *Radd* 1:315).

235 The following are also emphasized *sunnas* of the prayer: while standing, to keep the feet about four-fingers apart (*Imdād* 267); to lengthen the first *rakʿa* of only fajr, while for other prayers the first and second *rakʿas* should be approximately of similar length; to place one's hands on one's thighs when sitting, such that the fingertips are parallel to the knees, without grabbing the knees; to point with the right index finger when pronouncing the testification of faith in the *tashahhud*, raising it with *Lā ilāha* and lowering it back down with *illa 'Llāh*; for the imām when ending the prayer, to pronounce the second *salām* less audibly than the first one; for anyone, to begin with the right when turning the head with the closing *salāms*; and for the latecomer (*masbūq*), to wait until the imām says the second closing *salām* before rising to make up his missed *rakʿa*(s), to see if the imām needs to perform a forgetfulness prostration, since following the imām is mandatory (*wājib*). (*Hadiyya* 69–71; *Durr*, *Radd* 1:320–1, 332, 484; *Marāqī 'l-Falāḥ*, *Ṭaḥṭāwī* 1:375).

The following are emphasized *sunnas* that are specific to men, while women do the opposite. While bowing, men clutch the knees with the hands and spread the fingers wide, keep the legs straight without bending the knees, and bend over fully such that the head is even with the bot-

1. Before the *taḥrīma*, to raise the hands parallel to the ears, except for the free woman, who raises her hands parallel to the shoulders;[236]
2. To keep the fingers [slightly] spaced apart[237] [for the *taḥrīma*];
3. For the man, to place[238] the right hand over the left hand, under the navel; for the woman, to do so on her chest [underneath the breasts];
4. To pronounce the opening supplication of the prayer (*thanā'*);[239]
5. To pronounce the *taʿawwudh* [in the first *rakʿa* only] for the sake of recitation of Qur'ān;[240]

---

tom—yet without raising or lowering the head. Women, however, bend over just enough so the hands reach the knees, place them on the knees without clutching them, keep the fingers together, slightly bend the knees, and keep the elbows pressed against the body.

In prostration, men keep the abdomen at a distance from the thighs, the elbows from the sides, and the arms from the ground—unless it is crowded, as striking one's fellow Muslim is unlawful (*ḥarām*). Women keep all limbs close together, even the abdomen close to the thighs, and the forearms laid out on the ground.

The sitting position of men is *iftirāsh*, that is, to sit on the left foot while it is laid out on the ground, while keeping the right foot propped up, its toes directed toward the *qibla*. The women's sitting position is *tawarruk*, that is, to sit such that the buttocks rest directly on the ground rather than on the foot, keeping the right thigh over the left thigh, with the left foot coming out from under the right leg (*Hadiyya* 69–70; *Durr, Radd* 1:332).

Other general differences in the prayer between men and women include the following: she does not take the hands out of the sleeves with the opening *taḥrīma*; to alert the imām of a missed integral, she taps her hand instead of saying *Subḥāna 'Llāh*; she may not lead men as imām in congregational prayer; it is prohibitively disliked (*makrūh taḥrīman*) for women to pray in their own congregation without men, but if they do, she would stand in the middle of the first row as imām rather than ahead of it; if she joins the men in congregational prayer, she stands behind them; she does not have to attend the Friday prayer or the ʿĪd prayers, but they are valid for her if she does; it is not recommended for her to delay the fajr prayer to when light begins to appear; and she never recites aloud (*Hadiyya* 77; *Radd* 1:339).

236 Such that her fingertips are parallel to the shoulders (*Tanwīr, Durr* 1:324).

237 "Spaced apart" in this context means neither closed together tightly nor outstretched completely. It is also *sunna* for the *taḥrīma* to have the palms face the *qibla* and to keep the head straight rather than bending it down. Also, it is *sunna* for the man to have his thumbs touch the earlobes when raising the hands for the *taḥrīma* (*Hadiyya* 68; *Durr, Radd* 1:319, 324).

238 That is, when standing, immediately after the opening *taḥrīma*, without letting the arms down by one's sides (*Tanwīr, Durr* 1:327). This is also *sunna* for the standing position in the witr prayer while reciting *qunūt* as well as in the funeral prayer, as opposed to after rising from bowing or between the *takbīrs* of the ʿĪd prayers, wherein one instead lets the arms down by the sides (*Tanwīr* 1:328).

239 That is, immediately after the opening *taḥrīma*, unless the imām of congregational prayer starts reciting Qur'ān (*Durr* 1:328).

240 Thus, the follower in congregation does not do so, as it is prohibited for him to recite Qur'ān. The imām and one praying alone, however, pronounce both the *taʿawwudh* and the *basmala*, as they must recite Qur'ān in the prayer (*Durr, Radd* 1:329).

6. To pronounce the *basmala* before the Fātiḥa, in every *rakʿa* [except for the follower];
7. To say *āmīn* after the Fātiḥa, as well as *Rabbanā laka 'l-ḥamd* [(*taḥmīd*) after rising from bowing];
8. [To say the above (*thanā', taʿawwudh, basmala, āmīn*, and *taḥmīd*)] silently;[241]
9. For the imām, to say the *takbīrs* out loud;[242]
10. To say the *takbīrs* of going into bowing and prostration, as well as when rising from prostration;[243]
11. To recite the *tasbīḥ* three times [in both bowing and prostration];[244]
12. To recite the Fātiḥa[245] in the last two *rakʿas* [of a four-*rakʿa* prayer], and in the third *rakʿa* of maghrib;
13. To send blessings upon the Prophet ﷺ in the final sitting;
14. To supplicate afterwards, using words that do not resemble normal human speech [so as not to invalidate the prayer; see related note, p. 84];
15. To turn [one's head right and left] when making the closing *salāms*;

---

241 That is, such that one's voice can be heard by oneself yet not by others (see related note, p. 75).

242 And as appropriate for the congregation, as undue exaggeration is disliked (*Hadiyya* 68; *Radd* 1:319). The same ruling applies to *Samiʿa 'Llāhu liman ḥamidah* (*tasmīʿ*), which is said when rising from bowing, as well as both closing *salāms*. The follower in congregation and the one praying alone pronounce the *takbīrs* silently, meaning that the person alone can hear himself (*Durr* 1:319; *Imdād* 267).

243 Saying *Samiʿa 'Llāhu liman ḥamidah* when rising from bowing is also an emphasized *sunna*, specifically for the imām of congregational prayer and the one praying alone, but not the follower in congregational prayer (*Tanwīr, Durr* 1:334).

244 In the bowing position, one says *Subḥāna Rabbiya 'l-ʿAẓīm* ("Glory be unto my Lord, the Great") three times. In prostration, one says *Subḥāna Rabbiya 'l-Aʿlā* ("Glory be unto my Lord, the Sublime") three times (*Hadiyya* 69–70). To say them less than three times, or to omit them altogether, is worse than mildly disliked, yet not prohibitively disliked (*Radd* 1:320, 332). Also, if the imām in congregational prayer rises from bowing or prostration before the follower has pronounced the three *tasbīḥs*, the follower must follow him without delay. If, however, the imām rises from the first sitting position, or says the closing *salāms*, before the follower has finished the entire *tashahhud*, then the follower finishes the *tashahhud* before following the imām. If the imām says the closing *salāms* after the follower has finished the entire *tashahhud*, then the follower must immediately end the prayer (*Tanwīr, Durr* 1:333–4).

245 For these *rakʿas*, it is best to recite the Fātiḥa, followed in merit by saying *Subḥāna 'Llāh* three times, followed in merit by keeping silent for an equivalent time (of saying *Subḥāna 'Llāh* three times), yet keeping silent for even a moment is sufficient (*Hadiyya* 70). All of these fulfill the *sunna*—as there is no blame (*isā'a*) for remaining silent (*Badā'iʿ* 1:296)—yet the Fātiḥa is superior (*Radd* 1:343–4). (However, because reciting the Fātiḥa in these *rakʿas* is obligatory in other schools of thought, one should strive not to omit it.) Also, one is not to recite anything after the Fātiḥa in those *rakʿas*. If one does, it is deemed mildly disliked (*makrūh tanzīhan*) (*Durr, Radd* 1:308).

16. To intend to greet the congregation, guardian angels, and imām when making the closing *salāms*.

ETIQUETTE (*ĀDĀB*) OF THE PRAYER

Among them are the following:[246]

1. For the man, to take his hands out of his [loose, flowing] sleeves when performing the *taḥrīma*;
2. To direct one's glance toward the place of prostration when standing, the top of one's feet while bowing, the tip of one's nose while prostrating, the lap while sitting, and each shoulder when making the closing *salāms*;
3. To try one's best to refrain from coughing[247] and to keep one's mouth closed when yawning.[248]

SUPPLICATIONS OF THE PRAYER

The *tashahhud* is to recite the following:

> Greetings are for Allāh, as well as prayers and all things pure. Peace be upon you, O Prophet, as well as the mercy of Allāh and His blessings. Peace be upon us, and upon all the righteous servants of Allāh.
>
> I testify that there is no deity except Allāh, and I testify that Muḥammad is His servant and messenger [p. 191].

In the final sitting, one adds:

> O Allāh, send mercy upon Muḥammad and upon the family of Muḥammad, just as

246 Their omission does not entail any blame whatsoever; rather, it is more preferable to do them. Etiquette (*adab*) is synonymous with recommended (*mandūb*) (*Durr, Radd* 1:321).

247 So as to make sure one does not invalidate the prayer, since coughing for no reason—if it results in enunciated letters, like "*uh*"—would do so; the same ruling applies to burping (*Imdād* 284; *Majmaʿ al-Anhur* 1:91).

248 Otherwise if uncontrollable, one covers his mouth with his hand or sleeve (*Tanwīr* 1:321–2; *Imdād* 284; *Al-Durr al-Muntaqā* 1:91).

> You sent mercy upon Ibrāhīm and upon the family of Ibrāhīm; and send blessings upon Muḥammad and upon the family of Muḥammad, just as You sent blessings upon Ibrāhīm and upon the family of Ibrāhīm, in all of the worlds; indeed, You are Praiseworthy and Majestic [p. 191].

The final supplication is the following, or the like: Our Lord! Grant us much good in this life and much good in the next life, and protect us from the punishment of the Fire [p. 191].

The *qunūt* of the witr prayer is the following:

> O Allāh! Verily, we seek Your help and Your guidance. We ask for Your forgiveness and turn to You in repentance. We believe in You and place our trust in You. We praise You with every good praise; we thank You, and we do not reject You. We cast out and abandon anyone who disobeys You. O Allāh, You alone do we worship, and for Your sake alone do we pray and prostrate. To You alone do we earnestly strive and hasten. We hope for Your mercy and fear Your punishment; verily, Your true punishment will be meted out to the disbelievers.
>
> May Allāh send blessings and peace upon our Master Muḥammad, the unlettered Prophet, and upon his family and Companions [p. 192].

The follower [in a congregation of the witr prayer] recites the *qunūt* [as well], just as he does the *tashahhud*, with the imām.

One who is unable to recite this [i.e., the above *qunūt*] may simply say "O Lord!" (*Yā Rabb*) three times, or the like.

The opening supplication (*thanā'*) [of any prayer] is the following: Glory be to You, O Allāh, with Your praise. Blessed is Your Name; Exalted is Your honor. There is no deity besides You [p. 190].

THINGS THAT INVALIDATE THE PRAYER (*MUFSIDĀT*)

The following things invalidate the ritual prayer:

1. To utter a word [of human speech, as opposed to words of the prayer], even if out of forgetfulness;[249]

249 The least amount of speech that invalidates the prayer is two letters, or one letter that

2. Excessive movement;[250]
3. To eat, even if a little;[251]
4. To drink;
5. To clear one's throat [such that letters are uttered], without an excuse;[252]
6. To cry out loud [such that letters are uttered] or to moan, out of pain[253] or due to a calamity, as opposed to remembrance of Paradise or the Fire [which is excused];
7. To say *salām* to someone with the intention of greeting him;
8. To shake someone's hand;
9. To respond to someone's statement by saying *Lā ilāha illa 'Llāh*, or the like;[254]
10. To turn[255] one's torso away from [the direction of][256] the *qibla*;
11. To make supplication (*duʿā'*) using words that resemble our [normal human] speech;[257]
12. To elongate the letter *hamza* in the *takbīr*;

---

bears meaning (as opposed to one letter that does not), unless it is uncontrollable, such as when one is overcome by a cough, sneeze, burp, or yawn (*Hadiyya* 81). Yet coughing or the like without an excuse—that results in letters—does invalidate the prayer.

250 Excessive movement is defined as that due to which an onlooker from afar, who did not know from the onset that the person was praying, would be fairly certain that its doer was *not* performing ritual prayer. If the onlooker would be unsure, then the movement is not considered excessive. This criterion is the soundest opinion on the matter (*Marāqī 'l-Falāḥ*, *Ṭaḥṭāwī* 1:438; *Durr*, *Radd* 1:420).

251 If food is taken from outside the mouth, swallowing any amount breaks the prayer. If there is leftover food in the mouth, then swallowing the amount equivalent to the size of a chickpea breaks the prayer, while less than that is excused (*Marāqī 'l-Falāḥ* 1:439, *Durr* 1:418). This is the same criteria for breaking the fast.

252 If there is an excuse, such as if the phlegm was affecting his recitation, or if he cleared his throat to indicate to another that he was in the prayer, then the prayer is not invalidated (*Marāqī 'l-Falāḥ* 1:440; *Durr*, *Radd* 1:416; *Kanz*, *Tabyīn* 1:156).

253 Unless the person is ill and, therefore, cannot control the moaning or noise due to pain (*Ṭaḥṭāwī* 1:440, *Durr* 1:416; *Tabyīn* 1:156).

254 That is, to say anything in response to someone, even if with phrases from the Qur'ān or *dhikr* (*Marāqī 'l-Falāḥ* 1:442).

255 That is, by one's own volition without a valid excuse, in which case the prayer immediately breaks. If one is *pushed* such that his torso turns outside the direction of the *qibla*, then he must turn back toward the *qibla* within the time it takes to say *Subḥāna 'Llāh* three times in a measured pace; otherwise, the prayer is invalidated (*Radd* 1:421).

256 That is, more than 45 degrees on either side (*Majmaʿ al-Anhur* 1:83).

257 Namely, a *duʿā'* that is not found in the Qur'ān or Sunna, and that is possible to request from a human being. If it is found in the Qur'ān or Sunna, or if it is impossible to request from a human being, then the prayer is not invalidated (*Multaqā* 1:118; *Imdād* 335; *Radd* 1:416).

13. For one's nakedness [at least one-fourth of a limb] to be uncovered for the length of time it takes to perform an integral of the prayer;[258]
14. To carry an unexcused amount of filth [see p. 61];
15. [For the follower] to precede the imām by an integral [or completely miss one] which the imām does not perform afterwards *with* the follower, or which the follower does not repeat [afterwards];[259]
16. To miss an integral of the prayer and not make it up later before the end of the prayer.

All of the above invalidate the prayer if done before sitting, in the final sitting position, for the length of time it takes one to recite the *tashahhud*.[260]

THINGS THAT ARE DISLIKED IN THE PRAYER (*MAKRŪHĀT*)

1. To deliberately omit any mandatory (*wājib*) or *sunna* act;[261]

258 Namely, the time it takes for one to calmly recite three *tasbīḥāt* (i.e., *Subḥāna 'Llāh* three times). If one-fourth of a limb or more becomes exposed during the prayer for less than this time, it is excused. If less than one-fourth of a limb becomes exposed, for any duration of time, it is excused. If one-fourth or more is exposed at the onset of the prayer, the prayer's commencement—and hence the prayer itself—is deemed invalid. If one exposes his limb during the prayer (as opposed to a limb becoming exposed), the prayer is invalidated, no matter how small the exposure or how short the time period (*Ṭaḥṭāwī* 1:332, 455; *Durr, Radd* 1:273, 420).

The following is a classification of the limbs with regard to the prayer. The knee along with the thigh is deemed one limb, just as is a woman's ankle along with her shin. Her wrist is deemed part of her forearm, and her elbow part of her upper arm. Each ear by itself is deemed a separate limb. Each breast, if hanging low, is a separate limb. If firm and upright, both breasts are deemed part of the chest. The penis by itself is a limb, and the testicles together are a separate limb. The area between the navel and pubic region, horizontally around the entire waist, is deemed one limb. Each buttock is a separate limb, and the anus alone is deemed another limb.

Lastly, if multiple limbs simultaneously become exposed for the aforementioned time of three *tasbīḥāt*, then the prayer is invalid *if* the sum total of what is exposed equals one-fourth or more of the *smallest limb exposed*; otherwise, the prayer remains valid (*Marāqī 'l-Falāḥ, Ṭaḥṭāwī* 1:332–3).

259 That is, if the follower performs an integral before the imām and then moves on to another position *before* the imām performs that integral (such that there is not even a moment that both are in that position together)—and the follower does not *repeat* that integral for the remainder of the prayer—then his prayer is invalid. If, however, the imām performs it *while* the follower is still in that position—or if the follower *does* repeat it afterwards—then the follower's prayer is valid. If the follower completely misses an integral, he must perform it later, within the prayer, for the prayer to be valid (*Imdād* 344; *Marāqī 'l-Falāḥ* 1:455).

260 This sentence appears earlier in the Arabic published edition as well as in the manuscript, yet is placed here as it applies to all of the above nullifiers of prayer (see *Imdād* 343–4).

261 This serves as a general basis of why the remaining things are disliked, as they entail leaving

2. To fiddle around (*ʿabath*)[262] with one's garment or body, without excessive movement [as excessive movement also invalidates the prayer];
3. To wipe away pebbles on the ground, except once for prostration;
4. To crack one's knuckles;[263]
5. To place one's hands on one's hips;[264]
6. To turn one's neck;[265]
7. To sit with one's knees up;[266]
8. To lay one's forearms on the ground during prostration;[267]
9. To roll up one's sleeves;[268]
10. [For men] to pray in only a lower garment [that covers his nakedness], while having the ability to cover the whole body;[269]

---

either a mandatory requisite (*wājib*) or *sunna* of the prayer (*Marāqī 'l-Falāḥ* 1:466). Leaving out a mandatory requisite is prohibitively disliked (*makrūh taḥrīman*). Leaving out a *sunna* once is mildly disliked (*makrūh tanzīhan*) and entails doing wrong (*isā'a*), and could be sinful if habitual. If there exists a specific prohibition, its omission is prohibitively disliked (*makrūh taḥrīman*) (*Ṭaḥṭāwī* 1:464–5; *Radd* 1:70–1). Finally, it is mandatory (*wājib*) to repeat a prayer in which one intentionally did an act that is prohibitively disliked (*makrūh taḥrīman*) (*Durr*, *Radd* 1:307).

262 *ʿAbath* is defined as any movement that is of no benefit or purpose, and that is not of the actions of the prayer (*Marāqī 'l-Falāḥ* 1:466). To do so is deemed prohibitively disliked (*makrūh taḥrīman*). If, however, there is a reason or need, such as to wipe sweat or dirt off one's face if it distracts him, then it is not disliked provided the movement is not excessive, which would invalidate the prayer (*Ṭaḥṭāwī* 1:466; *Radd* 1:430).

263 This is deemed prohibitively disliked (*makrūh taḥrīman*) in the prayer. To do so outside the prayer, without any need, is deemed mildly disliked (*makrūh tanzīhan*) (*Ṭaḥṭāwī* 1:468; *Durr*, *Radd* 1:431–2; *Imdād* 352).

264 This is deemed prohibitively disliked (*makrūh taḥrīman*) (*Radd* 1:432; *Imdād* 353).

265 That is, while the torso remains facing the direction of the *qibla*; otherwise, the prayer would be rendered invalid. Turning one's neck alone is deemed prohibitively disliked (*makrūh taḥrīman*). Moving the eyes around while keeping the head straight is not disliked, but is better to avoid (*khilāf al-awlā*) (*Ṭaḥṭāwī* 1:469; *Durr*, *Radd* 1:432; *Imdād* 354).

266 That is, to place the buttocks on the ground and to elevate the knees, keeping them close to the chest, with one's hands on the ground in front of him, the way a dog sits. This is deemed prohibitively disliked (*makrūh taḥrīman*) (*Marāqī 'l-Falāḥ*, *Ṭaḥṭāwī* 1:471; *Radd* 1:432), whether sitting for *tashahhud* or between the two prostrations (*Hadiyya* 90).

267 This is deemed prohibitively disliked (*makrūh taḥrīman*) for men, yet *sunna* for women. However, it is not disliked for men if there is a valid excuse (*Radd* 1:432–3; *Majmaʿ al-Anhur* 1:123).

268 The author himself stipulates the rolling of the sleeves *to the elbows*, suggesting that to do so slightly without exposing the forearms is not disliked (*Nūr al-Īḍāḥ* 1:471, *Shurunbulāliyya* 1:106). Ibn ʿĀbidīn, however, considers rolling the sleeves to any extent disliked. He also maintains that the person in the prayer should roll them back down with slight movements (as excessive movements nullify the prayer) (*Radd* 1:430). This discussion, of course, pertains to men alone, since for a woman rolling the sleeves would entail exposing her nakedness (*ʿawra*), which would invalidate the prayer and be sinful.

269 This entails lack of consideration and respect for the prayer, as well as laziness, and is

11. To gather one's garment close to the body before going into prostration;[270]
12. To place a shawl on one's head or shoulders, letting its ends hang down below;[271]
13. To close one's eyes;[272]
14. To yawn;[273]
15. To stretch [one's arms, exposing the chest];[274]
16. To cover one's nose and mouth[275] [except when yawning];
17. To prostrate with the forehead covered;[276]
18. To prostrate on a picture [of an animate creature];[277]
19. To pray in a road, lavatory, or graveyard;[278]
20. To pray near filth;
21. To pray on stolen property, in a stolen garment, or after having made *wuḍū'* from stolen water;

---

therefore deemed prohibitively disliked (*makrūh taḥrīman*) (*Marāqī 'l-Falāḥ, Ṭaḥṭāwī* 1:472).

270 This is deemed prohibitively disliked (*makrūh taḥrīman*) (*Radd* 1:430), as it is a sign of arrogance (*Tabyīn* 1:164).

271 This includes wearing any garment in a manner not customarily worn, such as a coat or jacket on one's shoulders alone, without placing one's arms in the sleeves. It is deemed prohibitively disliked (*makrūh taḥrīman*). There is no difference between the garment being secure from falling down or not (*Ṭaḥṭāwī* 1:474; *Majmaʿ al-Anhur* 1:124; *Tabyīn* 1:164; *Durr, Radd* 1:429–30). This ruling would include a scarf around one's neck with its ends hanging below; hence, once should take it off before the prayer (*Imdād* 357).

272 This is deemed mildly disliked (*makrūh tanzīhan*), unless done for a legitimate reason, such as if it helps one to concentrate, in which case it is actually superior (*Marāqī 'l-Falāḥ* 1:479; *Hadiyya* 93; *Durr, Radd* 1:434).

273 If the yawn is natural and not deliberate, then there is no harm in it, yet one should still try to prevent it with his lips or, if necessary, his hand. If it is deliberate, it is deemed prohibitively disliked (*makrūh taḥrīman*), as it is a type of *ʿabath* (see p. 86) (*Radd* 1:433).

274 As long as there is no excessive movement, stretching is deemed mildly disliked (*makrūh tanzīhan*), as it is done out of laziness (*Marāqī 'l-Falāḥ, Ṭaḥṭāwī* 1:480).

275 This is deemed prohibitively disliked (*makrūh taḥrīman*), as it bears resemblance to Magians during their worship of burning coal (*Radd* 1:439).

276 This is deemed mildly disliked (*makrūh tanzīhan*), unless one has an excuse, such as if the ground is very hot, cold, or coarse (*Marāqī 'l-Falāḥ, Ṭaḥṭāwī* 1:481).

277 That is, at the place of prostration, where the face touches the ground, as that entails veneration for the picture and resembles worshipping it. This results in the most severe level of reprehensibility (*karāha*). It is not disliked, however, to pray with it underneath one's feet or where one sits, due to the implicit disdain therein (*Durr, Radd* 1:435–6; *Ḥalabī Kabīr* 359).

278 Praying on a road disturbs traffic; the lavatory is a place of filth and devils; and praying in a graveyard resembles the worship of Jews and Christians (*Marāqī 'l-Falāḥ, Ṭaḥṭāwī* 1:482).

22. To pray while having the urge to urinate or defecate, or while needing to relieve oneself from gas;[279]
23. To pray in work clothes;[280]
24. To pray in a garment on which there is a picture [of an animate creature];[281]
25. To pray with one's head uncovered, unless done out of humility;[282]
26. To pray when food has been served;[283]
27. To pray in the presence of a picture [of an animate creature];[284]
28. To pray around that which would distract the person;
29. To pray in a congregation while standing alone in a row;[285]
30. To pray in front of a furnace or ember;[286]
31. To pray in front of people sleeping;[287]
32. To wipe dirt [or sweat] off of one's face that does not distract him, during the prayer.[288]

---

279 This is deemed prohibitively disliked (*makrūh taḥrīman*), regardless of whether one is in such a state before commencing the prayer or during it. Therefore if it distracts him, he must break the prayer and relieve himself, unless he fears the prayer time will expire (*Radd* 1:431).

280 Namely, clothes that are usually dirty and worn out, or clothes that one normally wears in the house and are not suitable attire when meeting distinguished personalities. Praying in such clothes is deemed mildly disliked (*makrūh tanzīhan*) (*Marāqī 'l-Falāḥ*, *Ṭaḥṭāwī* 1:485–6; *Radd* 1:430).

281 As this resembles carrying an idol (*Tabyīn* 1:166), and as such is deemed prohibitively disliked (*makrūh taḥrīman*) (*Radd* 1:435).

282 This, of course, pertains to men alone, since for a woman it would entail exposing her nakedness (*ʿawra*), which would invalidate the prayer and be sinful.

283 That is, while one is hungry, such that it would distract him from the prayer. This is even considered an excuse for missing the congregation if one's desire is intense (*Marāqī 'l-Falāḥ* 1:404, *Durr* 1:374).

284 This is most severely disliked if the picture is in front of him (between him and the *qibla*), followed by above his head, followed by on his right or left—in all cases being prohibitively disliked (*makrūh taḥrīman*)—and lastly behind him, in which case it is mildly disliked (*makrūh tanzīhan*). It is not disliked in any case, however, if the picture is small to the extent that if on the ground, the details of its limbs would not be plainly visible to a standing person; nor if it is covered; if its head or face is severed; if it is missing a limb without which it could not live; or if the picture is of an inanimate object, such as a tree (*Durr*, *Radd* 1:435–6).

285 Rather, if there is a gap in the row in front of him, he should fill it in. Otherwise if there is no gap, then early jurists maintained that he should gently pull someone from that row. However, due to the widespread ignorance among people regarding the rules of the prayer, the later verdict (*fatwā*) is that one should not pull anyone but rather stand alone in his row (*Durr*, *Radd* 1:435).

286 As it resembles the worship of Magians, as opposed to praying in front of a candle or lamp, which is not disliked as it does not resemble their worship (*Marāqī 'l-Falāḥ* 1:491; *Majmaʿ al-Anhur* 1:127).

287 This is not disliked unless the one praying fears that they may cause him to laugh or feel embarrassed, or that he may pray toward one's face (*Marāqī 'l-Falāḥ* 1:491).

288 This is considered a type of *ʿabath*. If it distracts him during the prayer, or if he does so after

THINGS THAT ARE PERMISSIBLE IN THE PRAYER

It is recommended for one to place a barrier in front of him when praying.[289] If someone passes in front of him, he may take the dispensation of saying *Subḥāna 'Llāh* or gesturing [in order to ward off the passerby].[290] If someone passes in front of a woman praying, she may ward him off, yet without raising her voice.[291]

The following things in the ritual prayer are not disliked:

1. To fasten one's belt around the waist;
2. To strap a sword or the like on the belt, as long as its movement is not distracting;
3. To pray facing a copy of the Qur'ān; a sword; the back[292] of someone sitting,[293] even if speaking [quietly]; a candle; or a lamp;[294]
4. To kill a snake or scorpion, if one fears their harm, with no more than two strikes, even with turning away from the *qibla*.[295]

It is acceptable for one to pray on carpets or rugs.[296]

---

the prayer, it is not disliked (*Marāqī 'l-Falāḥ* 1:491).

289 That is, the imām or the one praying alone (*munfarid*). As for followers in a congregation, the barrier in front of the imām suffices them. The minimum size of a sufficient barrier is an object of a forearm's length and a finger's width. It is placed upright in front of the one praying, ideally 1.5 m ahead of him and aligned with one of his eyebrows, preferably the right. If not possible, one may lay it down instead, or spread a garment, or even draw a line in the ground lengthwise toward the *qibla*. It is mildly disliked (*makrūh tanzīhan*) to not use a barrier if one is praying in a place where he suspects people might pass in front of him (*Hadiyya* 96; *Marāqī 'l-Falāḥ* 1:496–8).

290 It is recommended to avoid warding off the passerby, and instead allow him to pass (*Marāqī 'l-Falāḥ* 1:498; *Durr* 1:428).

291 That is, such that it can be heard. Rather, she may clap her hands, tapping the back of the left hand with the inner side of the right hand (*Radd* 1:429).

292 To pray toward someone's face, however, would be prohibitively disliked (*makrūh taḥrīman*), as it resembles praying toward a picture. The one who transgressed would incur the sin (*Ṭaḥṭāwī* 1:501; *Durr*, *Radd* 1:433).

293 Or standing, as long as facing his back (see previous note) (*Durr*, *Radd* 1:438).

294 This is not disliked as it does not entail imitation of the Magians, who would worship burning coal rather than actual fire (*Ṭaḥṭāwī* 1:501).

295 If one does not fear their harm, it is disliked if with much movement. If one fears their harm, then it is not disliked even if it entails breaking the prayer, such as by excessive movement or turning the torso outside the direction of the *qibla* (*Imdād* 379; *Ṭaḥṭāwī* 1:502–3; *Radd* 1:438).

296 Although it is more preferable to pray directly onto earth or onto that which grows out of earth (*Imdād* 381).

BREAKING THE PRAYER

It is permissible to break the ritual prayer [even an obligatory prayer] if one is being robbed of something worth one *dirham* or more, even if it belongs to someone else. A shepherd may also break the prayer out of fear of a wolf for his sheep.

It is mandatory (*wājib*) to break the ritual prayer if one hears a call for help from someone in an emergency, or if one fears [with reasonable likelihood] that a blind person will fall into a well or the like.[297]

A midwife may delay her ritual prayer, even until after the time expires, out of fear for the baby or the mother in delivery.[298] The same ruling applies to a traveller who fears highway robbers.

ABANDONING THE PRAYER

One who abandons the ritual prayer altogether on purpose, out of laziness, is to be beaten[299] until he bleeds, and then imprisoned until he resumes praying. The same ruling applies to one who does not fast in Ramaḍān. He is not killed, however, unless he denies the obligation of something obligatory, or belittles it.

PRAYING ON A RIDING ANIMAL

Obligatory (*farḍ*) and mandatory (*wājib*) prayers[300] are invalid if performed on a riding animal [or in a vehicle], as is a prostration of recital *if* the verse was

297 It is not permissible to break the ritual prayer if one's parent is calling him for other than an emergency. An exception is for voluntary prayers: if the parent does not know that he is praying, he should break the prayer and respond; if the parent knows he is praying, then there is no harm in not responding and finishing the prayer first (*Hadiyya* 98).

298 That is, if the midwife fears that by her absence the baby might perish or lose a limb, then it is mandatory (*wājib*) for her to delay the prayer and remain to perform the delivery (*Hadiyya* 98; *Imdād* 383). Of course, she should take reasonable means beforehand to both perform the prayer on time and diligently fulfill her duty.

299 This section pertains to the duty of the government in dealing with religious negligence or apostasy; a Muslim citizen may not carry out such punishments on his own accord.

300 Like the witr prayer. This ruling also applies to the funeral prayer and the two-*rakʿa sunna* of fajr (*Hadiyya* 104; *Marāqī 'l-Falāḥ* 1:555; *Durr, Radd* 1:469).

recited [or heard] before mounting the animal,[301] except in cases of necessity,[302] such as muddy terrain,[303] fear of a robber [if one were to descend or stop], or inability to remount after descent.[304]

If a carriage on a camel is made stationary and connected to the ground by means of a wooden stick or the like, one may pray in it standing [as it takes the legal ruling of the ground].

If one is on an animal [or in a vehicle] and outside city limits, he may pray voluntary prayers, even emphasized *sunnas*, by head movements.[305] In such a case, any filth on the saddle or stirrups is excused.[306]

According to our school of thought, it is not valid to perform a ritual prayer while walking.

In general for voluntary prayers, even if able to stand, one may pray sitting yet while facing the *qibla*, both at the onset as well as in the middle of the prayer.[307]

---

301 If, however, the verse is recited or heard while on the animal (or vehicle)—and while outside of city limits—then its prostration may also be performed on it, that is, by head movements. Yet if the obligation occurs on the ground—or while inside city limits—then it cannot be performed by head movements on an animal (or vehicle) (*Ṭaḥṭāwī* 1:555; *Radd* 1:515).

302 In cases of necessity, the obligatory (*farḍ*) or mandatory (*wājib*) prayer may be performed by head movements while mounted. If possible, one must stop the animal and direct it toward the *qibla*. Otherwise if one cannot stop it, such as due to fear of an enemy, one may pray toward whichever direction the animal is facing, even if opposite the *qibla*, and even if while moving (*Marāqī 'l-Falāḥ*, *Ṭaḥṭāwī* 1:555; *Hadiyya* 105).

303 That is, such that one's face would become soiled from sinking into the mud, or one's prayer mat would become ruined in it. In fact, even if one did not have an animal to pray on, one would then stand in the mud and pray with head movements. However, dampness alone is not considered a necessity that would permit one to pray on an animal or with head movements while standing (*Marāqī 'l-Falāḥ* 1:555, *Hadiyya* 105).

304 With no one present that could help the rider remount (*Marāqī 'l-Falāḥ* 1:555, *Hadiyya* 105). Other examples of necessity include a woman's fear of a corrupt person (*fāsiq*); a sick person's fear of the illness worsening or the healing being delayed if he were to dismount and remount; or the flight of one's caravan or travel partners, such that if he were to stop to pray, he would be left alone, unable to catch up with them (*Marāqī 'l-Falāḥ* 1:555, *Hadiyya* 105).

305 To pray voluntary prayers on an animal (or in a vehicle), one must be outside city limits for the prayers to be valid. This applies to a traveller as well as a resident outside of his city. Moreover, one simply faces whichever direction the animal (or vehicle) is facing. This is valid for voluntary prayers, which includes emphasized *sunnas*, even without an excuse. An exception, however, is the two-*rakʿas* before fajr, which like obligatory and mandatory prayers must be performed on the ground (*Hadiyya* 104; *Marāqī 'l-Falāḥ* 1:551; *Durr*, *Radd* 1:469). Finally, the prayer is not invalidated by slight movements for steering the animal (or vehicle), which are permissible and not disliked. Excessive movements, however, would invalidate the prayer (*Durr*, *Radd* 1:470).

306 As well as on the animal itself, but not the person's own body or clothes (*Durr*, *Radd* 1:469–70).

307 That is, this ruling holds both for starting the prayer sitting, as well as for sitting in the middle of a prayer that one started off standing. In either case, doing so without any excuse is

If one prays [obligatory or mandatory prayers] in a ship while sitting,[308] even without an excuse, it is valid, yet he must turn toward the *qibla* every time it changes directions.

PRAYER OF THE TRAVELLER

The minimum period of travel whereby certain legal rulings take effect is three days [on camel].[309] Thus when a person has left his place of residence,[310] intending to travel at a medium pace to a place that he will reach in at least three days, then he does not fast [in Ramaḍān],[311] and he shortens the four-*rakʿa* obligatory prayers; he is not allowed to pray them as four *rakʿas*.[312] If he [does pray the full four *rakʿas* and] sits the first sitting [between the second and third *rakʿas*], then the prayer is valid, although he has committed a serious error;[313] otherwise, it is invalid.[314] He may not shorten any prayer aside from the four-*rakʿa* obligatory prayers.

---

permissible yet entails half the reward. This ruling pertains to performing voluntary prayers on the ground (*Marāqī 'l-Falāḥ* 1:548, 550).

308 However, he must perform bowing (*rukūʿ*) by bending his back and prostration (*sujūd*) on the ground. He may not simply pray with head movements without an excuse (*Hadiyya* 105; *Marāqī 'l-Falāḥ* 1:557).

309 That is, the least distance of travel for certain rulings to take effect is a camel journey of three days, which is roughly 48 mi (77 km). Reasonable estimation of this distance is sufficient; one does not have to be certain, as it is an approximation (*Ṭaḥṭāwī* 2:8; *Tabyīn* 1:209). Those rulings include the following: it becomes mandatory (*wājib*) to shorten the prayer; one has the option of not fasting in Ramaḍān (if outside city limits before fajr); the time period for wiping *khuffs* extends from one day to three days (see related section, p. 53); it is no longer mandatory to attend the Friday prayer or ʿĪd prayer, nor to perform the ritual sacrifice of ʿĪd al-Aḍḥā (*uḍḥiya*); it is forbidden for a woman to travel alone past this distance, as she must be accompanied by either her husband or a man of unmarriageable kin (*maḥram*) (see related note, p. 148); etc. (*Hadiyya* 108).

310 That is, having passed city limits (*Tanwīr* 1:525; *Kanz* 1:209).

311 That is, he has the option of not fasting, yet with the condition that he was outside city limits before the entrance of fajr. Otherwise, he must fast that day despite his journey (*Marāqī 'l-Falāḥ* 2:355; *Hadiyya* 175).

312 As it is mandatory (*wājib*) to shorten the obligatory prayers of ẓuhr, ʿaṣr, and ʿishā' to two *rakʿas*. The obligatory prayers of fajr and maghrib, as well as witr and emphasized *sunna* prayers, do not change (*Durr, Radd* 1:527).

313 That is, it is prohibitively disliked (*makrūh taḥrīman*) if done purposefully, or necessitates the prostration of forgetfulness (*sujūd al-sahw*) if done out of forgetfulness. This is because shortening the prayer to two *rakʿas* is mandatory, as is saying the closing *salāms* immediately after the final sitting, namely, the sitting after the second *rakʿa* (*Marāqī 'l-Falāḥ* 2:13; *Durr, Radd* 1:530).

314 That is, if he misses the first sitting altogether, the obligatory prayer is rendered invalid

If he is at a halt on the journey, while in a state of rest, he should pray the [emphasized] *sunna* prayers [along with the obligatory and mandatory prayers]. Otherwise, he may leave them[315] [and instead pray only the obligatory and mandatory prayers].

Once he reaches a city or village and intends on staying there for [at least] fifteen [full] days, he must complete [the four-*rakʿa* obligatory prayers, rather than shortening them] and must fast [if in Ramaḍān]. Otherwise [if he is still on the journey; or is residing somewhere—other than his normal place of residence—for less than fifteen days], then he does not [complete the four *rakʿas* nor fast. Rather, he must still shorten those prayers and may still choose to not fast in Ramaḍān].

The journey [of a traveller] ends upon entering [city limits of] his normal place of residence (*waṭan aṣlī*).

If he [the traveller] prays behind a resident [imām] within the prayer time, his prayer is valid, and he must pray the full four *rakʿas*; afterwards, it is not.[316]

In the opposite scenario, the prayer [of the resident follower] would be valid[317] in both cases—with the condition, however, that the resident does not complete the four *rakʿas* with his imām, the traveller [if the imām incorrectly performs four *rakʿas* instead of two], for if he completes it with him, his [the resident follower's] obligatory prayer is rendered invalid [and counts as a voluntary prayer instead].

A missed [four-*rakʿa*] prayer on a journey is made up as two *rakʿas* [even if one is no longer a traveller when making it up]. Likewise, a missed [four-*rakʿa*]

---

since he omitted an obligatory (*farḍ*) integral, namely, the *final* sitting of the two *rakʿas*. The four *rakʿas* are deemed a voluntary prayer, and he must re-pray his obligatory prayer (*Durr*, *Radd* 1:530).

315 Although some maintained that the two *rakʿas* of *sunna* before fajr are an exception to this general dispensation, meaning that it is still emphasized to pray them despite one's state of movement and being in a rush (*Durr* 1:532).

316 That is, after the time has expired, the traveller may not pray a four-*rakʿa* obligatory prayer in congregation behind a resident imām. If he does, his prayer (the traveller's) will not be valid (*Imdād* 445).

317 That is, in the opposite scenario—that of a resident praying as a follower behind a traveller imām—the resident's prayer is valid in both cases, i.e., both in the prayer time and after its expiration. In either case, because the traveller imām prays only two *rakʿas*, the resident follower does not say *salāms* with him, but rather rises to complete the remaining two *rakʿas*, as they are both obligatory for him. He does so without any recitation, and without performing a forgetfulness prostration (*sujūd al-sahu*) if any mandatory requisite (*wājib*) is omitted therein. Finally, it is recommended for the imām to say, immediately after the second closing *salām*, "Complete your prayer, for I am a traveller," although he should inform the congregation beforehand as well (*Marāqī 'l-Falāḥ* 2:16–7; *Imdād* 445–6; *Tanwīr*, *Durr* 1:530–1).

prayer while residing is made up as four *rakʿas* [even if one is on a journey when making it up]. The end of the prayer time is what is considered [for this and other legal rulings].[318]

A traveller in a permissible journey and one in a journey of disobedience are equivalent with regard to [legal rulings of the journey itself, such as] shortening [the prayer] and [the option of] not fasting.

PRAYER OF THE SICK PERSON

If it is difficult or impossible[319] for a sick person to stand in the prayer, he may pray the obligatory (*farḍ*) prayers sitting,[320] yet still bowing (*rukūʿ*) [by bending his head and back] and prostrating (*sujūd*) [normally on the ground]. If [normal prostration is also] impossible [or very difficult] then he prays by head movements [by bending his neck for each], making his head motion for prostration (*sujūd*) lower than that for bowing (*rukūʿ*).[321]

If sitting is impossible [or very difficult],[322] he may pray with head movements while lying down, either on his back or on his side [with his face directed

---

318 That is, if one is a traveller right before a prayer time expires, then he makes it up as two *rakʿas*; if a resident, then four *rakʿas* (*Marāqī 'l-Falāḥ* 2:17; *Imdād* 446; *Tanwīr* 1:532).

319 Because of, for example, intense pain associated with standing, or fear of worsening of one's illness or delay of its healing due to standing. As with all legal dispensations related to fear, the fear must have a reasonable basis, as opposed to being mere delusion. A reasonable basis may be (1) past experience, (2) a clear and obvious case, or (3) the medical opinion of a skilled, Muslim physician that is not an open sinner (*fāsiq*) (*Marāqī 'l-Falāḥ, Ṭaḥṭāwī* 2:20; *Imdād* 448; *Durr, Radd* 1:508).

320 He may sit in whichever position is easiest, even cross-legged for example. If, however, he is able to stand, even while reclining on a wall or support, then he *must* do so. This obligation to stand would apply if he is able to for at least some time without undue hardship, even if only for the time to recite the opening *taḥrīma* and one verse of the Qur'ān, after which he may sit for the rest of the prayer, as mentioned above. In either case, whether he can stand or not, both bowing (*rukūʿ*) and prostration (*sujūd*) *must* be performed; bowing by bending the back, and prostration by placing the forehead and hard part of the nose on the ground. If he is able to perform actual prostration as described, yet nevertheless prays with head movements, the prayer is invalid (*Marāqī 'l-Falāḥ* 2:21, *Hadiyya* 114; *Durr, Radd* 1:509).

321 He must bend his neck for both bowing and prostration, yet he does not have to exaggerate and bend the neck as far as possible. Rather, it is sufficient to slightly bend the neck for each, *as long as* the prostration is lower than the bowing. If it is not, the prayer is not valid. Also, he does not raise anything up to his face upon which to prostrate, as doing so is deemed prohibitively disliked (*makrūh taḥrīman*). He may pray with head movements while sitting or while standing, sitting being more preferable (*Marāqī 'l-Falāḥ, Ṭaḥṭāwī* 2:21–22; *Imdād* 449–50; *Durr, Radd* 1:509–10).

322 Whereby he cannot sit, even while leaning or reclining on a support, without undue hardship. If he can sit thereby yet does not, the prayer is invalid (*Marāqī 'l-Falāḥ* 2:23; *Imdād* 450; *Radd* 1:510).

toward the *qibla*].[323] If he is unable to perform head movements [then he does not pray], and if this state lasts for over a [full] day and night, then according to most scholars he becomes absolved of those obligatory prayers [meaning he does not have to make them up later]. Other scholars, however, maintained that he must make them up upon recovery.[324]

If one loses consciousness or sanity for a duration of five [obligatory (*farḍ*)] prayers [or less], he must make them up upon recovery; if longer,[325] he does not.

BEING ABSOLVED OF THE OBLIGATION OF PRAYING OR FASTING

If a sick person who was unable to perform obligatory fasts and obligatory prayers by head movements dies; or if a traveller dies on his journey [in which he missed fasts]; in either case having died before attaining unto alternative days,[326] then it is not necessary for either one of them to have left a bequest in his will for expiatory payment (*fidya*) [on behalf of those missed prayers or fasts].

If the two [i.e., the sick person recovering or the traveller residing for at least fifteen days] were able to pray or fast, yet did not perform those makeups [before death], then the two must leave a bequest in the will for the expiatory payment of a half *ṣāʿ* [2.2 kg][327] of wheat or a full *ṣāʿ* [4.4 kg] of barley, or its

323 To do so while lying on one's back is better than on one's side, although both are valid. If one lies on his back, he must place a pillow or the like under his head to direct his face toward the *qibla* rather than the sky, so as to enable himself to bend his neck for the actual head movements. In addition, he should ideally bend his knees—if he can without undue hardship—so that his feet are not extended toward the *qibla*, as that position is mildly disliked (*makrūh tanzīhan*) in general for someone able to refrain from doing so (*Marāqī 'l-Falāḥ* 2:23–4; *Imdād* 450–1; *Durr, Radd* 1:510).

324 The first position, which states that he becomes absolved of making up those prayers, is stronger and is the position of legal verdict (*fatwā*). If, however, that state lasted for five prayer times or less, those prayers would have to be made up upon recovery. In either case, one does not pray by eye or eyebrow movements, nor in one's heart (or mind) alone. If one does so, it is not valid as a ritual prayer (*Marāqī 'l-Falāḥ* 2:24–5; *Imdād* 452–3; *Tanwīr, Durr, Radd* 1:510–11).

325 That is, for the issue of someone unable to perform head movements, as well as this issue of losing consciousness, the point at which one becomes absolved of having to make up any missed prayers is by the expiration of the sixth missed prayer (*Marāqī 'l-Falāḥ* 2:26; *Imdād* 454).

326 That is, this ruling is on the condition that neither attained unto alternative days, meaning the sick person did not recover before death, or the traveller did not become a resident before death, for enough days to perform what was missed. A traveller becomes a resident either by entering city limits of his normal place of residence, or by residing elsewhere for at least fifteen days (*Imdād* 455).

327 There is some discrepancy in modern books as to how much weight a half *ṣāʿ* is equivalent to, ranging from 1.7 kg to 2.5 kg. Many contemporary scholars maintain that it is at least 2 kg, and this translation will use 2.2 kg as taught by our teacher, Shaykh Aḥmad al-Jammāl.

equivalent in cash, for each missed obligatory (*farḍ*) prayer, even witr,[328] and for each missed day of fasting.[329] This money is to be taken out from a third of his estate [before division of inheritance].[330]

If an heir of his, or another [third party], voluntarily pays on his behalf, then it is valid for the amount incumbent upon him. If the portion [i.e., a third of the deceased's estate] is not sufficient for that, then he [the executor of the will] may pay an indigent person (*faqīr*) with the intention of expiation and its payment, and then take back what he paid; as a result, the deceased will become absolved of that equivalent amount of prayers or fasts.[331]

It is valid to pay the expiatory payment (*fidya*) for multiple prayers [or fasts], all to one indigent person (*faqīr*), as opposed to the expiation for breaking an oath (*kaffārat al-yamīn*) or the like.[332]

One may not perform ritual prayer (*ṣalāt*) on behalf of another [as it will not count for him], and it will not reduce the amount of expiatory payment for his missed prayers.[333]

The expiatory payment is to be paid only to the indigent (*fuqarā'*), while [it is hoped that] Allāh will overlook the sins of His dead servant, by His limitless grace.

THE WITR PRAYER

The witr prayer[334] is mandatory (*wājib*). It consists of three *rakʿas*, prayed together with one set of *salāms*. In the third *rakʿa* before bowing, one recites

328 Since according to Abū Ḥanīfa, witr is in effect an obligation (*farḍ ʿamalī*) (*Marāqī 'l-Falāḥ* 2:30; *Imdād* 456).

329 Also including both obligatory (*farḍ*) and mandatory (*wājib*) fasts (*Imdād* 455).

330 It may be taken out by the executor of the will or by an heir, but not by any other third party (*Hadiyya* 117).

331 This is then repeated until the entire amount due—overall from each installment—has been transferred to the recipient, such that the deceased becomes absolved of everything incumbent upon him (*Marāqī 'l-Falāḥ* 2:32; *Imdād* 457; *Hadiyya* 118).

332 For which one may not give more than one expiatory payment per day to one recipient (*Imdād* 457).

333 This applies to both praying and fasting. For *ḥajj*, however, the heir of a deceased person may perform it on his behalf, even if without any bequest, in order to fulfill the deceased's *obligatory* (*farḍ*) requirement (*Hadiyya* 120).

334 The witr prayer is just like maghrib, except that it is mandatory (*wājib*) to recite the Fātiḥa and an additional *sūra* in the third *rakʿa* as well. After that, one says *Allāhu akbar* while raising the hands in the same manner as the opening *taḥrīma*; raising the hands for this *takbīr* is *sunna*.

the *qunūt*;[335] this is performed throughout the year. The description of the *qunūt* was already mentioned [see p. 83].

A group can pray the witr in congregation only in Ramaḍān,[336] wherein there is more reward for one to pray it in congregation than to do so alone, [even if] at the end of the night. If one joins the [congregation of the] imām in the third *rakʿa* [even if in the bowing position after the *qunūt* was performed], he does not recite the *qunūt* in that which he makes up [of missed *rakʿas*, since by catching the third *rakʿa* it is as if he recited it].

THE EMPHASIZED *SUNNA* PRAYERS

Those[337] consisting of two *rakʿas*:

- ☐ Before fajr,[338]
- ☐ After ẓuhr,

One then remains standing and recites the *qunūt*, which is mandatory (*wājib*), before bowing and finishing the prayer as normal. Both the *takbīr* and the *qunūt* are to be recited silently while standing, by the one praying alone and by both the imām and the follower if prayed in congregation. If the imām goes into the bowing position before the follower finishes (or starts) reciting the *qunūt*, then he should follow the imām if he fears missing the bowing position. Otherwise, he quickly makes any supplication to fulfill the requisite (see next note) and then joins the imām in bowing.

If one praying witr alone forgets the *qunūt* and then remembers it while bowing, or after having risen up from it, then he neither recites it in the bowing position nor returns to the original standing position in order to do so. Rather, he completes the prayer and performs the forgetfulness prostration (for having missed a mandatory requisite of the prayer) (*Hadiyya* 99–100; *Durr*, *Radd* 1:447–450).

335 Linguistically, *qunūt* means supplication (*duʿā'*). Hence, while the *sunna* is to recite the aforementioned supplication (see p. 83; for Arabic, p. 192), the mandatory (*wājib*) requisite can be fulfilled by any supplication. Examples are *Allāhumma 'ghfir lī* (three times), or *Rabbanā ātinā fi 'd-dunyā ḥasanataw wa fi 'l-ākhirati ḥasanataw wa qinā ʿadhāba 'n-nār*, or even *Yā Rabb* (three times) (*Marāqī 'l-Falāḥ*, *Ṭaḥṭāwī* 1:521; *Hadiyya* 99).

336 It is disliked (*makrūh*) to pray witr in congregation outside of Ramaḍān, unless there are only one or two followers in a congregation, whereby it is not disliked (*Hadiyya* 100, *Radd* 1:476).

337 "Emphasized" meaning that these prayers are close to the ruling of "mandatory" (*wājib*) with regard to sin, since omitting an emphasized *sunna*—persistently without any excuse—entails serious blame and misguidance (see related note, p. 42) (*Radd* 1:452).

338 This prayer is the most emphasized of all *sunna* prayers, according to the sound position. Yet some even deemed it mandatory (*wājib*), due to which, as opposed to the other *sunna* prayers and general voluntary prayers, one could not perform it while sitting or while in a vehicle outside city limits without a valid excuse. Also, it is the only *sunna* prayer that, if missed, can be made up after the time expires (*Durr*, *Radd* 1:453–4), yet only if the obligatory fajr prayer is also missed. In that case, the *sunna* prayer can only be made up after sunrise (and its accompanying time of about 15–20 minutes in which prayers are disliked) yet before midday (*zawāl*).

- [After] maghrib,
- [After ʿishā’].

Those consisting of four *rakʿas*:[339]

- Before ẓuhr,
- Before the Friday prayer,
- After the Friday prayer.

All of these four-*rakʿa* prayers are to be prayed with one [set of] *salāms*. Thus if one separates them [into two prayers of two-*rakʿas* each], then he has not performed the *sunna*; rather, they are merely voluntary prayers.

The recommended prayers [non-emphasized *sunnas*] (*mustaḥabbāt*) are the following:

- Four *rakʿas* before ʿaṣr,
- [Four *rakʿas*] before ʿishā’,
- [Four *rakʿas*] after ʿishā’,
- Six *rakʿas* after maghrib [with three sets of *salāms*].[340]

The following are general [non-emphasized] *sunnas*:

- Two *rakʿas* of greeting the mosque (*taḥiyyatul-masjid*) before sitting down,[341] in any time in which prayer is not disliked [see p. 71],
- Two *rakʿas* after performing *wuḍū’*, before the limbs dry,

---

339 Whether emphasized or non-emphasized, all *sunna* prayers of four-*rakʿas* are performed with one set of closing *salāms*. For the four-*rakʿa* prayers that are emphasized *sunnas*, one recites only the *tashahhud* in the first sitting, and then begins the third *rakʿa* with the *basmala* and Fātiḥa. For those that are non-emphasized *sunnas*, one follows the *tashahhud* in the first sitting with sending blessings upon the Prophet ﷺ before standing for the third *rakʿa*, which one then begins with the opening supplication (*thanā’*) and seeking refuge (*taʿawwudh*) before the *basmala* and Fātiḥa (*Marāqī ’l-Falāḥ* 1:532; *Hadiyya* 101; *Imdād* 405; *Tanwīr*, *Durr* 1:454).

340 The two *rakʿas* of emphasized *sunnas* after maghrib can be counted among these six *rakʿas* (*Hadiyya* 100).

341 That is, preferably before one sits down. Also, any other prayer—whether obligatory, *sunna* or otherwise—fulfills this *sunna* of greeting the mosque, as does entering the mosque with the intention of praying in the congregation if one does so *immediately* upon entering. If one needs to enter the mosque multiple times in a day, then performing this prayer once that day fulfills the *sunna* for every entry. If one cannot perform this prayer—for any reason, such as the time being one in

- ☐ Four to twelve *rakʿas* of late morning[342] (*ḍuḥā*) prayers,
- ☐ Any voluntary (*nafl*) prayer,
- ☐ The prayer of making a decision (*ṣalāt al-istikhāra*) [p. 192],
- ☐ The prayer of need (*ṣalāt al-ḥāja*) [p. 193],
- ☐ The night prayer before the two days of ʿĪd,
- ☐ The night prayer during the last ten nights of Ramaḍān,
- ☐ The night prayer during the first ten nights of Dhū 'l-Ḥijja,
- ☐ The night prayer of mid-Shaʿbān [the 15th of Shaʿbān].

THE NIGHT VIGIL OF RAMAḌĀN (*TARĀWĪḤ*)

The *tarāwīḥ* prayers are [an emphasized] *sunna* for both men and women. They consist of twenty *rakʿas* [performed in sets of two] with ten [sets of] *salāms*. They are valid only after the ʿishā' prayer [until fajr], and they may be performed before the witr prayer.[343]

One should [ideally] rest after every four *rakʿas* for approximately their length [i.e., the length of time taken to perform those four *rakʿas*].

It is a communal *sunna* (*kifāya*)[344] for men to pray them in congregation,

---

which prayer is disliked, or if one is in a state of ritual impurity—then it is recommended that he instead glorify Allāh and send blessings upon the Prophet ﷺ (*Ṭaḥṭāwī* 1:536; *Durr, Radd* 1:456–7).

342 That is, from after sunrise (and its accompanying time of about 15–20 minutes in which prayers are disliked) until before midday (*zawāl*) (*Durr* 1:459).

343 If missed, they may not be made up. Moreover, it is mildly disliked (*makrūh tanzīhan*) for one without an excuse to perform them while sitting. It is prohibitively disliked (*makrūh taḥrīman*) for one to delay joining the prayer until the imām bows, if out of laziness, but not if due to a valid excuse such as old age or weakness. It is also disliked for one to perform them while feeling overcome by sleep; rather, he should wait until he feels awake. Lastly, it is mildly disliked (*makrūh tanzīhan*) to perform the witr prayer or voluntary prayers in congregation outside of Ramaḍān if done in a manner of calling others to it, namely, for four people to pray behind an imām (*Hadiyya* 106–7; *Durr, Radd* 1:473, 475–6).

344 That is, if some members of the community perform these prayers in congregation in the mosque, the entire community is deemed to have fulfilled the *sunna*. In that case, if one person in the community performed them in his home, he would have left a more virtuous deed. Even if he performed them in congregation in his home, he would have missed the merit of doing so in the mosque. If, on the other hand, these prayers are not performed in congregation at all in the mosque, then the entire community would have abandoned this emphasized *sunna*, for which there is serious blame and, with persistence, would be sinful (*Durr, Radd* 1:473–4). To summarize, every Muslim should strive his utmost to perform them in congregation in the mosque due to the immense reward entailed therein, especially since reward is multiplied many times over in the holy month of Ramaḍān.

as well as to recite the entire Qur'ān (*khatm*) [in these prayers, once over the course of the month]. If, however, the lengthy recitation entailed therein is too burdensome for the congregation, the imām should reduce this burden by reciting short *sūras* like al-Kawthar and *Qul Huwa 'Llāhu Aḥad* (al-Ikhlāṣ) over their entirety.[345]

PRAYING INSIDE THE KAʿBA

It is valid to pray both obligatory (*farḍ*) and voluntary (*nafl*) prayers inside the Kaʿba and on top of it.[346]

For [a congregation] either inside the Kaʿba or on top of it, it is valid if one directs his back toward other than the imām's face.[347]

It is valid for one outside the Kaʿba to pray as a follower behind an imām inside it.[348]

If the congregation forms a circle outside the Kaʿba, it is valid, except[349] for those on the same side [of the Kaʿba] as the imām while closer to it.

---

345 The basis of this ruling is that a larger congregation entails greater merit than lengthier recitation (*Radd* 1:475). Similarly, if the prayers prove burdensome for the congregation, the imām may suffice with *Allāhumma ṣalli ʿalā Muḥammadiw wa ʿalā āli Muḥammad* ("O Allāh, send blessings upon Muḥammad and upon the family of Muḥammad") in the final sitting after *tashahhud*. However, he should not recite extremely fast. Nor should he omit the *sunnas* of the opening supplication (*thanā'*), seeking of refuge (*taʿawwudh*), mentioning the Name of Allāh (*basmala*), the three *tasbīḥs* of bowing and prostration, or resting between each set of four *rakʿas*. Nor should he omit the mandatory requisite (*wājib*) of remaining still for at least a moment in every position of the prayer (*Hadiyya* 106; *Durr* 1:475).

346 Although to pray on top of the Kaʿba is deemed mildly disliked (*makrūh tanzīhan*) due to the lack of respect entailed therein (*Marāqī 'l-Falāḥ*, *Ṭaḥṭāwī* 2:4; *Tanwīr*, *Durr* 1:612).

347 If the follower's back is directed toward the imām's face, however, the follower's prayer is invalid, as in any case when the follower is ahead of the imām (*Marāqī 'l-Falāḥ*, *Ṭaḥṭāwī* 2:4; *Imdād* 434–5; *Durr*, *Radd* 1:613–14).

348 That is, as long as the follower is able to know of the imām's movements, whether by seeing him if the door were open, or by hearing his *takbīrs*. Otherwise if the follower had no way of knowing the imām's movements, the follower's prayer would be invalid (*Marāqī 'l-Falāḥ* 2:5; *Imdād* 435; *Radd* 1:613).

349 This word is missing in the Arabic published edition, yet is correctly added here as noted in *Nūr al-Īḍāḥ*. The upshot is that those on the same side as the imām must be behind him, as opposed to followers on other sides of the Kaʿba, who may be closer to it than the imām (*Marāqī 'l-Falāḥ* 2:5; *Imdād* 435).

MAKING UP MISSED PRAYERS (*QAḌĀ'*)

Maintaining correct order (*tartīb*) between a missed prayer and a current prescribed prayer, as well as between missed prayers themselves, is necessary (*mustaḥaqq*).[350]

However, this order is no longer mandatory in one of three situations:

- If the recommended[351] time [of the current prescribed prayer] is about to expire [in which case one prays the current prescribed prayer before making up the missed prayer],
- Forgetfulness,[352]
- If the number of missed prescribed prayers, *excluding* witr, becomes six [or more].

Hence, that which one prays [of current prescribed prayers], even witr, is invalid yet suspended.[353]

350 That is, it is in effect an obligation (*farḍ ʿamalī*), meaning that if not performed in order the prayers *themselves* are rendered invalid (*Marāqī 'l-Falāḥ* 2:34; *Imdād* 458; *Durr*, *Radd* 1:487).

351 Ibn ʿĀbidīn, however, explains that the position of all three Imāms of the Ḥanafī school—Abū Ḥanīfa, Abū Yūsuf, and Muḥammad—is that expiration of the *entire* prayer time is what is considered, not just that of the *recommended* time. This is the position that should be relied upon (*Radd* 1:488).

352 That is, if one forgets that he missed any prayer(s) and therefore prays the current obligatory prayer, he does not have to make up that current obligatory prayer upon remembering his missed prayer(s) (*Al-Durr al-Muntaqā* 1:146). For example, if one prays witr thinking he had prayed ʿishā', and then recalls that he had actually not prayed ʿishā', then he performs ʿishā' alone, and need not repeat witr. The same ruling would apply if one prayed ẓuhr and then later ʿaṣr, only to realize that he had performed ẓuhr alone without *wuḍū'*, then he need only repeat ẓuhr, not ʿaṣr (*Radd* 1:489).

353 That is, if none of the three aforementioned situations is present—i.e., one prays current obligatory prayers, each when its time is not about to expire, despite remembering his missed prayer, which is less than six—then that which he prays of current prayers, obligatory or witr, is invalid yet suspended. "Suspended" means it can potentially become valid. This occurs by the expiration of the fifth obligatory prayer after the missed prayer (such that the total, excluding witr, is six), in which case all five of the suspended prayers are made valid. If, however, he makes up the missed prayer before the expiration of the fifth prayer after the missed prayer, then all of those current obligatory prayers are rendered voluntary (*nafl*) in description, and he must make them all up to fulfill the obligation (*Marāqī 'l-Falāḥ*, *Ṭaḥṭāwī* 2:37; *Imdād* 460; *Multaqā*, *Majmaʿ al-Anhur* 1:144; *Tabyīn* 1:190; *Durr*, *Radd* 1:491). For example, if one misses fajr on Monday and then prays the remaining prayers of that day while remembering it, those remaining prayers (i.e., ẓuhr, ʿaṣr, maghrib, ʿishā', and witr) are invalid yet suspended. If he makes up Monday's fajr before sunrise on Tuesday, those prayers are rendered voluntary, and they all must be made up (in their correct order) to fulfill their obligation. If, however, he does not make up Monday's fajr by sunrise on Tuesday, then those other

It is not necessary [in the intention of making up a missed prayer] to specify the exact prayer; rather, it is sufficient to intend *a* ẓuhr or *an* ʿishāʾ that one owes.[354] This ruling also applies to fasting.

One who did not immigrate to Muslim lands after his conversion to Islam is excused [from the obligation of making up missed prayers or fasts] due to his ignorance of the Sacred Law (*sharīʿa*).[355]

CATCHING THE CONGREGATIONAL PRAYER

Prayer in congregation[356] surpasses its performance alone by twenty-five degrees [in terms of merit].

Thus if the congregation commences after one had already begun the obligatory prayer alone,[357] he should break it with one *salām* while standing and then

prayers are rendered valid (at sunrise), and he need only make up Monday's fajr (*Durr* 1:491). Witr is unique in that it must be performed in order, but is not given consideration in this ruling of six missed prayers absolving one of the obligation of correct order (*Imdād* 460).

354 That is, if one has missed multiple ẓuhr prayers, for example, he does not have to specify the day of the prayer in his intention when he makes it up—such as "*the* ẓuhr of Sunday, May 9th, 2004," or even "the earliest—or most recent—ẓuhr that I owe." Rather, he may simply intend "*a* ẓuhr that I owe." This is the opinion mentioned in *Kanz al-Daqāʾiq*, and is deemed to be the sounder position (*aṣaḥḥ*) by Imām Shurunbulālī in *Marāqī ʾl-Falāḥ* (2:40), as well as others. The same ruling applies to missed fasts of Ramaḍān, as stated in the text above. The other position in the school is that *some* type of specification is required for the validity of makeups, whether the particular day of that prayer, or for example "the earliest—or most recent—ẓuhr that I owe." This opinion entails greater precaution and should therefore be acted upon, yet the former opinion is valid and hence followable.

355 This ruling is not applicable, however, if Islamic knowledge is available in his land (*Radd* 1:493–4), which is the case with most places around the world today.

356 For a congregation of healthy men, the imām must be a sane, adult male that can recite Qurʾān and that is free from any chronic excuses (see related section, p. 59) (*Hadiyya* 73). Some conditions to be a valid follower in congregational prayer include: the follower's heel cannot be in front of the imām's heel; the follower cannot pray a *stronger* prayer than the imām, such as an obligatory (*farḍ*) prayer behind an imām praying a *sunna* or voluntary prayer, including *tarāwīḥ*; the follower cannot pray an obligatory prayer *different* from that of the imām; and finally, the follower cannot pray behind a latecomer (*masbūq*) of another congregational prayer when the latter is making up his missed *rakʿa*(s) (*Hadiyya* 74).

357 This ruling applies only if one is praying in the same vicinity where the congregation commences. If, however, one is in his house while the congregation commences in the mosque, or one is in a mosque while the congregation is in another, then he does not break his prayer in any case. Finally, if a funeral prayer commences while one is praying a voluntary prayer, he should break it to catch the funeral prayer and then make up the voluntary prayer later (as it is mandatory in general to make up broken voluntary prayers) (*Marāqī ʾl-Falāḥ*, *Ṭaḥṭāwī* 2:43; *Imdād* 467).

join the congregation, as long as he had not yet performed the first prostration [for a four-*rakʿa* prayer], or [even] if he had performed the first prostration for prayers that do not have four *rakʿas* [i.e., fajr or maghrib].[358]

For those prayers specifically [i.e., the four-*rakʿa* prayers, if he had already performed the first prostration], he should add a second *rakʿa* such that it becomes a [two-*rakʿa*] voluntary prayer, and then join the congregation, intending the obligatory prayer.

If he had completed three[359] [of the four *rakʿas*], he should finish the prayer [i.e., all four *rakʿas*] and then join the congregation with the intention of performing a voluntary prayer, except for ʿaṣr.[360]

Regarding the [four *rakʿas* of] *sunna* before the Friday prayer or before ẓuhr, one should break the prayer after only two *rakʿas*.[361]

If one [enters the mosque and] finds the imām already performing the obligatory prayer in congregation, he should not pray any *sunna*, except for the two *rakʿas* before fajr,[362] as long as he feels reasonably sure that he will not miss the congregation [upon quickly finishing the *sunna*].[363]

---

358 For fajr or maghrib, if he performs the prostration of the second *rakʿa*, he should finish the prayer by himself. He may *not* join the congregation afterwards, even with the intention of performing a voluntary prayer (*Marāqī ʾl-Falāḥ* 2:44–5; *Imdād* 467).

359 That is, by prostration. If, however, he had only *stood* for the third *rakʿa* upon commencement of the congregation, and had not yet prostrated for that *rakʿa*, then he should break the prayer while standing, with one *salām* (*Marāqī ʾl-Falāḥ* 2:46).

360 As it is prohibitively disliked (*makrūh taḥrīman*) in general to pray voluntary prayers after ʿaṣr (*Marāqī ʾl-Falāḥ* 2:46).

361 That is, if the imām of the Friday prayer rises to the pulpit—or if the congregation of ẓuhr commences—while one is praying that *sunna* prayer, then he should end the prayer after two-*rakʿas* and then must re-pray those four *rakʿas* of *sunna* after the prayer. Yet if he had already performed the prostration of the third *rakʿa*, he would quickly complete the entire four *rakʿas* of the *sunna* prayer with short recitation (*Hadiyya* 107). There is, however, another sound opinion that he may complete the four *rakʿas* in any case (*Marāqī ʾl-Falāḥ*, *Ṭaḥṭāwī* 2:47; *Imdād* 469).

362 The *sunnas* should not be performed amid the congregation, which would be disliked as it entails differing with the congregation (and would cause confusion with his recitation). Rather, it is most preferable for him to perform them in his house. Otherwise if he is in the mosque, then in another room. If there is no other room available in the mosque, then behind a pillar away from the rows of congregation. It is most severely disliked to perform them amid the congregation, followed by performing them directly behind the rows without any barrier (*Marāqī ʾl-Falāḥ*, *Ṭaḥṭāwī* 2:47–8; *Durr*, *Radd* 1:481).

363 Otherwise, if it is likely that by praying the *sunna* prayer he will miss the congregation altogether—not even catching it in the final sitting before the first *salām*—then he joins the congregation without praying the *sunna*, as the merit of congregational prayer exceeds that of even the two *rakʿas* before fajr. Moreover, those two *rakʿas* in general are not made up if missed, unless the obligatory prayer itself is missed as well. In this case, the *sunnas* are to be made up with it only if

The *sunna* prayer before ẓuhr is made up within its prayer time, before its two-*rakʿa sunna*.[364]

The merit of praying in congregation is attained by catching even the final *tashahhud* with the congregation,[365] yet by doing so one is not considered praying in congregation.[366]

One may pray voluntary prayers before any obligatory prayer as long as he feels reasonably sure that he will not miss performing the obligatory prayer in its time.[367]

If one prays the obligatory prayer by himself, after which its congregation begins, it is not disliked to leave the mosque, except for ẓuhr and ʿishāʾ, in which case he should pray with the congregation, intending four *rakʿas* of voluntary prayer.

It is disliked[368] for one to leave a mosque in which the *adhān* has been performed before praying with its congregation, except for a valid excuse.[369]

---

done before midday (*zawāl*) of that day. If fajr is made up after midday, the *sunnas* cannot be made up and only the obligatory prayer is performed (*Hadiyya* 108, 123; *Marāqī 'l-Falāḥ* 2:49; *Imdād* 472).

364 That is, aside from the two *rakʿas* of *sunna* before fajr, the only other *sunna* prayers that can be made up are the four *rakʿas* before ẓuhr and those before the Friday prayer, which if missed are to be prayed after the obligatory prayer. According to one opinion, they should be performed before the *sunna* prayers that follow the obligatory prayer, and according to another opinion, after those *sunna* prayers. Both opinions are sound and followable, the first being slightly stronger. Either way, this can no longer be done once the prayer time of ẓuhr expires (*Hadiyya* 123; *Marāqī 'l-Falāḥ* 2:49–50; *Imdād* 473; *Durr, Radd* 1:482–3).

365 In general, the latecomer of a congregational prayer makes up the *rakʿa*(s) he missed in the following manner: with respect to Qur'ānic recitation, he starts at the beginning of the prayer, yet with respect to sitting and *tashahhud*, he starts at the end of the prayer. So for maghrib, if he caught one *rakʿa* of the congregation, he would make up two *rakʿas*, both with recitation of the Fātiḥa and a *sūra*, with a sitting and *tashahhud* in between. For the four-*rakʿa* prayers, if he caught one *rakʿa* of the congregation, he does the same, followed by another *rakʿa* with just the Fātiḥa, without sitting before it (*Durr* 1:401).

366 That is, with regard to oaths, vows, and the like (*Marāqī 'l-Falāḥ* 2:50–1).

367 Or even in the congregation, let alone praying alone within the prayer time (*Ṭaḥṭāwī* 2:51). For this ruling, "voluntary prayers" include emphasized *sunnas* (*Durr* 1:445; *Radd* 1:483).

368 This is deemed prohibitively disliked (*makrūh taḥrīman*) (*Durr* 1:479; *Ṭaḥṭāwī* 2:55).

369 Such as one who has a pressing need and intends on returning if possible; or one who has to pray elsewhere in order to attend a lesson there; or one who is an imām of another congregational prayer elsewhere, and his absence would cause the people to disperse and not pray in congregation (*Durr, Radd* 1:480; *Marāqī 'l-Falāḥ, Ṭaḥṭāwī* 2:55; *Imdād* 476). Finally, it is not disliked if one leaves the mosque after having prayed alone, as he would have responded once to the call to prayer. An exception is if the congregational prayer commences for ẓuhr or ʿishāʾ while he is still there, in which case he should not leave despite having prayed alone, but rather join with the intention of performing a voluntary prayer (*Imdād* 476–7).

An obligatory prayer is not repeated after its performance.[370]

If one joins the congregation while the imām is in the bowing position, says the *taḥrīma*,[371] then remains standing until the imām raises his head, he did not catch that *rakʿa* of the prayer.[372]

If a follower bows before his imām, yet *after* the imām had recited the minimum obligatory amount by which a *rakʿa* is valid,[373] and the imām then catches him [the follower] in it [bowing], the follower's bowing is valid; otherwise, it is not.[374]

370 That is, after one has prayed an obligatory (*farḍ*) prayer, he may not repeat it due to mere delusion of invalidity or to seek extra reward, as it is prohibitively disliked (*makrūh taḥrīman*) to do so (*Durr*, *Radd* 1:469).

371 The entire *taḥrīma* must be recited while in the standing position. Otherwise, the entrance into the prayer is invalid, rendering the prayer itself invalid (see related note, p. 75).

372 When joining a congregation while the imām is in the bowing position, one catches that *rakʿa* only if, after saying the *taḥrīma* while standing, he reaches the bowing position while the imām is also in the bowing position (*Durr* 1:484). That is, for even a moment, each person is bent such that if he were to extend his hands, they would reach his knees.

373 That is, one verse of the Qur'ān (*Imdād* 475).

374 That is, if either the imām had not recited the obligatory amount before the follower's bowing, or he did not bow while the follower was still in that position, then the follower's bowing is invalid. In that case, the follower's prayer would be invalid if he did not repeat the bowing with or after the imām (*Imdād* 476).

THE PROSTRATION OF FORGETFULNESS (*SUJŪD AL-SAHW*)

It is mandatory (*wājib*) to perform two prostrations, along with an extra *tashahhud* and two *salāms*, for the omission of one or more mandatory (*wājib*) requisites[375] of the prayer due to inattentiveness [or forgetfulness].[376]

---

375 Hence, there is no prostration of forgetfulness for omitting a *sunna* (*Ikhtiyār* 1:111), nor for omitting an integral, since its omission renders the entire prayer invalid (*Marāqī 'l-Falāḥ* 2:60). There is also no forgetfulness prostration for omitting a phrase of remembrance (*dhikr*), except for omitting the mandatory requisite of Qur'ānic recitation (see p. 78), all or part of any *tashahhud*, or the *qunūt* altogether in witr (*Mukhtār* 1:111; *Ṭaḥṭāwī* 2:60; *Tabyīn* 1:193–4).

Examples of cases in which the forgetfulness prostration is mandatory include the following: performing an extra integral of the prayer, such as an extra bowing, prostration, standing, or sitting (*Ikhtiyār* 1:111); reciting a verse of Qur'ān while bowing, standing afterwards, sitting, or in prostration (*Mukhtār* 1:111; *Multaqā* 1:148); forgetting to recite even one verse of the Fātiḥa, or at least three verses or its equivalent after the Fātiḥa, in the first or second *rakʿa*; repeating the Fātiḥa in either of those *rakʿas*; or reciting a full verse of Qur'ān before the Fātiḥa (*Ṭaḥṭāwī* 2:60). Also, failing to rise immediately after completing the *tashahhud* in the first sitting necessitates a forgetfulness prostration—if one remains seated afterwards for the length of time to say *Allāhumma ṣalli ʿalā Muḥammad*, he must prostrate, while less than that is excused (*Durr, Radd* 1:313, 498; *Tabyīn* 1:193). In addition, for the imām of congregational prayer, a forgetfulness prostration is due for reciting aloud in a *rakʿa* of silent recitation or vice-versa (see related section, p. 79), with less than one verse of Qur'ān being excused (*Ṭaḥṭāwī* 2:60–1; *Ikhtiyār* 1:111; *Radd* 1:498; *Tabyīn* 1:194). Also, if one remains silent for the length of time it takes to say *Subḥāna 'Llāh* three times in a measured pace during any part of the prayer, while thinking—even if about the prayer itself or a deficiency therein—or while inattentive, then a forgetfulness prostration is due. However, if one continues verbally making remembrance of any sort while thinking or while inattentive, even recitation of Qur'ān, then prostration is not mandatory (*Marāqī 'l-Falāḥ*, *Ṭaḥṭāwī* 2:76–7). Finally, a follower in congregation never performs the prostration of forgetfulness unless the imām does so, in which case he must follow the imām. If the follower makes any mistakes that would otherwise necessitate a prostration, they are excused. The latecomer performs the prostration with his imām, whether the imām makes the mistake before or after he joins. If the latecomer himself makes a mistake while making up his missed *rakʿa*(s), then he would perform his own prostration at the end of his prayer (*Hadiyya* 124; *Durr, Radd* 1:498–9).

376 Hence, even if one were to accidentally omit *all* the mandatory (*wājib*) requisites of the prayer, it is not sinful and he would have to perform only one prostration of forgetfulness, which consists of two prostrations, followed by an additional *tashahhud* and two *salāms*. These are the mandatory (*wājib*) acts of the prostration of forgetfulness itself. The *sunnas* of it are: to do so after the first (normal) *salām* of the prayer, and to send blessings upon the Prophet ﷺ and make the closing *duʿā'* after the additional *tashahhud* in the sitting that follows the prostration of forgetfulness.

Therefore, if one omits one or more mandatory (*wājib*) requisites in a prayer, he continues the prayer and sits the final sitting at the end of the last *rakʿa*, wherein he recites only the normal *tashahhud*. He then makes one *salām*, turning his head to the right. He then performs the two extra prostrations and sits in a second final sitting, wherein he recites the *tashahhud*, blessings upon the Prophet ﷺ, and closing *duʿā'*, followed by two *salāms* to end the prayer.

If, however, one omits one or more mandatory (*wājib*) requisites of the prayer *intentionally* and without a valid excuse, then it is sinful. He cannot perform a forgetfulness prostration. Rather, in order to rectify the deficiency in the prayer, it is mandatory (*wājib*) for him to repeat the entire

It is *sunna* to perform the prostration of forgetfulness after the first *salām*; thus if one does so before the *salām*, it is mildly disliked (*makrūh tanzīhan*).

One becomes absolved of performing the forgetfulness prostration if a time in which prayers are disliked enters—such as the changing of the sun [after ʿaṣr]—or if the time expires such that the prayer is broken—such as sunrise [for fajr].

If one thinks he has finished a four-*rakʿa* prayer, [says the closing *salāms*,] stands up and then realizes he had actually been in the first sitting [having prayed only two *rakʿas*], he should complete it[377] and then perform the prostration of forgetfulness. If someone else joins his prayer, it is valid.

If one begins to rise for the third *rakʿa* [in a three or four-*rakʿa* prayer] and then realizes he had not performed the first sitting, he should return to the sitting position.[378] The same ruling applies to the final sitting [i.e., he returns to it if omitted] as long as he had not prostrated. If, however, he performs the prostration of the extra *rakʿa* [in this latter case], his obligatory (*farḍ*) prayer is invalidated [and becomes a voluntary prayer]. He then adds another *rakʿa* such that the extra two *rakʿas* constitute an [additional] voluntary prayer for him, and then performs the prostration of forgetfulness.[379]

---

prayer. The same ruling applies if one does something that is prohibitively disliked (*makrūh taḥrīman*) related to the prayer (see related section, p. 85).

In either case, if he fails to repeat the prayer before the time expires, then he has incurred another sin. Afterwards, according to Ibn ʿĀbidīn, it remains mandatory (*wājib*) for him to repeat the prayer, yet according to Imāms Ḥaṣkafī and Ṭaḥṭāwī, it is merely recommended (*Hadiyya* 124; *Marāqī 'l-Falāḥ*, *Ṭaḥṭāwī* 2:59–61; *Durr*, *Radd* 1:486–7).

377 That is, he should resume the prayer and perform its last two *rakʿas*. This is possible as long as he had not done an action contrary to the prayer, such as eating or speaking—i.e., with words that would otherwise nullify the prayer (see p. 83), while words of remembrance or Qur'ānic recitation are excused. Turning the torso away from the *qibla* direction also prevents one from resuming the prayer (*Hadiyya* 126; *Durr*, *Radd* 1:505; *Imdād* 492; *Shalabī* 1:199).

378 It is mandatory (*wājib*) to return to the sitting position as long as he had not fully stood up. If he was closer to the sitting position when he returned to it—meaning that his knees were still bent upon recalling and sitting back down—he does not perform the prostration of forgetfulness. If, however, he was closer to the standing position when he recalled—meaning that he had straightened his legs yet his back was still bent—he still returns to the sitting position yet performs the prostration of forgetfulness.

If his back was also straight though, he would have fully stood up and thus would not be allowed to return to the sitting position. Rather, he completes the prayer (having fully omitted the first sitting), and performs the forgetfulness prostration. If he had fully stood up and nevertheless returned to the sitting position before completing the prayer, then the prayer remains valid yet he would have incurred sin (*Hadiyya* 125; *Marāqī 'l-Falāḥ* 2:66–8; *Durr*, *Radd* 1:499–500; *Imdād* 486–7).

379 That is, once he performs the first prostration of the fifth *rakʿa*—the extra *rakʿa* added—after having omitted the final sitting after the fourth *rakʿa*, the *entire* prayer automatically turns into a voluntary prayer consisting of four *rakʿas*. Now that he is in the midst of a fifth *rakʿa*, he may if he

If one needed to perform the prostration of forgetfulness but rather said the closing *salāms*, after which another person joined his prayer as a follower, then the follower's joining will be valid only if he [the original person praying] performs the forgetfulness prostration.

If one does not frequently have doubts[380] in the prayer, then a doubt in the prayer would invalidate it. If, however, it is frequent, he should make a reasonable estimation (*taḥarrī*) [and adhere to it].[381] Otherwise, he should assume the lower number and sit after every *rakʿa* that could possibly be the last one.[382]

THE PROSTRATION OF RECITAL (*SAJDAT AL-TILĀWA*)

The prostration of recital is mandatory (*wājib*),[383] yet it can be delayed unless the verse is recited in the prayer; [384]

---

wishes add a sixth *rakʿa* so as to perform a second voluntary prayer consisting of two *rakʿas*. In any case though, after completing this prayer, he must still perform the obligatory (*farḍ*) prayer that he was originally performing. The same ruling applies to adding a third *rakʿa* in fajr, or a fourth in maghrib. An exception, however, is that one does not add the second extra *rakʿa* in maghrib, so as to keep the total number of *rakʿas* even (at four). Finally, as opposed to what is stated in the text above, one does *not* perform a forgetfulness prostration afterwards according to the sounder position (*aṣaḥḥ*) (*Hadiyya* 125; *Marāqī 'l-Falāḥ*, *Ṭaḥṭāwī* 2:69–71; *Imdād* 488–9; *Durr*, *Radd* 1:501–2).

380 This ruling refers to the first time in one's life as an adult that one has doubt during the prayer regarding the number of *rakʿas* that have been performed, like if unsure whether one had prayed two or three *rakʿas*. Doubt in this context refers to equivalency of two matters, that is, a 50-50 split without inclination toward one option over the other. If, however, one has such a doubt after having completed the prayer—or after having sat the final sitting for the length of time it takes to recite the *tashahhud* (i.e., after having performed the last integral of the prayer)—then the doubt is given no due consideration and is of no consequence. Only reasonable surety or certainty would be given consideration (*Durr*, *Radd* 1:505–6; *Imdād* 494; *Marāqī 'l-Falāḥ*, *Ṭaḥṭāwī* 2:78–9; *Hadiyya* 126).

381 According to most scholars, frequent occurrence of doubt is established with the second time it occurs in one's life as an adult. It is also important for one who has doubt during the prayer to not stop verbally making remembrance or reciting Qur'ān while thinking and making his reasonable estimation, so as not to necessitate a forgetfulness prostration by remaining silent for the time it takes to say *Subḥāna 'Llāh* three times in a measured pace (see related note, p. 106) (*Durr*, *Radd* 1:506–7; *Hadiyya* 126–7).

382 That is, if he is unable to make an estimation, he assumes the lower number of *rakʿas*, performs a sitting after each *rakʿa* since any one could be an even *rakʿa*, and performs a forgetfulness prostration at the end (*Durr*, *Radd* 1:506–7; *Marāqī 'l-Falāḥ*, *Ṭaḥṭāwī* 2:80–2; *Imdād* 495).

383 Even for one in a state of major ritual impurity (*junub*), who must perform it after becoming pure. However, it is not mandatory on a child or a woman in menstruation or postnatal bleeding, neither by reciting nor by hearing the verse (*Tanwīr*, *Durr* 1:516). Also, it is prohibitively disliked (*makrūh taḥrīman*) to skip or avoid a verse of prostration and instead recite the rest of a *sūra* (*Tanwīr*, *Durr* 1:523).

384 If the verse is recited in the prayer, its prostration is mandatory therein, as it is deemed a part of the prayer itself. It cannot be performed after the prayer. Hence, finishing the prayer with-

Its legal cause is recitation of any one of fourteen specific verses, that are found in the following *sūras*: al-Aʿrāf, al-Raʿd, al-Naḥl, al-Isrā', Maryam, al-Ḥajj, al-Furqān, al-Naml, al-Sajda, Ṣād, Fuṣṣilat, al-Najm, al-Inshiqāq, and Iqra' Bismi (al-ʿAlaq) [see p. 194]. However, hearing[385] the verse is a condition [for the prostration to be mandatory], even if it were recited in a language other than Arabic *if* the listener understood its meaning.[386]

It can be fulfilled by an extra bowing or an extra prostration in the prayer [if the verse is recited in that prayer]. The normal bowing of the prayer can also suffice, yet only if one intends the prostration of recital thereby, while the normal prostration of the prayer will suffice even if not accompanied by such an intention, as long as it [i.e., the normal bowing or the normal prostration] is performed immediately[387] after its recital.[388]

Joining the congregation in a *rakʿa* in which the imām had recited a verse of prostration [and had already prostrated for it] is effectively like joining him in it [i.e., the prostration];[389] otherwise, he must perform his own prostration[390] if he heard it from the imām.

---

out prostrating for the verse is sinful, and even within the prayer its delay is sinful (*Imdād* 497–8; *Durr, Radd* 1:517–8; *Badā'iʿ* 1:448).

385 Hence, it is not mandatory on one who did not hear its recital, even if he were present at the place of recital (*Radd* 1:513–4). Also, it is not mandatory if one hears an echo of the recital (*Marāqī 'l-Falāḥ* 2:92; *Tanwīr* 1:517). Based on this ruling, one does not have to prostrate for hearing a recording, but does for a live broadcast.

386 That is, with respect to *hearing* a verse of prostration, if it is recited in a language other than Arabic, the prostration is not mandatory unless one understood its meaning. If recited in Arabic, however, one must perform the prostration whether he understood it or not, unless he does not know Arabic and did not *know* that it is a verse of prostration. With respect to *reciting* a verse of prostration in a language other than Arabic, the prostration is mandatory whether one understood it or not (*Hadiyya* 128; *Radd* 1:514).

387 That is, if one recites more than three additional verses afterwards, it is too late for the normal bowing or normal prostration to fulfill the prostration of recital. It would then have to be performed within the prayer with an extra bowing or an extra prostration. If three additional verses are at the end of the *sūra*, such as in al-Inshiqāq or al-Isrā', the normal bowing or prostration can still suffice after those final three verses (*Radd* 1:519). In general, an immediate extra prostration is most preferable (*Hadiyya* 129).

388 If the imām in a silent prayer recites a verse of prostration, he should fulfill the obligation by the normal prostration of the prayer. Otherwise, it is disliked for him to recite such a verse in a silent prayer, for he will either omit the mandatory prostration altogether or perform an extra prostration to fulfill the obligation, which in turn will confuse the congregation (*Hadiyya* 135; *Durr, Radd* 1:519).

389 Therefore, he does not have to perform its prostration, neither within the prayer nor outside of it (*Marāqī 'l-Falāḥ, Ṭaḥṭāwī* 2:100; *Hadiyya* 130; *Durr, Radd* 1:518).

390 That is, if he misses that *rakʿa*, and had heard the verse of prostration from the imām, then he must perform his own prostration *outside* of the prayer (*Durr, Radd* 1:518).

One prostration suffices for the recital of a verse of prostration multiple times if [that verse is] repeated in the same sitting.[391]

If a verse of prostration is recited before the prayer, then one's prostration for it within the prayer suffices; the opposite, however, does not hold.[392]

It is recommended for one to recite it silently if someone else is present and not paying attention.[393] It is also recommended for one to stand before performing its prostration.[394]

All the conditions of the prayer are stipulated for the validity of the prostration of recital, except the opening *taḥrīma.*

It is performed in the following manner: one prostrates once between two *takbīrs,* both of which are *sunna.* One does not raise the hands, recite *tashahhud,* or say closing *salāms.*

THE PROSTRATION OF GRATITUDE

There is difference of opinion as to whether the prostration of gratitude is legislated [i.e., recommended without being disliked] or disliked.[395] If one desires to express gratitude, he should pray two *rakʿas* out of gratitude to Allāh, Glorious and Exalted.

---

391 One must perform a separate prostration if a different verse of prostration is recited, even if in the same sitting. If the same verse is repeated in the same sitting, then one prostration suffices. If it is repeated in different sittings, a separate prostration is mandatory per sitting. Legally, a change of sitting can be actual or effective. An actual change of sitting occurs by moving three or more steps if one is outside in an open area, while two steps or less is not a change of sitting. An actual change also occurs by switching to a different room if one is indoors, or by leaving the mosque. One room or mosque, however, is considered one area whereby moving around does not affect one's sitting. An effective change occurs by engaging in an unrelated action between recitations, like eating three or more bites of food, taking three or more sips of a drink, or speaking with three or more words. Less than that does not affect one's sitting, nor does engaging in remembrance of Allāh (*dhikr*), standing up, sitting down, or just remaining silent while seated, even if for a long time (*Marāqī 'l-Falāḥ, Ṭaḥṭāwī* 2:102–5; *Hadiyya* 131–2).

392 That is, if the verse is recited in the prayer, its prostration must be performed within that prayer, not outside the prayer (*Hadiyya* 130; *Tanwīr, Durr* 1:518).

393 If he does not know whether those around him are prepared to prostrate, or feels it will be difficult for them, he should recite it silently. If someone else is preoccupied with some work and therefore does not hear the recital, it is not mandatory for him to prostrate (*Hadiyya* 133).

394 And according to some, to stand up again afterwards (*Durr* 1:515).

395 The relied-upon position and that of legal verdict (*fatwā*) is that it is recommended in general, especially when one receives a manifest blessing or is protected from a calamity, yet disliked specifically after the prayer, so that ignorant people do not deem it to be mandatory (*wājib*) or a *sunna* (*Hadiyya* 135; *Durr, Radd* 1:524).

An important note regarding a method of warding off every harm and stress
Imām Nasafī and others have stated, "If one recites all [fourteen] verses of prostration in one sitting, and performs a separate prostration for each verse, then Allāh Most High will take care of all his worries [in both this life and the next]" [p. 194].

THE FRIDAY PRAYER (*JUMUʿA*)

The Friday prayer is an individual obligation (*farḍ ʿayn*), with its conditions,[396] namely:

- ☐ Being male,
- ☐ Being a freeman,
- ☐ Residence in a city, or [even] in its outskirts according to the sounder position (*aṣaḥḥ*) [i.e., within city limits],[397]
- ☐ Sound health,[398]
- ☐ Safety from any oppressor [i.e., general safety of passage],
- ☐ Sound eyesight,[399]
- ☐ Ability to walk.[400]

---

396 That is, attending the Friday prayer is obligatory on every Muslim that fulfills these conditions. If one of these conditions is not met, it is not obligatory. Rather, one may either attend nevertheless, as it still takes the place of ẓuhr—and if a man, may even lead the Friday prayer—or pray ẓuhr elsewhere (*Mukhtār* 1:126; *Tanwīr*, *Durr* 1:548).

397 Hence, the Friday prayer is not obligatory on travellers—even if staying in a city (unless residing therein for 15 days)—nor on those that reside well outside city limits (*Marāqī 'l-Falāḥ*, *Ṭaḥṭāwī* 2:115–6; *Tanwīr*, *Durr* 1:553).

398 That is, to be free from an illness that prevents one from leaving on his own (without help from another), or an illness that would worsen by going out. The same ruling applies to one taking care of an ill person who would be left unattended if the caretaker would leave for the prayer, as well as to a very old, debilitated man (*Marāqī 'l-Falāḥ*, *Ṭaḥṭāwī* 2:117; *Hadiyya* 136; *Durr*, *Radd* 1:547).

399 Ibn ʿĀbidīn maintains that the Friday prayer is obligatory on someone with poor eyesight yet who normally walks around town, knows its roads and goes to (for example) the marketplace alone without undue hardship, and can therefore go to the mosque without having to ask anyone for help (*Radd* 1:547–8).

400 That is, if one is unable to walk on his own, then he is absolved of the obligation, even if he finds someone or something to carry him (*Radd* 1:547–8). Another excuse that absolves one from the obligation of attending the Friday prayer, or any congregational prayer for that matter, is heavy rain, snow, hail, or mud (whereby there is undue hardship in going to the mosque) (*Marāqī 'l-Falāḥ*, *Ṭaḥṭāwī* 2:117; *Hadiyya* 137; *Durr* 1:548).

The conditions of its validity[401] are the following:

- ☐ A city, or its outskirts,[402]
- ☐ The head of state or one appointed by him [to lead the prayer],[403]
- ☐ The time of ẓuhr,[404]
- ☐ A sermon (*khuṭba*) that precedes it, delivered intentionally, also in the time of ẓuhr,[405]
- ☐ The presence of even one person to listen to the sermon, that person being among those with whom the Friday prayer is valid,[406]
- ☐ General permission [for Muslims to join its congregation],[407]
- ☐ A congregation of [at least] three men other than the imām, even if they are slaves or travellers.[408] The condition is that they remain in the prayer with the imām until he prostrates—that is, if they [break the prayer and] leave him alone after he has made prostration, he is to complete the two *rakʿas* of the Friday prayer on his own; otherwise, it is rendered invalid.[409]

---

401 That is, if even one of these conditions is not fulfilled, the Friday prayer itself is rendered invalid.

402 That is, the Friday prayer is valid only if performed in a town or city—within city limits—as opposed to in a small village or open desert. Within a city, it may be performed in multiple places (*Kanz, Tabyīn* 1:217–8; *Imdād* 520; *Multaqā* 1:165, 167; *Durr, Radd* 1:541).

403 If for some reason there is no ruler, or there is no permission from him, yet nevertheless a group of Muslims congregate and agree on someone to lead the Friday or ʿĪd prayers, it is valid (and, hence, obligatory to attend) (*Ṭaḥṭāwī* 2:119–20; *Durr, Radd* 1:540–1).

404 Hence, the Friday prayer is not valid if performed before the prayer time, and is invalidated by the expiration of the prayer time (*Hadiyya* 138; *Kanz, Tabyīn* 1:219; *Multaqā* 1:166, 169; *Tanwīr* 1:543).

405 Hence if there is no sermon, or if the sermon is delivered before the time of ẓuhr, or if it is delivered after the prayer, then the Friday prayer itself is rendered invalid, even if the prayer is performed in the time of ẓuhr (*Shalabī* 1:219; *Durr* 1:543).

406 That is, a sane adult that is male, even if a traveller or if ill, as opposed to a woman or child (*Marāqī 'l-Falāḥ* 2:122–3; *Hadiyya* 139; *Radd* 1:543). Imāms Ḥaṣkafī and Shurunbulālī mention that the presence of one such person is sufficient for the sermon, whereas most scholars mention that a congregation (i.e., at least three men) is necessary. Ibn ʿĀbidīn seems to incline toward the latter opinion (*Durr, Radd* 1:543).

407 That is, no Muslim may be barred from joining the Friday prayer; otherwise, the prayer itself is rendered invalid. Ibn ʿĀbidīn, however, suggests that if those that are barred are still able to attend the Friday prayer elsewhere, then it is valid (*Radd* 1:546).

408 That is, a condition for the prayer itself is a congregation of at least three men, even if they did not attend the sermon. They may be people who are not obligated to attend, such as travellers or people that are ill, as opposed to women or children, who would not fulfill the condition regardless of their number, even if accompanied with two men (*Hadiyya* 140; *Durr, Radd* 1:545–6).

409 That is, if they leave him before the first prostration, the prayer is rendered invalid, so he

Any vicinity that has its own governor (*amīr*) and judge (*qāḍī*) carrying out the law and establishing penal punishments (*ḥudūd*) is considered a valid city (*miṣr*) for the Friday prayer.

The minimum obligation for a valid sermon is one *tasbīḥa* or one *tahlīla*.[410] It is *sunna* [for the one delivering it (*khaṭīb*)] to perform two sermons, with a sitting in between, in a state of ritual purity and while standing.[411]

It is mandatory (*wājib*) to hasten (*saʿy*)[412] to the Friday prayer, at the first call to prayer, leaving any sort of distraction [unrelated to preparation for the prayer].

Once the imām emerges [from his quarters, or if there are no quarters, once he stands to ascend the pulpit (*mimbar*)], one may not pray or speak [until after the prayer].[413] It is disliked to eat, drink, fiddle around, or turn to and fro during the sermon.

It is also disliked to leave the city after the [first] call to prayer (*adhān*) without having prayed the Friday prayer.[414]

---

instead prays four *rakʿas* of ẓuhr (*Hadiyya* 140; *Radd* 1:545–6; *Multaqā, Majmaʿ al-Anhur* 1:168).

410 That is, to say *Subḥāna 'Llāh* once (*tasbīḥa*), or *Lā ilāha illa 'Llāh* once (*tahlīla*); the same applies to *al-Ḥamdu li 'Llāh* once (*taḥmīda*). However, to do so with any of these phrases alone is disliked. Ibn ʿĀbidīn states that it seems to be mildly disliked (*tanzīhan*), which is the opinion of Imām Ṭaḥṭāwī (*Marāqī 'l-Falāḥ, Ṭaḥṭāwī* 2:127; *Hadiyya* 139; *Durr, Radd* 1:543).

411 All of these, however, are not conditions for its validity. In addition, it is disliked for the sermons to be excessively long, as well as to not contain recitation of at least one Qur'ānic verse, blessings upon the Prophet ﷺ, and exhortation to piety (*taqwā*) (*Durr, Radd* 1:544; *Multaqā, Majmaʿ al-Anhur* 1:168).

412 Hastening to the Friday prayer is actually obligatory (*farḍ*) (*Hadiyya* 141; *Imdād* 532; *Radd* 1:552), as is leaving anything at the first call to prayer (*adhān*) that would impede one from hastening to it (*Imdād* 533; *Radd* 1:552), including trade if attending the prayer is obligatory on *either* the buyer or seller. If, however, both parties are exempted from attending, then it is not sinful to conduct business at that time (*Marāqī 'l-Falāḥ, Ṭaḥṭāwī* 2:133).

413 Everything that is prohibited in the prayer itself is prohibited during the sermon, as remaining silent and listening to it is mandatory (*wājib*). Hence, one does not reply to a greeting or to a sneeze, command to good or forbid evil, or even say *Subḥāna 'Llāh*. One does not make supplication (*duʿā'*) or respond to it with *āmīn*, except within one's heart. *Any* type of speech during the sermon is deemed prohibitively disliked (*makrūh taḥrīman*). Likewise, when the imām ascends the pulpit, he should not greet the congregation. When he commands them to send blessings upon the Prophet ﷺ, they do so internally without saying it. They should not even raise their hands during his supplication (*Marāqī 'l-Falāḥ* 2:135–6; *Hadiyya* 141; *Durr, Radd* 1:550–1).

414 With the exception of someone who, intending to embark on a journey, would miss his caravan were he to pray the Friday prayer, and is unable to undertake the journey by himself (*Hadiyya* 141; *Radd* 1:553). Otherwise, to do so is prohibitively disliked (*makrūh taḥrīman*) for those on whom attending is obligatory (*farḍ*), yet permissible for those excused (*Ṭaḥṭāwī* 2:137).

The Friday prayer takes place of the ẓuhr prayer, [even] for one excused from attending, like a traveller or person that is ill.

If one joins [the congregation of] the Friday prayer in the *tashahhud* [i.e., in the final sitting], or [even] in the prostration of forgetfulness,[415] he completes it as the Friday prayer.[416]

THE ᶜĪD PRAYER

The two ᶜĪd prayers are mandatory (*wājib*) on the one for whom the Friday prayer is obligatory (*farḍ*), with its same conditions, except for the sermon, which is a *sunna* for them.[417]

On the Day of Fiṭr [1st of Shawwāl], it is recommended (*mustaḥabb*)[418] to eat an odd number of dates or something else [sweet], perform the *ghusl*, apply scent, use the toothstick (*siwāk*), wear one's finest clothes, and pay the charity of the end of Ramaḍān (*ṣadaqat al-fiṭr*)[419]—based on one's ability—before leaving for the prayer area (*muṣallā*).

One should head out walking, silently[420] reciting the *takbīrs* until the beginning of the ᶜĪd prayer. He should [ideally] return [back home] from a different route.

It is disliked to pray voluntary prayers in the mosque [i.e., ᶜĪd prayer area] in any case, as well as in one's home before the ᶜĪd prayer.[421]

Its time starts after the sun has risen one [or two] spear's length [above the

415 Although later scholars preferred that the imām of the Friday or ᶜĪd prayers not perform the prostration of forgetfulness, so as not to confuse the large congregation. If he does so nevertheless, it is valid and not disliked, but merely less preferable (*Ṭaḥṭāwī* 2:139; *Hadiyya* 140; *Radd* 1:550).

416 That is, when he rises to make up the missed *rakᶜa*(s), he completes the two *rakᶜas* since it remains the Friday prayer and does not become ẓuhr.

417 As opposed to that of the Friday prayer, the sermon of the ᶜĪd prayer is a *sunna*, and is to be delivered after the prayer itself. Hence, if it is omitted or performed before the prayer, there is heavy blame incurred, yet the ᶜĪd prayer is still valid and would not be repeated (*Shalabī* 1:219; *Durr*, *Radd* 1:555).

418 The sound position (*ṣaḥīḥ*) is that these things are actually emphasized *sunnas*, specifically for men (i.e., those attending the prayer) (*Radd* 1:556).

419 This charity is actually mandatory (*wājib*). What is *sunna* is to give it—as well as to do all of the above, including eating something—*before* leaving for the prayer area (*Durr*, *Radd* 1:556–7). Today many Muslims give this charity at the prayer area itself before the prayer, which is also valid.

420 As opposed to the *takbīrs* of ᶜĪd al-Aḍḥā, which are recited aloud on the way to the prayer area (*Radd* 1:557).

421 That is, it is mildly disliked (*makrūh tanzīhan*) to perform voluntary prayers at the prayer

horizon—namely, after the time period in which prayers are disliked] until midday (*zawāl*). If there is a valid excuse, it may be delayed until the following day.[422]

The way of performing the prayer is the following:

One makes the intention of performing the ʿĪd prayer. The follower makes the additional intention of being a follower. Then [after the opening *taḥrīma*] both the imām and congregation recite the opening supplication (*thanāʾ*), after which they all pronounce three extra *takbīrs*, raising their hands for each one.[423] Next the imām says the *taʿawwudh* and the *basmala* silently, and then recites the Fātiḥa and a *sūra* [aloud]. It is preferred for the *sūra* to be *Sabbiḥi ʾsma Rabbika ʾl-Aʿlā* [Sūrat al-Aʿlā]. He then bows [and finishes the *rakʿa* like normal].

When he stands for the second *rakʿa*, he begins with the *basmala* [silently], followed by the Fātiḥa and [preferably] Sūrat al-Ghāshiya [both recited aloud]. He then performs three extra *takbīrs* [all of which are mandatory (*wājib*)] in this second *rakʿa*, raising his hands for each one. This method is more preferable than performing the extra *takbīrs* of the second *rakʿa* before the recitation.[424]

After the prayer, the imām delivers two sermons in which he teaches [the congregation] the rules pertaining to the charity of the end of Ramaḍān (*ṣadaqat al-fiṭr*).

The rules of Aḍḥā [the 10th of Dhul-Ḥijja] are similar to those of Fiṭr, yet [with the following exceptions]: eating is delayed[425] until after the prayer; the *takbīrs* on the way [to the prayer, as well as at the prayerarea] are said aloud; and the rules of the ritual sacrifice (*uḍḥiya*)[426] as well as the *takbīrs* of the three

---

area, both before and after the ʿĪd prayer, as well as to do so at one's home beforehand. It is not disliked at one's home afterwards, but rather recommended (*Durr, Radd* 1:558).

422 By agreement of our scholars, the ʿĪd prayer may be performed in multiple places within one city. In addition, it may be delayed up to midday (*zawāl*) of the following day—but no later—for a valid excuse, such as heavy rain, or lack of visibility of the crescent moon. If delayed without a valid excuse, the prayer is invalid (*Marāqī ʾl-Falāḥ, Ṭaḥṭāwī* 2:159; *Hadiyya* 143; *Tanwīr, Durr* 1:561–2).

423 Each *takbīr* is mandatory (*wājib*); raising the hands for each *takbīr*, in the manner one does for the opening *taḥrīma*, is *sunna*. Between each *takbīr*, one keeps his arms to his sides. One does not raise the hands for the *takbīr* of bowing (*Marāqī ʾl-Falāḥ* 2:155; *Hadiyya* 142; *Durr, Radd* 1:561).

424 Both methods are allowed, as well as adding more *takbīrs*, such as the common method of seven in the first *rakʿa* and five in the second *rakʿa*. In any case, it is mandatory (*wājib*) for the congregation to follow the imām, unless he does more than sixteen *takbīrs* total, in which case they remain silent (*Marāqī ʾl-Falāḥ* 2:155–6; *Hadiyya* 143; *Durr, Radd* 1:559).

425 That is, it is recommended to delay eating until after the prayer, even for children and, based on the practice of the Companions, babies that suckle. Yet it is not disliked to eat beforehand, not even mildly (*tanzīhan*), as it relates more to etiquette (*adab*) (*Durr, Radd* 1:562).

426 It is recommended (*mustaḥabb*)—but not mandatory (*wājib*), even for the one perform-

days after ʿĪd al-Aḍḥā (*tashrīq*) are taught in the sermon.[427] This ʿĪd prayer may be delayed up to three days if there is a valid excuse.[428]

According to the Imām [Abū Ḥanīfa], the *takbīrs* of *tashrīq* are mandatory (*wājib*) from fajr of ʿArafa until ʿaṣr of Naḥr [i.e., the Day of ʿĪd], after[429] each obligatory (*farḍ*) prayer performed in a congregation that is not disliked, on both the imām that is a resident in the city as well as his followers in each congregation.

The two [companions—Abū Yūsuf and Muḥammad] maintained that these *takbīrs* are mandatory (*wājib*) on even the one praying alone, the traveller, and the resident of a village;[430] [and that they are to be recited] until ʿaṣr of the fifth day after the Day of ʿArafa. This is the opinion that is acted upon (*bihī yuʿmal*).[431]

There is no harm in reciting the *takbīrs* after the ʿĪd prayer [itself].

They [the *takbīrs* of tashrīq] are to say:

> Allāh is the greatest, Allāh is the greatest; There is no deity except Allāh. Indeed, Allāh is the greatest, Allāh is the greatest; For Allāh is all praise [p. 195].

It is recommended to add:

> Allāh is indeed the Greatest; Much Praise is for Him; Glory be to Him, with much praise, morning and evening. There is no deity except Him alone; He fulfilled His

ing the ritual slaughtering—to refrain from cutting nails and trimming hair in the first ten days of Dhū 'l-Ḥijja (*Radd* 1:565).

427 The *takbīrs* of *tashrīq* should also be taught in the sermon of the Friday prayer before ʿĪd, as it is mandatory (*wājib*) to say them starting on fajr of the Day of ʿArafa (the day before ʿĪd), as explained above (*Marāqī 'l-Falāḥ* 2:161–2; *Radd* 1:562).

428 That is, it is valid up to midday (*zawāl*) on the 12th of Dhū 'l-Ḥijja, even without an excuse, although in that case the delay would entail doing wrong (*isāʾa*); with a valid excuse, there is no blame (*Durr, Radd* 1:562).

429 That is, from fajr of the 9th until ʿaṣr of the 10th, the Day of ʿĪd, for a total of eight prayers (*Durr* 1:564). To fulfill the requisite, they must be recited immediately after each prayer, without a break of something contrary to the prayer, such as leaving the mosque or speaking, even if by accident or out of forgetfulness (*Durr, Radd* 1:563).

430 That is, on everyone that must perform the prescribed daily prayers (*Radd* 1:564).

431 This is also the position of legal verdict (*fatwā*). It is to be recited from fajr of the 9th until ʿaṣr of the 13th, for a total of twenty-three prayers. It must be recited *once* immediately after every obligatory (*farḍ*) prayer—including the Friday prayer and, if it is the general practice of the Muslims in one's area, the ʿĪd prayer—but not after witr, *sunna* or voluntary prayers. It must be recited by everyone, male or female, whether praying in congregation or by oneself. Women, however, should recite it silently. If the imām forgets to recite it, the follower must do so nevertheless. The latecomer to a congregation recites it after making up his missed *rakʿa*(s) (*Marāqī 'l-Falāḥ, Ṭaḥṭāwī* 164–5; *Imdād* 550; *Durr, Radd* 1:563–4).

promise, gave victory to His servant, strengthened His soldiers, and [He] alone defeated the confederates. There is no deity except Him. We worship none but Him, practicing the religion solely for His sake, even if the disbelievers hate it. O Allāh, send blessings upon our Master Muḥammad, and upon the family of our Master Muḥammad, and upon the Companions of our Master Muḥammad, and upon the wives of our Master Muḥammad; and send abundant peace on them all [p. 196].

Imitating the pilgrims' standing of the Day of ʿArafa is not an act of worship.[432]

THE PRAYER OF ECLIPSE (*KUSŪF WA KHUSŪF*)

It is *sunna* to pray two *rakʿas* similar to a voluntary prayer when there is a solar eclipse (*kusūf*), performed [in congregation] with the imām of the Friday prayer, yet without the call to prayer (*adhān*), call to commencement (*iqāma*), loud recitation, or sermon.

It is *sunna* to prolong its recitation, bowing, and prostration. Afterwards, the imām should make supplication (*duʿāʾ*). He may either sit facing the *qibla*, or stand facing the congregation, the latter being preferred. The congregation should continue saying *āmīn* as he supplicates until the sun fully appears.

If the imām does not attend the prayer, they should pray separately, as they should [normally] for a lunar eclipse (*khusūf*), darkness during the daytime, strong winds, or any general catastrophe or terror.

THE PRAYER FOR RAIN (*ISTISQĀʾ*)

[During a time of drought] it is recommended (*mustaḥabb*) for members of the community to leave the city for it [i.e., the prayer for rain] for three days, on foot and in shabby clothes, in a state of humbleness and reverence for Allāh Most High. They should give some charity every day before going out.

It is recommended [for the entire community to go out, and hence even] to take with them their animals, as well as the elderly and the children.

432 Hence, it should not be performed, as it is not from the *sunna* but rather an innovation in religion, and is therefore deemed prohibitively disliked (*makrūh taḥrīman*) (*Marāqī 'l-Falāḥ*, *Ṭaḥṭāwī* 2:161–2; *Imdād* 548; *Radd* 1:562).

Everyone should pray however much he wishes, [but] individually. Afterwards, they make supplication and seek forgiveness from Allāh Most High. The imām then stands facing the *qibla*, raising his hands, while the people remain sitting, responding with *āmīn* to his supplication, [ideally] of that which has come in the Noble Sunna, [such as]:

> O Allāh! Bless us with abundant and pleasant rainwater that will deliver us [from this calamity], immediately rather than delayed; one that fills the entire horizon and pounds hard on the earth, completely covering our lands, lasting as long as is needed [p. 196].

It is not *sunna* for the imām to turn his garment.[433]

Non-Muslims may not attend this prayer.

THE PRAYER OF FEAR (*ṢALĀT AL-KHAWF*)

If there is intense fear[434] due to an enemy [attack], a group of Muslims should block off the enemy while another group performs half the prayer in congregation [with the imām], i.e., [one *rakʿa* of a two-*rakʿa* prayer, or] two *rakʿas* of a three or four-*rakʿa* prayer.

After finishing, this group [excluding the imām] goes out to the enemy while the second group comes forth and prays the remainder of the prayer with the imām, after which he alone makes the closing *salāms*. This second group then goes back to the enemy, while the first group returns to finish the prayer, which they do without any recitation. After making their *salāms*, they go back to the enemy while the second group comes back and finishes their prayer, with recitation.

If the fear intensifies even more, everyone prays separately, while riding [their conveyances], with head movements toward any direction possible.

433 As opposed to all three other schools of thought (*Al-Durr al-Muntaqā* 1:140).

434 This prayer is designed to accommodate Muslims defending their lands from an enemy in a situation where each group among the Muslims wants to pray behind the imām, and altogether they only want one imām; in such a case, the fear prayer is legislated, in order to prevent any internal disputation. Otherwise if there is no potential disputation, then it is best for each group to pray in its own congregation with its own imām (*Marāqī 'l-Falāḥ* 2:188; *Durr, Radd* 1:569; *Tabyīn* 1:232; *Majmaʿ al-Anhur* 1:177).

It is recommended to carry one's weapons while performing the prayer of fear.

THE FUNERAL PRAYER (*JANĀZA*) AND BURIAL

It is *sunna*[435] to direct the person on his deathbed (*muḥtaḍar*) toward the *qibla*, such that he faces it while on his right side. It is permissible, however, to do so while he is lying on his back [with his feet directed toward the *qibla*], yet his head should be [slightly] raised with something.[436]

Then the *shahāda* should be recited in his presence, so that he may pronounce it. This is referred to as *talqīn*, and it is also performed after his burial.[437]

When the person dies, his jaws should be closed and fastened, and his eyes should be shut. The one closing his eyes should say:

> In the Name of Allāh, and on the way of the Messenger of Allāh ﷺ. O Allāh, make his affair smooth for him; ease for him that which is to follow; make him felicitous by his meeting You; and make that which he has gone off to better than that which he has left [p. 197].

Next, his nakedness (*ʿawra*)[438] should be covered. The rest of his clothes are then removed, and he is given *wuḍū'* except for the rinsing of the mouth and nose. Then the entire body will be washed [a *ghusl* of ideally three complete washes to fulfill the *sunna*] with water and, if possible, lotus-tree leaves (*sidr*) or the like [otherwise, warm water alone suffices]. [Before the *ghusl*, however,] his beard and hair are washed with mallow leaves (*khiṭmī*) or [any type of] soap. [Next, when actually performing the *ghusl*] the body is washed from its

---

435 That is, as long as it is not difficult for him. Otherwise, he is left alone in whichever position he is in, or placed in the position that is least cumbersome for him (*Tanwīr* 1:570; *Ṭaḥṭāwī* 2:189).

436 Such that his face is directed toward the *qibla* rather than the sky (*Marāqī 'l-Falāḥ* 2:190; *Radd* 1:570).

437 *Talqīn* of the person on his deathbed is recommended, so that his final words before death are *Lā ilāha illa 'Llāh*. He should not be commanded to recite it. Rather, it should merely be recited in his presence, and in a gentle manner as he is already in a difficult state (*Marāqī 'l-Falāḥ* 2:191; *Durr* 1:570–1). As to its performance for the deceased after burial, there is a difference of opinion among the Ḥanafī scholars. The author maintains that it is legislated and should therefore be performed. At the very least, if done by some, it should not be denounced by others, as there is benefit in it for the deceased (*Durr*, *Radd* 1:571).

438 That is, from the navel to the knees, although according to another opinion, covering the private parts alone suffices (*Radd* 1:574).

right side first, followed by the left [thus comprising the first two washes].[439] He is then made to sit up, and his abdomen is gently wiped [to remove any of its contents]. Thereafter, pure water is poured over his body [for the third and final wash of the *ghusl*].[440] The body is then dried with a cloth. His hair should not be combed, and his nails should not be trimmed. The funeral shrouds should be perfumed with incense an odd number of times and then wrapped around the body. A mixture of fragrant substances (*ḥanūṭ*) is placed on his hair and beard, and camphor on his feet, knees, hands, forehead, and nose [(*masājid*)—the limbs upon which he would prostrate, so as to honor them].

The man's funeral shrouds according to the *sunna* (*kafan al-sunna*) consist of a long shirt (*qamīṣ*), an inner shroud (*izār*), and an outer shroud (*lifāfa*), [all preferably taken] from [the quality or standard of] that which he would wear in his life [for the Friday or ʿĪd prayers]. Shrouds made from white cotton are most preferred. Both the inner and outer shrouds should cover the body from the top of the head to the bottom of the feet.[441] The long shirt[442] should not have any sleeves, gore, or opening at the neck,[443] and its ends should not be hemmed.

It is disliked to place a turban on the head [of the deceased].

The inner shroud is wrapped [first] from the left side, then from the right side. If it is feared that the shrouds will open up [e.g., if the burial site is far], they should be tied.

The inner and outer shrouds [alone] are sufficient [to fulfill the obligation for a man] (*kafan al-kifāya*).

To fulfill the *sunna* for a woman's shrouds (*kafan al-sunna*), the face should

---

439 As the author mentions in his *Imdād*, the body is first placed on its left side for the first complete wash, which starts on the right side of the body and ends on the left side ("the side touching the plank"). It is then placed on its right side for the second wash, which starts on the left side of the body and ends on the right side ("the side touching the plank") (573).

440 Both the Arabic published edition and the manuscript mention here that water is poured "over the right and left sides" of the body. What is meant—as mentioned by the author himself in *Imdād al-Fattāḥ* (573)—is that the body is laid on its left side for the third and final complete wash. Each wash was of the entire body, so as to fulfill the sunna of three complete washes. For the inserted brackets above, see *Imdād* (573) and *Baḥr* (2:302–3).

441 Yet with the outer shroud being a little longer so as to facilitate the tying of the shrouds (*Imdād* 577).

442 Its length should be from the base of the neck to the bottom of the feet (*Imdād* 576).

443 Rather, it is sufficient to have only enough space for the head to get through, instead of making an extended slit further down the chest like normal shirts (*Ṭaḥṭāwī* 2:216).

also be wrapped in a head covering (*khimār*), and her breasts should be tied with a separate clothe (*khirqa*).

For the minimally sufficient shroud (*kafan al-kifāya*) for a woman, the head covering is enough [in addition to the two main shrouds].

Her hair is tied into two braids, which are placed on her chest above the long shirt; then the head covering above it yet underneath the outer shroud;[444] and lastly, the extra cloth for her breasts over the outer shroud.[445]

The bare minimum shrouds (*kafan al-ḍarūra*) [for either gender] is based on whatever is available.

The Funeral Prayer (*janāza*) is a communal obligation (*farḍ kifāya*).[446]

It is performed by saying [in one's heart], "I intend to pray for the sake of Allāh Most High, and to supplicate for the deceased." The follower should additionally intend to pray behind the imām.

One then says the first *takbīr*[447] [to commence the prayer] and recites the opening supplication (*thanā'*), although it is permissible to recite the Fātiḥa.[448] He then makes the second *takbīr*, after which he sends blessings upon the Prophet ﷺ. Next, he makes the third *takbīr* and says:[449]

---

444 That is, underneath both the inner and outer shrouds (*Ṭaḥṭāwī* 2:217; *Radd* 1:579).

445 The ideal way to shroud the man is to spread the outer shroud, and then the inner shroud above it. The long shirt is then laid on top with the upper flap of it rolled up. The body is placed on top of this arrangement and first wrapped in the long shirt, and then the inner shroud is wrapped around the body, left side first (so the right side is on top). Finally, the outer shroud is wrapped in the same manner (left side first).

For the woman, the outer and inner shrouds are similarly spread (outer first, then inner above it). The long shirt is then laid on top with the upper flap of it rolled up. Her body is placed on top of this arrangement and then wrapped in the long shirt. Before the two shrouds (inner and outer) are wrapped around her, however, the *khimār* is placed over her head and face. Then both shrouds (inner and outer) are wrapped over the body, left side first, one at a time (like with the man). Lastly, placed above the outer shroud, the *khirqa* is used to tie her breasts, left side first. Some scholars, however, maintained that it is tied beneath the outer shroud (*Durr*, *Radd* 1:579; *Marāqī 'l-Falāḥ*, *Ṭaḥṭāwī* 2:217).

446 That is, if even one person in the community fulfills the obligation, the entire community is absolved of it. The same ruling applies to the preparation of the body (i.e., its washing), its shrouding, and its burial (*Hadiyya* 144). If no one performs these rights, however, then the entire community is sinful for having abandoned them.

447 This is the only *takbīr* in which one raises the hands (*Tanwīr* 1:585). Also, all four *takbīrs* are said aloud, while the closing two *salāms* are said silently (*Hadiyya* 146).

448 After the first *takbīr*, one may say the Fātiḥa with the intention of *duʿā'*, but not with the intention of recitation of Qur'ān, as that is deemed prohibitively disliked (*makrūh taḥrīman*) (*Durr*, *Radd* 1:586).

449 After the third *takbīr*, one may say any *duʿā'* regarding affairs of the afterlife, ideally supplicating for oneself, one's parents, the deceased and all Muslims. It is preferable, however, to recite

> O Allāh, forgive him and have mercy on him. Give him well-being, and pardon him. Honor his place of residence, and make his entrance expansive. Wash him with water, ice, and snow. Purify him from sins just as a white garment is purified from filth. Replace his abode with a better one, his family with a better one, and his spouse with a better one.[450] Enter him into Paradise, and save him from the punishment of the grave and that of the Fire [p. 197].

He then says the fourth *takbīr*, followed by the closing [two] *salāms*.

One does not seek forgiveness [in the *janāza* prayer] for a deceased child or insane person [as neither bears legal responsibility]; rather, one says:

> O Allāh, make him one who is sent forth[451] on our behalf, as well as a reward and a stored treasure for us. Make him an intercessor for us, and accept his intercession [p. 197].

If the deceased is buried without a funeral prayer, then it is to be performed over his grave, unless the body has disintegrated [which is known by estimation].

The funeral prayer is performed over a miscarried fetus (*siqṭ*) if most of it came out while it was alive[452] before dying. Otherwise, the fetus is washed, wrapped in a cloth, and buried without a funeral prayer.

The most deserving of leading the funeral prayer is the head of state, followed by his representative, the judge, the local imām, and finally the guardian (*walī*).[453]

The funeral prayer is not performed over rebels or highway brigands.[454]

---

a *duʿā'* that has been transmitted from the Prophet ﷺ, such as the one mentioned above (*Durr*, *Radd* 1:585). Also, according to the sound position of the school, there is no *duʿā'* after the fourth *takbīr*, although some scholars deemed it good to recite a short one (*Hadiyya* 146; *Radd* 1:585).

450 Ibn ʿĀbidīn mentions that what is meant by replacement of family and spouse is a replacement of their qualities, not a replacement of their entities; i.e., they will be the same people, yet with improved characteristics and traits (*Radd* 1:585).

451 That is, sent forth to the Watering Pool of the Prophet ﷺ (*ḥawḍ*) to make ready its water for them, or sent forth to prepare beneficial things for his parents in the Everlasting Abode (*Durr*, *Radd* 1:587).

452 That is, by displaying some sign of life such as crying or movement of a limb. In that case, the body is washed, and the funeral prayer is performed. Also, the baby would inherit, be inherited from, and be named. Otherwise if there is no sign of life, the body is washed, given a name, wrapped in a clothe and buried without any funeral prayer (or inheritance) (*Hadiyya* 148).

453 The order of guardians in leading the funeral prayer is that of marriage and inheritance, yet with the father first (i.e., father, son, brother, then paternal uncle) (*Imdād* 586; *Durr* 1:590; *Ṭaḥṭāwī* 2:232).

454 That is, if killed during combat. If they are subdued by the government and then killed, the

It is permissible to wash and bury a non-Muslim relative without having to adhere to the *sunna* way of doing so; alternatively, the body may be given to the people of his religion.[455]

One funeral prayer may be performed over an entire group of deceased, yet a separate prayer for each individual body is more preferable.

When carrying the bier, it is recommended to [first] place the front right side then the back right side on the right shoulder, followed by the front left side then the back left side on the left shoulder.[456]

It is recommended to move fast when carrying the body, yet not so fast as to cause it to wobble. It is more preferable to walk behind the procession than in front of it. It is disliked to raise one's voice with *dhikr* or the like,[457] as well as to sit down before the body is lowered into the grave.[458]

The grave is dug the length of at least half a body's length into the ground; it is dug in an L-shape (*laḥd*)[459] [with the niche facing the *qibla*], rather than straight down (*shaqq*), except in soft earth.[460]

The one lowering the body [into the ground, within the niche] says: "In the Name of Allāh, and on the way of the Messenger of Allāh ﷺ."

The body is directed toward the *qibla* while on its right side [according

---

funeral prayer is performed over them (*Imdād* 594). In the Arabic published edition, this sentence is repeated toward the end of the section, yet has been translated only once in the present work.

455 Moreover, the Muslim relative may follow the funeral procession from afar (*Imdād* 594).

456 That is, it is recommended that each carrier rotate around all four corners of the bier, holding each corner for ten steps, for a total of forty steps. The carrier begins at the front right corner (from the perspective of the deceased, who is placed on his back, with the direction of his head considered "front") and places it on his right shoulder. Then he moves to the back right corner of the bier (where the right foot of the deceased is), also to be carried on his right shoulder. He then moves to the front left corner, and lastly the back left corner, both of which he carries on his left shoulder (*Marāqī 'l-Falāḥ* 2:250–1).

457 Raising one's voice with *dhikr* or the like, such as Qur'ānic recitation, is either prohibitively disliked (*makrūh taḥrīman*) or mildly disliked (*makrūh tanzīhan*); both are mentioned by Ibn ʿĀbidīn without preference of either opinion. Instead, one should keep a prolonged silence or make *dhikr* to oneself (*Radd* 1:598).

458 Sitting down before the body is lowered into the grave is deemed prohibitively disliked (*makrūh taḥrīman*) (*Radd* 1:597).

459 The L-shape (*laḥd*) is the *sunna* way of digging a grave, namely, that a hole is dug into the ground, and then within the hole at the side facing the *qibla*, a niche is dug into which the body is placed, such that the body lies under a "ceiling" of earth (*Radd* 1:599).

460 In which case a straight grave (*shaqq*) may be dug, or if L-shaped, a coffin may be used. Otherwise, if there is no particular need, the use of a coffin is disliked (*makrūh*) (unless required by law) (*Radd* 1:599). However, some dirt should be spread out on the floor of the coffin if used (*Tabyīn* 1:245).

to the *sunna*]; the knots of the shrouds are untied; and unbaked bricks[461] are laid against it [i.e., against the niche, thereby sealing it off within the grave].

The grave of a woman, not that of a man, is covered before her body is placed in it.[462]

Dirt is poured into the grave, and then rounded on its top [with an elevation of a hand's span or a bit more, to resemble the hump of a camel].

It is prohibited to build a structure over the grave for the sake of decoration.[463]

If there is a legitimate necessity, it is permissible to bury multiple bodies in one grave; in that case, sand and dirt are used to make a barrier between each [body].

It is not permissible to transfer the corpse after its burial [once the grave has been filled with dirt], unless the land turns out to have been confiscated.[464]

It is recommended to visit graves and to recite Sūra Yāsīn, even if sitting next to them, due to that which has been narrated, namely: "Whoever visits graves and recites Sūra Yāsīn, then on that day Allāh will lighten [the punishment] for them, and he [the reciter] will have as many good deeds as there are deceased in that graveyard." [465]

It is disliked to sit at graves for other than reciting Qur'ān [or making *dhikr*]; to step on them;[466] or to pluck out moist grass[467] from the graveyard.

---

461 There seems to be a transcription error here in both the Arabic published edition as well as the manuscript. The correct sentence, taken from the author's *Nūr al-Īḍāḥ*, has been translated instead (see *Marāqī 'l-Falāḥ* 2:258, *Imdād* 600).

462 That is, in order to provide extra concealment, it is recommended (*mustaḥabb*) to cover a woman's grave with a garment or sheet while her body is being placed therein, until the unbaked bricks are laid against the niche. This does not apply for a man's grave, unless done for another reason such as rain or snow (*Marāqī 'l-Falāḥ* 2:260; *Radd* 1:600).

463 The author does mention in his *Imdād al-Fattāḥ* that some scholars deemed it good to place some bricks or stones over the grave so as to protect it from being dug up (602).

464 As for transferring the body before its burial, there is no harm in it if within a reasonable distance, which jurists estimated to be about 2.3 mi (3.72 km). This estimation was based on the fact that traditionally, the graveyard of a town might have been that distance away from the town itself. From this reasoning, some scholars deduced that what is disliked is to transfer the body to another town altogether (*Imdād* 604; *Radd* 1:602). Based on the latter opinion, even if the graveyard of a large city today is at a far distance from its city, it would not be disliked to transfer the body there, as opposed to transferring it to another city, which would be disliked.

465 This ḥadīth is narrated by the Ḥanbalī scholar Abū Bakr ʿAbd al-ʿAzīz (Ṣāḥib al-Khallāl) with his chain of narrators (*sanad*) in *Kitāb al-Sunan*, on the authority of Anas ﷺ (*Mirqāt al-Mafātīḥ* 4:174).

466 Unless while reciting Qur'ān, making *dhikr*, or praying for their inhabitants while walking on them (*Hadiyya* 151; *Radd* 1:606).

467 Since moist grass is always engaged in the glorification of Allāh, by which the deceased

MARTYRS (*SHUHADĀ'*)

A martyr[468] is one who is killed by enemy combatants, rebels, highway brigands, or robbers in his house at night, even if killed by a heavy object; or [one who is] killed unjustly by a Muslim with a sharp object.

The martyr is buried with his blood and in his clothes, and is prayed over without being washed. His weapons, armor, winter coat, and padded garments are removed. If, however, he was killed while in a state of major ritual impurity or as a child, then his body is washed.

The same is true for one whose death becomes *prolonged*[469] after the battle ends, whether by eating, drinking, sleeping, being given medicine, having a prayer time elapse while being conscious, or being transferred from the battlefield while alive, unless out of fear of being trampled upon by animals.

Anyone killed by penal punishment (*ḥadd*) or retaliatory punishment (*qiṣāṣ*) is washed after death.

---

find repose and by which His mercy descends (*Imdād* 609).

468 This section deals with martyrs in a legal sense, in relation to rulings of this life, such as not washing the body. With regard to the afterlife, only Allāh Most High knows who will be among the martyrs since the matter is based solely on one's intention, although it is hoped that these people will be granted that rank. However, there are many other ways of dying that are considered martyrdom with regard to the afterlife, as related in numerous ḥadīths (*Majmaʿ al-Anhur* 1:188; *Durr*, *Radd* 1:611).

469 This "prolonging" of death (*irtithāth*) is defined as either experiencing some comfort of life or becoming legally obligated to do something, namely, the ritual prayer. The body of someone whose death was "prolonged" is washed (*Marāqī 'l-Falāḥ* 2:285, *Majmaʿ al-Anhur* 1:189).

Fasting (Ṣawm)

[The legal definition of] fasting is to withhold from eating, drinking, and sexual intercourse during daylight hours,[470] with an intention of fasting, performed by one capable and required to do so.

Its types are seven—obligatory, mandatory, *sunna*, recommended, voluntary, prohibitively disliked, and mildly disliked.

1. Obligatory (*farḍ*): the fasting of Ramaḍān, during the month (*adāʾ*) as well as makeups (*qaḍāʾ*); fasts of expiation (*kaffāra*); and vowed fasts (*mandhūr*), the latter two according to the more apparent position (*aẓhar*) [in terms of strength];[471]

2. Mandatory (*wājib*): makeups of broken voluntary (*nafl*) fasts;

---

470 Namely, from true dawn until sunset; i.e., it is lawful for the one intending on fasting to continue eating until true dawn (*fajr ṣādiq*), even if false dawn (*fajr kādhib*) comes in. At true dawn, however, one must stop eating, even if one is in the middle of the meal, to the extent that even the morsel or sip in one's mouth must be expelled and not swallowed, so as not to invalidate the fast.

As for the ḥadīth, "If one of you hears the call [to prayer] while his [drinking] vessel is in his hand, let him not place it down until having fulfilled his need from it" (*Mustadrak, Abū Dāwūd, Aḥmad*)—indeed, the eminent masters of ḥadīth have clearly stated that it is not rigorously authenticated (*ṣaḥīḥ*) by either of its two chains of transmission. Moreover, what is meant by "the call [to prayer]" in the ḥadīth is that of Bilāl ⬥, which used to be given well before true dawn so as to alert people that dawn was approaching. It does not refer to the call of prayer *at dawn*, which used to be performed by Ibn Umm Maktūm ⬥ (*Nafaḥāt* 163–4). This is of utmost importance, as unfortunately many people invalidate their fasts by eating or drinking past true dawn, based on a gross misinterpretation of the above ḥadīth.

Finally, with respect to modern tables of prayer timings, the 18-degree time for fajr is more precautionary and should therefore be used, especially for fasting.

471 The more accurate position in the school is that the fasts of expiation and vows are mandatory (*wājib*) rather than obligatory (*farḍ*) (*Ṭaḥṭāwī* 2:296–7; *Hadiyya* 153; *Durr, Radd* 2:82).

3. *Sunna*: the fasting of the Blessed ʿĀshūrāʾ [tenth of Muḥarram][472] along with the ninth;[473]
4. Recommended (*mandūb*): fasting three days of every month;[474] or Mondays and Thursdays; or six days of Shawwāl, yet spread out;[475]
5. Voluntary (*nafl*): any other day of fasting as long as its reprehensibility is not established [see next two categories];
6. Prohibitively Disliked (*makrūh taḥrīman*): fasting on [any one of] the two days of ʿĪd, or the Days of Tashrīq;[476]
7. Mildly Disliked (*makrūh tanzīhan*): e.g., to single out[477] fasting on Saturday, [Friday,][478] *Nayrūz* or *Mahrajān*,[479] unless it happens to coincide with one's habit;[480] or to fast consecutively (*ṣawm al-wiṣāl*).[481] It is [also] disliked to fast daily [for the entire year] (*ṣawm al-dahr*).[482]

---

472 Ibn ʿĀbidīn inclines toward considering it recommended (*mandūb* or *mustaḥabb*) rather than *sunna* (*Radd* 2:83).

473 Or with the eleventh. If the tenth is fasted alone it is mildly disliked (*makrūh tanzīhan*), as that entails resemblance of the Jews. The *sunna*, therefore, is to conjoin with it either the day before or after (*Marāqī 'l-Falāḥ* 2:299; *Durr, Radd* 2:84).

474 It is a separate recommended (*mandūb*) act to make those three days the 13th, 14th, and 15th of the month (*Nūr al-Īḍāḥ* 2:297).

475 Although to fast them consecutively, immediately after ʿĪd al-Fiṭr, is also acceptable (*Ṭaḥṭāwī* 2:298).

476 The Days of Tashrīq are the three days after ʿĪd al-Aḍḥa, namely, the 11th, 12th, and 13th of Dhū 'l-Ḥijja.

477 That is, without fasting the day before or after it as well (*Ṭaḥṭāwī* 2:299).

478 Although some scholars considered it recommended to fast on Friday, even if singled out (*Durr, Radd* 2:83), which would perhaps explain why the author left it out of this text, although he did include it in *Nūr al-Īḍāḥ* as being mildly disliked if singled out for fasting (*Imdād* 621, *Marāqī 'l -Falāḥ* 2:299).

479 Nayrūz and Mahrajān are the spring and autumn holidays of the Persians (*Marāqī 'l -Falāḥ* 2:300). They are celebrated on the days of the astronomical vernal and autumnal equinoxes.

480 Such as if one fasts every other day—or if one fasts the first of every month—and then that day corresponded with one of the above days (*Radd* 2:84).

481 *Ṣawm al-wiṣāl* is to fast for two or more days consecutively without eating in between, while *ṣawm al-dahr* is to fast daily yet with breaking the fast every night (*Marāqī 'l -Falāḥ* 2:300).

482 Both *ṣawm al-wiṣāl* and *ṣawm al-dahr* are deemed mildly disliked (*makrūh tanzīhan*), and regarding the latter, it is disliked even if one does not fast on the five days on which it is prohibited to fast (see type six in text above) (*Hadiyya* 154; *Durr, Radd* 2:84).

THE INTENTION OF FASTING

[All types of fasts require an intention.][483] The following types of fasts require an intention and specification of the "type" of fast [as well as that the intention be made the previous night before fajr, yet after maghrib (*tabyīt*)]:

- ☐ Makeups (*qaḍā'*) from Ramaḍān,
- ☐ Makeups from voluntary (*nafl*) fasts that one invalidated,
- ☐ Fasts of expiation (*kaffāra*),
- ☐ Unspecified vows (*nadhr muṭlaq*).[484]

The following types of fasts require neither specification of the type of fast, nor that the intention be made the previous night before fajr; rather, the intention may be made any time from the previous night[485] until [before] *ḍaḥwa kubrā*:[486]

- ☐ Ramaḍān fasts during the month (*adā'*),
- ☐ Specified vows (*nadhr muʿayyan*),[487]
- ☐ Voluntary (*nafl*) fasts.

THE CRESCENT MOON (*HILĀL*)

The beginning of the month of Ramaḍān is established either by sighting the crescent moon,[488] or by the completion of thirty days of Shaʿbān.

One may not fast on the Day of Doubt (*yawm al-shakk*),[489] except as a voluntary fast.[490]

---

483 This section has been somewhat paraphrased in translation for more fluidity.

484 That is, vows made to fast, without specifying a particular day.

485 For the previous night, the intention must be made *after* maghrib, not beforehand (*Durr* 2:85).

486 *Ḍaḥwa kubrā* is determined by dividing the time between the entrance of fajr and that of maghrib by half. If the intention of fasting *the entire day* is performed *before ḍaḥwa kubrā*, the above three types of fasts are valid; otherwise, they are not. Another way of determining *ḍaḥwa kubrā* is to divide the entire prayer time of fajr, from true dawn until sunrise, by half; this amount of time before midday (*zawāl*) is *ḍaḥwa kubrā* (*Ṭaḥṭāwī* 2:303; *Hadiyya* 154; *Radd* 2:85).

487 That is, vows made to fast, in which a particular day was specified when making the vow.

488 That is, at night, as day sightings are given no consideration (*Durr*, *Radd* 2:95–6).

489 *Yawm al-Shakk* refers to the day after the 29th of Shaʿbān, yet for one reason or another the crescent moon is not sighted by reliable witnesses. Hence, there is doubt as to whether it is the 30th of Shaʿbān or the 1st of Ramaḍān (*Marāqī 'l-Falāḥ* 2:306; *Tabyīn* 1:317).

490 One may fast on this day *only* if with a *firm* intention of the fast being voluntary (*nafl*).

For the beginning of Ramaḍān, if there is an obstruction in the sky [such as cloudiness or fog], then the sighting of one upright person is sufficient, even if a slave or woman.

For the completion of Ramaḍān (*fiṭr*), however—if there is an obstruction in the sky—there must be at least two free male witnesses, or one male and two females.

If there is no obstruction in the sky, then there must be a large body of people that sight the new crescent.[491]

Moonsighting for ʿĪd al-Aḍḥā [i.e., the month of Dhū 'l-Ḥijja], as well as every lunar month, takes the same ruling[492] as that of ʿĪd al-Fiṭr [i.e., the month of Shawwāl].

THINGS THAT INVALIDATE THE FAST (*MUFSIDĀT*)

Actions of one who is fasting are divided into four categories:[493]

1. Those that require a makeup as well as expiation,
2. Those that require a makeup without expiation,
3. Those that require nothing [and are not disliked],
4. Those that require nothing yet are disliked.

Those that require a makeup as well as expiation

If one eats or drinks something of nutritional value [i.e., something customarily eaten][494] or something for medicinal purposes; or if one has sexual intercourse

Otherwise it is disliked, prohibitively (*taḥrīman*) if done with a firm intention of fasting Ramadān, and mildly (*tanzīhan*) if (a) with a firm intention of a makeup obligatory (*farḍ*) fast or a makeup mandatory (*wājib*) fast, or (b) with a mixed intention, i.e., of fasting Ramaḍān if it turns out to be Ramaḍān, or a voluntary or mandatory fast otherwise. In any of the above cases, if it does in fact turn out to be the first of Ramaḍān, the fast fulfills the obligation of Ramaḍān. If it turns out to be Shaʿbān, it counts for what was intended if the intention was firm, or for a voluntary fast if the intention was mixed. Finally, *if* one makes no intention of fasting but rather hesitates, intending that if it turns out to be Ramaḍān then it is a fast, yet if Shaʿbān it is not a fast, *then* it is indeed not a fast, even if it turns out to be Ramaḍān, as there was no intention whatsoever (*Hadiyya* 156–7; *Durr*, *Radd* 2:88–9).

491 This applies to any month, its start or end (*Ṭaḥṭāwī* 2:316).

492 Namely, the requirement of two free male witnesses, or one male and two females, if there is an obstruction in the sky; and a large body of people if there is no obstruction (*Marāqī 'l-Falāḥ* 2:317).

493 This section has been rearranged in translation for clarity.

494 As opposed to, for example, stones, or uncooked dough or flour, as ingesting such things

in either of the two passages [front or rear]; *on purpose*,[495] then he must make up the fast as well as perform expiation, which is to free a slave; if he does not have one, he must fast two consecutive months; if he is genuinely unable, then he must feed sixty poor people, a half *ṣāʿ* [2.2 kg] of wheat [or give its equivalent monetary value] to each person.[496]

If, however, he does one of the above—namely, if he eats, drinks, or has intercourse—*out of forgetfulness*,[497] then he neither has to make up the fast nor perform expiation.

Those that require a makeup without expiation

- ☐ Use of a suppository;[498]
- ☐ Something not normally eaten [nor used for medicinal purposes], like dirt, reaching the body cavity;
- ☐ Accidentally swallowing water while rinsing the mouth;[499]
- ☐ Being coerced to break one's fast;

---

only necessitates a makeup, not expiation (*Hadiyya* 165; *Durr, Radd* 2:103; *Kanz, Tabyīn* 1:326). Yet doing so without a valid excuse would still be sinful.

495 This stipulation applies to any one of the three acts, namely, eating, drinking or intercourse. It serves to exclude doing so out of forgetfulness (in which case the fast is not nullified), by mistake, or under coercion (the latter two cases requiring a makeup yet no expiation) (*Radd* 2:108). For this entire chapter, *any* action mentioned as nullifying the fast only does so if one did that act *while remembering* that he was fasting.

496 Expiation is mandatory only if one had made the intention to fast before fajr; and only if no sickness severe enough to otherwise absolve one from fasting, nor menstruation or postnatal bleeding, occurred later that day before maghrib. If one of those did occur that day, or if the intention were made after fajr that day, then no expiation is required. Of course, breaking one's fast without a valid excuse would still be gravely sinful (*Hadiyya* 168). Finally, expiation is legislated only for breaking fasts in Ramaḍān, not outside of the month, even if makeups for Ramaḍān (*Kanz, Tabyīn* 1:329; *Radd* 2:107).

497 Forgetfulness in this context means forgetting that one is fasting, not forgetting that such an act breaks the fast, which would still invalidate the fast. If one breaks the fast out of forgetfulness, such as by eating or drinking, then although the fast is not nullified he must stop that act immediately upon remembering that he is fasting. If he fails to do so and continues eating or drinking, the fast would be nullified. If someone else sees the person eating or drinking, he must remind him of the fast, as it is prohibitively disliked (*makrūh taḥrīman*) to not remind him, unless the person is weak such as a very old person (*Hadiyya* 160; *Durr, Radd* 2:97; *Tabyīn* 1:322).

498 Both the vagina and the anus are deemed passageways into the body through which the entrance of a foreign substance could vitiate the fast; the distance within each that the substance would have to reach to do so is the size of a suppository. Hence, placing anything wet with water, oil or the like, even a wet finger, that distance inside either orifice vitiates the fast. Likewise, the complete insertion of a solid substance, such that it disappears, into either orifice vitiates the fast (*Durr, Radd* 2:99).

499 Or accidentally ingesting water while rinsing the nose (*Tabyīn* 1:329).

- ☐ Eating [even if intentionally], in the daytime, for a fast in which the person did not make the intention before fajr;
- ☐ Ejaculation due to touching or kissing;[500]
- ☐ Someone pouring water into the body cavity of a sleeping person [i.e., the sleeping person must make up the day without expiation];
- ☐ Self-induced vomiting[501] [a mouthful or more].[502]

Those that require nothing and are not disliked

- ☐ Blood cupping (*ḥijāma*) or drawing blood, as long as it does not weaken him;[503]

---

500 As opposed to ejaculation due to looking or thinking, or having a wet dream, neither of which vitiate the fast (*Kanz, Tabyīn* 1:322–3).

501 The only other case whereby vomiting breaks the fast is if one naturally vomits a mouthful or more, and then purposefully reswallows it; in that case, the fast must be made up, yet there is no expiation (*Ṭaḥṭāwī* 2:325; *Hadiyya* 164–5; *Durr, Radd* 2:111). The criteria of a mouthful is that one's mouth cannot withhold the vomit without strain (*Hadiyya* 26).

502 The following also necessitate a makeup without expiation:

- Depositing oil (or medicine) into the ear, whether intentionally or not (*Marāqī 'l-Falāḥ* 2:338). With regard to depositing *water* into the ear, there is agreement that it does not break the fast if unintentional. If done intentionally, the opinion given preference in the *Hidāya* (1:123), *Tabyīn* (1:329) and other texts, is that it does not invalidate the fast. This is deemed a sound and followable position (*Radd* 2:98).
- *Unintentionally* ingesting rain, snow or blood (from outside the mouth) that enters one's mouth on its own (*Marāqī 'l-Falāḥ* 2:339, *Ṭaḥṭāwī* 2:324). The same applies to tears or sweat if one *tastes* the saltiness throughout the mouth, and then unintentionally swallows (*Durr, Radd* 2:103). If one *intentionally* does any of the above, then both a makeup and expiation are required (*Marāqī 'l-Falāḥ* 2:339, *Ṭaḥṭāwī* 2:324; *Hadiyya* 166). If one bleeds from within the mouth, then if the saliva becomes red or pink as a result and is swallowed, the fast is broken and must be made up without expiation; if the saliva is yellow or clear, it may be swallowed and the fast remains valid (*Tabyīn* 1:325).
- Ingesting leftover food in one's mouth that amounts to the size of a chickpea or more (*Marāqī 'l-Falāḥ, Ṭaḥṭāwī* 2:326, 344); if it amounts to less, the fast is not invalidated and hence no makeup is required (*Marāqī 'l-Falāḥ, Ṭaḥṭāwī* 2:326).
- *Intentionally* inhaling or ingesting smoke (*without* enjoyment or benefit), dust, water vapor, steam (such as from cooking or a bath), or a fly (*Marāqī 'l-Falāḥ, Ṭaḥṭāwī* 2:343; *Hadiyya* 166). If one inhales smoke with enjoyment or for benefit, then both a makeup and expiation are required (*Marāqī 'l-Falāḥ* 2:329; *Hadiyya* 166). If, however, one *unintentionally* inhales or ingests smoke, dust, water vapor, steam, or a fly (e.g., if such things are in the air, and one is simply trying to breathe), then the fast is not invalidated and hence no makeup is required (*Radd* 2:97). This criteria applies to inhaling anything with a *physical* body, such that one can actually see it in the air. However, if one intentionally inhales scented air that has no *physical* body, such as the scent of musk or a flower, then the fast is not invalidated and hence no makeup is required (*Radd* 2:97).

503 As it is disliked to do anything that one thinks will weaken him to the point of breaking

- ☐ Using the toothstick (*siwāk*), even if used at the end of the day [rather, it is a *sunna*];
- ☐ Rinsing the mouth or the nose [without any water proceeding down the throat];
- ☐ Placing a wet garment on one's body [or taking a bath] due to heat.[504]

Those that require nothing yet are disliked

If one tastes some food or chews on it [*without swallowing*], without a valid excuse;[505] or if one kisses [his spouse] while not feeling secure [from ejaculation or intercourse], it is disliked. If, however, one feels secure from engaging in intercourse or from ejaculation due to the kissing, it is not disliked.[506]

The following actions are recommended (*mustaḥabb*) for the one fasting:

- ☐ To have the pre-dawn meal (*suḥūr*) [due to the blessing therein, even if only a sip of water];
- ☐ To delay it [until shortly before fajr, yet while being certain not to swallow anything after fajr enters];[507]
- ☐ To hasten in breaking one's fast, unless it is a cloudy day [i.e., one must be certain that maghrib has indeed entered].

The following actions during the day necessitate withholding (*imsāk*) from

---

the fast, lest he do so due to that weakness (*Hadiyya* 171; *Radd* 2:114).

504 The following are also permissible and not disliked when fasting: the entrance of water, oil or the like into the urethra of the male organ (*Durr*, *Radd* 2:100); being in a state of major ritual impurity when true dawn enters (*Durr*, *Radd* 2:101); oiling one's moustache or body, as absorption through skin pores does not vitiate the fast; or applying antimony (*kuḥl*) or the like in the eyes, as absorption through the eyes does not vitiate the fast (*Durr*, *Radd* 2:113; *Tabyīn* 1:323–4). Based on the latter two cases, modern injections and eyedrops are permissible while fasting and do not vitiate the fast (*Al-Jāmiʿ fī Aḥkām al-Ṣiyām* 48–9, *Maqālāt Fiqhiyya* 207).

505 Tasting or chewing on food without swallowing is mildly disliked (*makrūh tanzīhan*), unless there is a valid excuse, such as a woman tasting the food she cooks because her husband is unkind, in which case it is not even mildly disliked (*Hadiyya* 163; *Tabyīn* 1:330; *Radd* 2:112).

506 Kissing here does not refer to mouth-to-mouth, which is always disliked (as one might swallow the other's saliva, which would vitiate the fast). It is also disliked for the two spouses to lie down or hug while naked. However, to do so while clothed, or to kiss other than mouth-to-mouth, is based on the criterion mentioned above in the text, namely, that it is not disliked as long as they both feel secure from ejaculation or intercourse (*Ṭaḥṭāwī* 2:347; *Radd* 2:112–3).

507 If, however, one has doubt as to whether the time of true dawn has entered or not, it becomes disliked to eat (*Radd* 2:114).

anything that would vitiate the fast, for the remainder of that day [i.e., it is mandatory (*wājib*) to do so]:

- ☐ If one breaks the fast [whether accidental, on purpose, or under coercion];
- ☐ If a traveller arrives to his place of residence, and was not fasting on his journey [since if he were fasting, then he must remain fasting *a fortiori*];
- ☐ If a woman in menstruation or postnatal bleeding becomes pure;
- ☐ If a non-Muslim embraces Islam;
- ☐ Or if a child becomes an adult [by puberty or by age].[508]

The first three cases require a makeup, as opposed to the last two.

EXEMPTIONS FROM FASTING

The following people are exempted from fasting in Ramaḍān:

- ☐ A sick person who fears that the illness will worsen;[509]
- ☐ A pregnant woman or nursing woman, with the condition for each that she have a legitimate fear[510] for the baby or for herself;[511]
- ☐ One who is undergoing severe thirst from which he fears death;

508 Normally, puberty for a boy is by ejaculation (such as a wet dream), and for a girl is by menstruation. If either a boy or girl has not yet reached puberty, then upon completion of fifteen lunar years (fourteen solar years and seven months), he or she legally becomes an adult; this is the position for legal verdict (*fatwā*) (*Durr, Radd* 5:97).

509 This also includes a sick person who fears prolongation of his illness, or even a healthy person who fears becoming ill due to the fast (*Tabyīn* 1:333). In either case, the fear of course must be a *genuine fear*, not just mere delusion (see next note).

510 For the sick person, pregnant woman, and nursing woman, the condition for permissibility of breaking the fast is not simply a delusion of potential harm, but rather a legitimate fear, recognized by the Sacred Law (*sharīʿa*). This entails either (1) past experience, even if of someone else with the same sickness; (2) an obvious sign of potential harm; or (3) an opinion of a qualified, Muslim physician who does not sin in public. The same would apply for a healthy person that has a legitimate fear, based on one of the above indications, of becoming ill (*Ṭaḥṭāwī* 2:355, *Durr* 2:116). Ibn ʿĀbidīn adds that if one were to break the fast without one of the above indications, then he would have to perform expiation, while most people are unfortunately completely unaware of this ruling (*Radd* 2:116).

511 There is a typo here in the Arabic published edition; it reads *nufasā'* (woman in a state of

- Or a traveller,[512] yet for him to fast is more preferable if it does not harm him.

If one who breaks the fast due to a valid excuse [as listed above] passes away before having the chance to make up the days missed, then it is not mandatory to make up those days.[513]

When making up fasts in general, one does not have to perform them consecutively.

The *fidya* payment for a very old person who is unable to fast[514] is a half *ṣāᶜ* [2.2 kg] of wheat [or its equivalent monetary value] for each day.[515]

A person performing a voluntary fast may break it without an excuse, according to one narration.[516]

Entertaining guests is a valid excuse for both the host and the guest.[517]

If one breaks a voluntary fast after having started it [in any case], it is mandatory (*wājib*) for him to make it up, except for the days in which it is prohibited to fast, namely, the two days of ᶜĪd and the three Days of Tashrīq.

If a person makes an unspecified vow to fast; or a vow to fast upon fulfillment of a particular condition, which then occurs; then he must fulfill his vow. And Allāh knows best.

---

postnatal bleeding), which does not make sense and should rather read *al-nafs* (herself) as in the manuscript.

512 With the condition that he initiates the journey and is outside city limits, or is already a traveller, at the onset of fajr. Otherwise if he is resident when fajr enters, then he *must* fast that day, even if he travels after fajr. If he still breaks his fast then there is no expiation, although it is sinful (*Marāqī 'l -Falāḥ, Ṭaḥṭāwī* 2:355). Finally, unlike the above categories, the traveller cannot break the fast after having started it (*Radd* 2:122–3).

513 That is, he does not need to stipulate *fidya* payment on their behalf in his will if it seems that he will die before being able to make them up.

514 With the condition that his inability to fast continue until death; otherwise once able, the missed fasts would have to be made up. The same ruling would apply to someone with a chronic illness, likewise whose recovery is not expected for the remainder of his life, and were he to recover, he would have to make up the missed fasts (*Ṭaḥṭāwī* 2:358–9; *Hadiyya* 173; *Radd* 2:119).

515 The *fidya* payment is mandatory (*wājib*) (*Hadiyya* 173; *Durr* 2:119).

516 According to the stronger narration, however, one must have a valid excuse to break a voluntary fast (*Durr, Radd* 2:121). In any case, it would have to be made up if broken.

517 Breaking the fast in such circumstances would be permissible only if the following conditions are met:

- The host would be offended if the guest did not eat, or the guest would feel uncomfortable eating by himself;
- The person is confident that he will make it up;
- The fast is broken before *ḍaḥwa kubrā* (see related note, p. 129) (*Durr, Radd* 2:121–122).

SPIRITUAL RETREAT IN THE MOSQUE (*IʿTIKĀF*)

The spiritual retreat[518] is of three types:

1. Mandatory (*wājib*): when one makes a vow to perform it;
2. Emphasized Communal (*kifāya*) Sunna:[519] the last ten nights of Ramaḍān;
3. Recommended (*mustaḥabb*): any other retreat.

Fasting is a condition for the validity of the vowed spiritual retreat [the first type] only.

The minimum period of time to fulfill a voluntary retreat [the third type] is a moment, with its intention, [and as with all types of spiritual retreat, is valid only] in a mosque of congregation.[520]

One may not leave his place of retreat except for a legitimate need based on the Sacred Law, such as to pray the Friday prayer in the main community mosque;[521] or for a natural need, such as to urinate; or due to an emergency, such as if forced to leave under coercion. [In any of these cases] he should immediately enter another mosque [upon fulfilling the need]. If there were no valid excuse, then the spiritual retreat would be invalidated by his leaving the mosque.

The woman performs the spiritual retreat in that area of her house which she in general has designated for her prayer (*ṣalāt*).[522]

---

518 The spiritual retreat may not be performed without its intention; nor by one in a state of major ritual impurity, menstruation, or postnatal bleeding (*Marāqī 'l-Falāḥ*, *Ṭaḥṭāwī* 2:374–5; *Durr*, *Radd* 2:129).

519 That is, if any member(s) of the community performs it, the *sunna* is fulfilled, such that there is no sin on the others for leaving it without a valid excuse. Yet if no one performs it, then the entire community is in blame for leaving it, and potentially in sin if habitually left (*Radd* 2:129).

520 That is, a mosque with an *imām* and a *mu'adhdhin*. Some stipulated that all five prayers must be performed there in congregation, while others did not. The two companions (Abū Yūsuf and Muḥammad) maintained that any mosque would suffice, and some scholars preferred this opinion as it is easier, especially in latter times (*Durr*, *Radd* 2:129).

521 In such a case, one should leave for the main community mosque with enough time to pray the *sunna* prayers before and after the Friday prayer, and then immediately return to the mosque of his retreat. If he remains in the main community mosque for his retreat, then it is valid yet mildly disliked (*makrūh tanzīhan*) (*Marāqī 'l-Falāḥ* 2:377; *Imdād* 676; *Hadiyya* 184; *Durr*, *Radd* 2:132–3).

522 In general, it is recommended for a woman to designate a place in the house for prayers, just as it is recommended for a man to do so for his voluntary prayers. The woman's retreat then should be in her designated prayer area. If she nevertheless did it in the mosque, it would be valid

It is permissible[523] for the man performing the spiritual retreat to eat, drink, sleep, and even buy or sell[524] in the mosque, provided the commodity for sale is not brought inside the mosque, as to do so is disliked.[525] It is also disliked to remain silent,[526] or to speak other than good.

It is unlawful (*ḥarām*) to have sexual intercourse or to engage in any foreplay; moreover, the retreat is invalidated by intercourse, or by ejaculation due to foreplay.[527]

If one makes a vow to perform the spiritual retreat for a certain number of days, he must remain in his retreat during the accompanying nights as well; similarly, a vow of nights necessitates their accompanying days. This type of retreat [in either case] must be performed in consecutive days and nights, not separately, even if he did not explicitly stipulate consecutiveness in the vow. If he makes a vow for two days, he must perform his retreat for the accompanying two nights as well.[528]

---

yet mildly disliked (*makrūh tanzīhan*), or according to some (*Badā'iʿ*), merely contrary to what is optimal (*khilāf al-afḍal*). Also, her retreat is not valid in any part of her house aside from her designated prayer area; if she does not have a designated prayer area, it is not valid anywhere in her house. She may, however, simply designate such an area in her house when she desires to perform the retreat. When performing the retreat in her designated prayer area, she may not leave that area until the retreat is over. Finally, she should get her husband's permission first before doing her retreat. Once he grants it to her, he is not allowed to renege on his permission and have intercourse with her (*Durr, Radd* 2:129; *Tabyīn* 1:350).

523 Such that if he left the mosque for these actions, the retreat would be invalidated (*Marāqī 'l -Falāḥ* 2:379).

524 That is, it is not disliked for one performing the spiritual retreat to conduct a purchase or sale in the mosque if the transaction is for something he or his dependents need, as long as the commodity is not brought inside. It is disliked, however, to conduct a transaction in the mosque if merely for his usual business, even if the commodity is not brought inside the mosque (*Marāqī 'l -Falāḥ* 2:379–380; *Durr* 2:134; *Tabyīn* 1:351).

525 That is, prohibitively disliked (*makrūh taḥrīman*) (*Ṭaḥṭāwī* 2:380).

526 That is, it is disliked to remain silent if one believes that silence *in and of itself* is an act of worship—as that belief is prohibited—as opposed to remaining silent in order to guard one's speech without believing that it is an act of worship, in which case it is not disliked (*Marāqī 'l-Falāḥ* 2:380; *Tabyīn* 1:352).

527 The retreat is not invalidated by ejaculation due to thinking or looking (*Tabyīn* 1:352–3).

528 Meaning that he begins at maghrib (*Marāqī 'l -Falāḥ* 2:382). In general, one enters the mosque for the retreat before maghrib of the first night, and leaves after maghrib of the last day (*Tabyīn* 1:353).

Almsgiving (Zakāt)

Zakāt is defined as the transfer of ownership (*tamlīk*) of a portion[529] of wealth—specified by the Lawgiver—to a particular person,[530] with its intention.[531]

It is obligatory (*farḍ*) on every free Muslim who is legally responsible,[532] and who possesses the quantum (zakātable amount) (*niṣāb*)[533]—whether in

529 Namely, 2.5% of one's wealth that is equal to or above the zakātable amount (*niṣāb*) (see note below), upon which one lunar year has elapsed (*Hadiyya* 197; *Durr* 2:3).

530 That is, a Muslim of one of the categories of eligible recipients listed below.

531 Because it is an act of worship rather than a tax, *zakāt* is not valid without its intention, which must be present either (a) when one pays it to the recipient, (b) when one gives it to one's agent appointed to pay it on one's behalf, or (c) when one sets it aside to be paid as *zakāt* in the future. If one pays it without its intention, then it does not fulfill one's *zakāt* obligation, *unless* one later intends it as such while it is still intact, in the recipient's possession. Moreover, the recipient does not have to know that it is one's *zakāt* payment. One may, for example, call it a "gift" or "loan" while paying it to the recipient, all the while intending it to fulfill the *zakāt* obligation (and then later forgive the "loan") (*Imdād* 681; *Hadiyya* 202; *Durr, Radd* 2:11–12; *Kanz, Tabyīn* 1:257).

532 That is, adult and sane, as otherwise one is not legally responsible (*Hadiyya* 198; *Durr, Radd* 2:4; *Tabyīn* 1:252).

533 *Niṣāb* is of two types: *niṣāb wujūb al-zakāt* and *niṣāb ḥirmān al-zakāt*. The first type, mentioned above, refers to the minimum amount of wealth upon which *zakāt* is due, specifically from one's monetary wealth (i.e., gold, silver, cash, etc.), livestock, or trade goods, with the conditions mentioned above. The second type, *niṣāb ḥirmān al-zakāt*, is the minimum amount of wealth by which one would become ineligible to receive *zakāt*, though he may not have to pay it either. It is the same *amount* of wealth as the first type, yet is considered from *any type of wealth* other than one's basic personal needs (*Sharḥ al-Wiqāya* 1:230–231, *Lubāb* 168, *Durr* 2:73). For example, the combined value of a person's monetary wealth, livestock, and trade goods (i.e., categories of wealth for which *zakāt* is due) is below the quantum. Yet he owns an extra piece of land that was not purchased for resale (and hence not a trade good—see related note below, p. 140), and that land is of a value—when added to the previous amount (i.e., categories of wealth for which *zakāt* is due)—that causes his *total wealth* to be above the quantum. This person would have *niṣāb ḥirmān al-zakāt*, such that he would be ineligible to receive *zakāt*, yet would not have *niṣāb wujūb al-zakāt*, such that he would not be obligated to pay *zakāt*.

Hence, the central condition shared by all eligible recipients is possessing less than *niṣāb ḥirmān al-zakāt*, while the condition by which one is obligated to pay *zakāt* is possessing more than *niṣāb*

monetary wealth or in trade goods whose value is equivalent to the *niṣāb* of wealth[534]—over which a full lunar year (*ḥawl*) has passed, in excess of any debts[535] and of basic personal needs.[536]

The *niṣāb* of gold[537] is 20 *mithqāls*,[538] for which one pays half a *mithqāl*. The *niṣāb* of silver is 200 *dirhams*, for which one pays 5 *dirhams*. For any amount above the *niṣāb*, if it increases to a fifth of the *niṣāb*, one pays its proportionate amount due, yet pays nothing if less than a fifth.[539]

The value of trade goods[540] is combined with one's gold and silver, both of which are also added together by value.

---

wujūb al-zakāt. Finally, one who possessed *niṣāb ḥirmān al-zakāt* would still have to pay *ṣadaqat al-fiṭr* (see related section, p. 143) and perform the *uḍḥiya* (see related chapter, p. 169).

534 This sentence comes later in the Arabic published edition and in the manuscript, yet is as above in the author's larger works *Imdād* (681) and *Marāqī 'l-Falāḥ* (2:391).

535 That is, debts that would reduce his wealth below the *niṣāb*. Otherwise, if one still possesses *niṣāb* despite one's debts, *zakāt* remains obligatory (on the wealth that exceeds the debts). Moreover, what is meant above is debts owed to humans, not those owed for religious obligations such as expiation (*kaffārā*), vows (*nudhūr*), the obligation of *ḥajj* and the like; such debts are not deducted when calculating one's zakātable wealth (*Ikhtiyār* 1:150; *Hadiyya* 198; *Tabyīn* 1:254–5). Finally, money set aside for general expenses, such as food, rent, education, or family provisions (*nafaqāt*), is likewise *not* deducted (*Badā'iʿ* 2:101).

536 Basic personal needs (*ḥawā'ij aṣliyya*) refer to personal items that are not zakātable, such as one's house(s); furniture; clothing; vehicle(s); equipment used for one's profession; or any other personal belongings, like books or even property, not purchased with the intention of resale. If something is purchased with the intention of resale, it is deemed a trade good and is hence zakātable (*Ikhtiyār* 1:151; *Ṭaḥṭāwī* 2:392; *Durr, Radd* 2:8–9; *Tabyīn* 1:253).

537 *Zakāt* is due on gold and silver in *any* form, whether minted coins, raw nuggets, jewelry (whether worn or not worn, contrary to other schools), or household decorative pieces (*Imdād* 681; *Kanz* 1:277). There is no *zakāt* due, however, on precious stones such as rubies, diamonds or emeralds, regardless of their value, unless they are one's trade goods (see note below) (*Durr, Radd* 2:14; *Tabyīn* 1:277).

538 A *mithqāl* is roughly equivalent to 4.374 g; therefore, the *niṣāb* (minimum zakātable amount) is approximately 87.48 g of gold, or its equivalent monetary value (*Imdād al-Awzān* 17, 31). This value is the quantum used to determine whether or not one is obligated to pay *zakāt*, or eligible to receive it (see discussion at beginning of chapter and related note on two types of *niṣāb*).

539 For example, if someone owned 450 *dirhams* of silver, then he would pay 11 *dirhams* of *zakāt*—10 on the 400 and 1 on the extra 50—since the extra 50 *dirhams* is more than 1/5 of the *niṣāb* (i.e., 40). The proportionate amount of *zakāt* on the 50 *dirhams* is 1 *dirham*, since 1 *dirham* is owed for 40, and the extra 10 does not amount to another 1/5. If, however, he had 430 *dirhams*, he would pay 10 *dirhams*, as the extra 30 does not amount to 1/5 of the *niṣāb*. If he had 480 *dirhams*, he would pay 12 *dirhams*; and so on.

540 A trade good refers to any non-monetary item purchased with the intention, *at the time of purchase*, of resale. If one does not intend resale at the time of purchase, then the item is not deemed a trade good with regard to *zakāt*, and is hence not zakātable. That is, even if later after the purchase he intends resale, or even if it was purchased for personal use yet with the intention that *if he later found a good deal, he would sell it*, *zakāt* is not due on the item. Rather, once he actually

The *zakāt* of livestock—i.e., camels, cattle, sheep, and goats—is based on the quantum allotted for them, as delineated in its relevant section [in other works of jurisprudence].

ELIGIBLE RECIPIENTS OF *ZAKĀT*

1. An indigent person (*faqīr*),[541] i.e., possessing less than the *niṣāb*,[542] whether by actual gold and silver or by valued goods, even if he is healthy and earning a living;[543]
2. A poor person (*miskīn*), i.e., one who has no wealth at all;
3. A slave working to free himself (*mukātab*);
4. A person in debt;[544]
5. A soldier cut off from his troop;
6. A pilgrim cut off from his group;

sells the item, *zakāt* would be owed on the money collected from the sale. Likewise if one gains ownership of a non-monetary item without a sale contract, such as by inheritance, then it is not zakātable, as there was no contract with which the intention of resale could be conjoined. Finally, if one purchases a non-monetary item with the intention of resale, whereby it is deemed a trade good and is zakātable, and then later changes his intention and decides to not sell it and instead uses it for personal use, it is no longer deemed a trade good for *zakāt* (*Ṭaḥṭāwī* 2:396; *Durr, Radd* 2:10,13, 14; *Tabyīn* 1:256–7).

541 The basis of eligible recipients is the Qur'ānic verse, "Charity is only for the indigent; the poor; workers who collect it; those whose hearts are to be reconciled; slaves [working to free themselves]; people in debt; in the way of Allāh; and wayfarers—a mandate from Allāh, and Allāh is All-Knowing, Ever-Wise" (9:60). No person outside of these categories is eligible to receive *zakāt*, as the verse *limits* them as recipients with the particle "only" (*Tafsīr Abī 'l-Suʿūd* 4:76). By scholarly consensus, the category of "those whose hearts are to be reconciled" is no longer applicable for *zakāt*, from the time of the Caliphate of Abū Bakr (*Tabyīn* 1:299). Moreover, the condition for all categories is, as noted from the definition of *zakāt* above in the text, transfer of ownership (*tamlīk*) (to an individual from one of the above categories). Therefore, one cannot pay *zakāt* to build institutions such as mosques or hospitals; for general public welfare such as fixing roads or bridges; or for sponsoring someone's education or pilgrimage; without first "transfering ownership" to a poor individual. The phrase "in the way of Allāh" in the verse cannot be applied to such endeavors. Rather, it is interpreted to refer to soldiers or pilgrims, specifically the indigent among them. They are mentioned separately, despite being included in the first category of "the indigent," since they have an extra need, having been cut off from their troop or group (*Durr, Radd* 2:62; *Kanz, Tabyīn* 1:298, 300).

542 That is, *niṣāb ḥirmān al-zakāt* (see related note, p. 139).

543 Although it is better for one who is able to earn a living not to take *zakāt* (*Badā'iʿ* 2:159).

544 Such that his debts take his wealth below the *niṣāb* (*Mukhtār* 1:175; *Tabyīn* 1:298).

7. A wayfarer who, despite possessing wealth in his homeland, has nothing [i.e., less than the *niṣāb*] with him on his journey;[545]
8. One who works as a state *zakāt* collector.[546]

The one paying *zakāt* can choose to give it to recipient[s] of all of the above categories, or any one category of them, regardless of whether or not recipients of other categories are present.[547]

Zakāt may not be given to any of the following:

1. A non-Muslim;
2. A wealthy person (*ghanī*), i.e., one who possesses the *niṣāb* in any form of wealth;[548]
3. A Hāshimite, or a freed slave of a Hāshimite, although Imām Ṭaḥāwī maintained that they are eligible recipients;
4. One's parent or grandparent;
5. One's child or grandchild;[549]
6. One's wife or husband;
7. One's slave, even one working to free himself;
8. One's partially-freed slave;
9. To pay for a deceased person's funeral shroud;
10. To pay off a deceased person's debt;[550]
11. Or to purchase a slave to be freed.

If one pays *zakāt* after having made an honest effort to ensure the recipient was eligible, and then finds out the recipient was not eligible,[551] then it is valid

545 With the condition that he has no access to his wealth back home (*Tabyīn* 1:298).

546 Who is paid out of the *zakāt* funds enough to fairly suffice him and in proportion to the amount of work he performs as *zakāt* collector (*Mukhtār* 1:174; *Tabyīn, Shalabī* 1:297). This, however, only applies to someone appointed by the government, not to one working for an independent organization, for example.

547 Even if just to one person, from only one category (*Tabyīn* 1:299).

548 Aside from personal belongings (*Marāqī 'l -Falāḥ* 2:399; *Lubāb* 165); i.e., *niṣāb ḥirmān al-zakāt* (see related note, p. 139).

549 As for indigent siblings, aunts, uncles, and other relatives, it is not only permissible but rather preferable for one to pay *zakāt* to them (*Ṭaḥṭāwī* 2:399).

550 If, however, one were to pay off a debt of an indigent person (*faqīr*), *upon his command* and with the intention of paying *zakāt*, then it is valid, as the creditor effectively serves as the debtor's agent in collecting *zakāt* (*Ikhtiyār* 1:178; *Durr, Radd* 2:62).

551 For example, if the recipient turns out to be wealthy; a non-Muslim in Muslim lands; the

[such that he does not have to pay it again], unless the recipient turns out to be his slave, even one who is working to free himself.

It is disliked to give an amount of wealth to an eligible recipient such that he would then own the *niṣāb* [and hence no longer be eligible to receive *zakāt* in the future].[552] It is preferred, however, to give enough to a recipient such that he need not ask for money for food.[553]

It is disliked to pay one's *zakāt*, after the completion of the lunar year,[554] to a recipient in another land,[555] unless the recipient is a relative; one who is needier; one who is stricter in adherence to the religion; or one who is more beneficial to the Muslims through [for example] teaching.

It is more preferable to pay *zakāt* to relatives, starting with the nearest of kin; then to one's neighbors; then to one's district; then to members of one's profession; and then to fellow citizens.

CHARITY AT THE END OF RAMAḌĀN (*ṢADAQAT AL-FIṬR*)

Ṣadaqat al-fiṭr is mandatory (*wājib*) on every free Muslim who is legally responsible (*mukallaf*),[556] possessing the *niṣāb*,[557] in excess of any debts and of basic personal needs.

---

donor's father, son, or spouse; or a Hāshimite. In such cases, it is valid *as long as* the donor had made an honest effort to ensure the recipient was eligible (*Ṭaḥṭāwī* 2:400; *Durr*, *Radd* 2:67–8).

552 That is, the recipient receives enough wealth whereby once his lunar year is up, he would retain enough of that wealth such that he could no longer receive *zakāt*. Thus, if the recipient is given enough such that he owns *niṣāb*, yet after paying off his debts or after spending on his dependents he still has less than *niṣāb* (and remains an eligible recipient), then it is not disliked (*Ikhtiyār* 1:178; *Marāqī 'l-Falāḥ* 2:400; *Durr* 2:68).

553 This sentence is incomplete in the Arabic published edition, yet its missing words have been filled in from the manuscript as well as the author's well-known commentary, *Marāqī 'l-Falāḥ* (2:400).

554 Yet if one does so before completion of the lunar year, it is not disliked (*Ṭaḥṭāwī* 2:400).

555 According to Imām Ṭaḥṭāwī, it is prohibitively disliked (*makrūh taḥrīman*), even to a place less than the travelling distance away (48 mi or 77 km) (2:400); while according to Ibn ʿĀbidīn, it would appear to be mildly disliked (*makrūh tanzīhan*) (*Radd* 2:68). In either case, it would still be valid (*Ikhtiyār* 1:179; *Radd* 2:68). Finally, in general, one should avoid paying *zakāt* to someone that he knows will use the money for sinful acts, although it would still be valid if the person were an eligible recipient (*Ṭaḥṭāwī* 2:400).

556 That is, adult and sane, as otherwise one is not legally responsible (*Hadiyya* 198; *Durr*, *Radd* 2:4; *Tabyīn* 1:252).

557 That is, *niṣāb ḥirmān al-zakāt* (see related note, p. 139).

It is mandatory on behalf of oneself, one's child who is a minor,[558] one's slave used for personal service, one's slave promised freedom upon owner's death (*mudabbar*), and one's female slave with whom he bore a child (*umm al-walad*), even if the slave is non-Muslim.

It is not mandatory on behalf of one's slave working for his freedom; one's child [son or daughter] who is an adult;[559] one's wife;[560] a co-owned slave; or a runaway slave, kidnapped slave or imprisoned slave—except after their return.[561]

The amount due is a half *ṣāᶜ* [2.2 kg] of wheat, flour, or *sawīq* [a mix of wheat and barley], or one *ṣāᶜ* [4.4 kg] of dates, raisins, or barley, which equals eight *riṭls* according to the Iraqi standard.

It is permissible to pay by monetary value of one of the above amounts; this is actually superior when one can find what he needs—i.e., in times of ease—as it is more expedient in fulfilling the needs of the indigent. If, however, it is a time of difficulty [like famine], then wheat, barley, or any staple good is superior to monetary currency.

The time in which *ṣadaqat al-fiṭr* becomes mandatory is when fajr comes in on the Day of ᶜId al-Fiṭr. Therefore, if one dies or becomes indigent *before* that time; or if one becomes Muslim, or attains wealth thereby possessing *niṣāb*, or is born *after* that time; then it is not mandatory for him.

It is preferable to pay it before leaving for the ᶜId prayer area (*muṣallā*), yet it is valid if one pays it beforehand or afterwards,[562] although delaying it is disliked.[563]

---

558 That is, who is indigent (*faqīr*), from the father's wealth or, if the father is not alive or is himself indigent, the paternal grandfather's wealth (*Hadiyya* 213; *Shurunbulāliyya* 1:193). This ruling differs from that of the ritual sacrifice of ᶜĪd al-Aḍḥā (*uḍḥiya*), which does not have to be performed by the parent on behalf of his indigent child (see p. 169).

559 The father also does not have to pay it from his own wealth on behalf of his wealthy child who is a minor; rather, the obligation is on the child's wealth. If the parent or guardian does not pay on his behalf, the child himself must pay it for those missed years once he reaches puberty (*Durar*, *Shurunbulāliyya* 1:193; *Tabyīn*, *Shalabī* 1:307).

560 If one does pay on behalf of his wife or adult children, *without* their permission or knowledge, it counts on their behalf *if* they are his dependants (*Hadiyya* 213; *Hidāya* 1:113; *Tabyīn* 1:307). For *zakāt* however, if one pays on behalf of someone else—even if a spouse or dependant—it would fulfill the other person's obligation *only* if that person gave him permission, or at the very least *knew* of the payment, at the time or beforehand.

561 Whereupon the master must pay on their behalf for those years in which they were absent (*Tanwīr* 2:75).

562 Even to the end of one's life (*Ṭaḥṭāwī* 2:404; *Hadiyya* 212).

563 That is, mildly disliked (*makrūh tanzīhan*), but not prohibitively disliked (*makrūh taḥrīman*) (*Radd* 2:72, 78).

Every person should pay it to one indigent person (*faqīr*), even if to a non-Muslim resident of Muslim lands (*dhimmī*). One may not split it between two indigent persons (*faqīrs*), although there is disagreement among the jurists on this matter.[564]

It is permissible for a group of people to pay their combined *ṣadaqat al-fiṭr* to one recipient, according to the sound position (*ṣaḥīḥ*).

564 Most jurists, however, maintain that it is permissible, which is the sound position (*ṣaḥīḥ*). Yet even according to this position, it is still more preferable to give it to one indigent person, so as to better fulfill his need (*Ṭaḥṭāwī* 2:404; *Durr*, *Radd* 2:78; *Durar*, *Shurunbulāliyya* 1:196).

The Greater Pilgrimage (Ḥajj)

Ḥajj is defined as visiting a particular place, while in a state of pilgrim sanctity (*iḥrām*), in its appointed months—namely, Shawwāl, Dhū 'l-Qaʿda, and the first ten days of Dhū 'l-Ḥijja.[565]

It is obligatory (*farḍ*) to perform *ḥajj* once [in a lifetime], and as soon as one is able to (*ʿalā 'l-fawr*), according to the sounder position (*aṣaḥḥ*).

The person on whom it is obligatory[566] is anyone who is free; Muslim; legally responsible (*mukallaf*);[567] and able—at the time when the people of his locality leave for the *ḥajj*—to afford[568] provisions and transportation for the actual journey and other expenses, for both going and returning, [in excess of] expenses for one's dependants [until his return], and [in excess of one's] other basic necessities.[569]

The obligatory requirements for its performance[570] are a sound, healthy

565 One cannot perform *ḥajj* before the 9th of Dhū 'l-Ḥijja; however, certain rites may be performed earlier in the above months, such as the mandatory *saʿy* conjoined with the Ṭawāf of Arrival (see related note, p. 148) (*Radd* 2:150; *Kanz, Tabyīn* 2:49–50).

566 That is, if one does not meet all of the conditions mentioned in this paragraph, *ḥajj* is not obligatory on him at all—neither to perform it himself, nor to pay for someone else to perform it on his behalf or leave such a bequest in his will (as opposed to the next paragraph) (*Shalabī* 2:5).

567 That is, adult and sane, as otherwise one is not legally responsible (*Hadiyya* 198; *Durr, Radd* 2:4; *Tabyīn* 1:252).

568 "Affording" in this context refers to one's personal ownership of wealth. Hence, *ḥajj* is not obligatory on one who is lent the requisite money for provisions and transportation, nor on one for whom those expenses are paid for by another (*Radd* 2:142).

569 That is, just like in *zakāt*, such as one's house, furniture, equipment for one's profession, etc. (*Marāqī 'l-Falāḥ* 2:407; *Hadiyya* 221; *Durr, Radd* 2:143).

570 That is, if any one of the conditions in this paragraph is not fulfilled, it is no longer obligatory on the person to perform *ḥajj himself*; however, he must instead pay for someone else to perform it on his behalf, or leave such a bequest in his will. The same of course applies to a woman (*Radd* 2:142; *Tabyīn, Shalabī* 2:4–6).

body;[571] prevention of any physical barrier on the journey [to Makka]; safety of passage based on reasonable assumption; and, [for a woman] to not be in her waiting period (*ʿidda*), and to be accompanied by her husband or unmarriageable kinsman (*maḥram*) who is trustworthy, sane, and an adult.[572]

HOW TO PERFORM THE RITES OF *ḤAJJ*

When one intends to enter the state of pilgrim sanctity (*iḥrām*)[573] at one of the

---

571 That is, one that is free of any disease or condition that would impede the person's ability to travel, such as paralysis or blindness. The same ruling would apply to being wrongly imprisoned (*Hadiyya* 221; *Durr, Radd* 2:142; *Tabyīn* 2:3).

572 If the journey to *ḥajj* entails travelling the legal distance by which prayers are shortened (i.e., roughly 48 mi or 77 km), then the woman must be accompanied by either her husband or a man of unmarriageable kin (*maḥram*), i.e., one whom she may never marry, whether by blood relationship, nursing, or marriage (such as father-in-law, with whom she may travel unless there is fear of falling into sin). In either case, the one who accompanies her must be trustworthy, sane, an adult or at least an adolescent, and not an open sinner (*fāsiq*), as he would not be trustworthy in protecting her. This condition applies even to elderly women. In addition, she must be able to afford the provisions of both herself and her kinsman (*maḥram*) accompanying her, but not that of her husband if he instead takes her. It is deemed prohibitively disliked (*makrūh taḥrīman*) for her to travel and perform *ḥajj* without her husband or appropriate kinsman, yet the *ḥajj* itself would still be valid (*Hadiyya* 221; *Ikhtiyār* 2:202; *Durr, Radd* 2:145–6; *Tabyīn, Shalabī* 2:5–6).

573 The obligatory (*farḍ*) integrals of *ḥajj* are three, which are not valid unless performed in the following order: (1) Entering the state of pilgrim sanctity (*iḥrām*). This entails (a) making an intention (*niyya*) and, immediately afterwards without engaging in another unrelated action, (b) reciting the *talbiya*, or any other *dhikr* in its place. However, reciting a *dhikr* other than the *talbiya* is mildly disliked (*makrūh tanzīhan*) as it entails leaving a *sunna*. In either case, the condition is that the *dhikr* be *uttered* on the tongue, not merely intended in the heart (*Radd* 2:158–9). (2) The Standing (*wuqūf*) at ʿArafāt. "Standing" in this context means being present there even for a moment, between midday (*zawāl*) of the 9th of Dhū 'l-Ḥijja (the Day of ʿArafa) until right before fajr of the 10th (the Day of Sacrifice). This pillar will not be valid if the pilgrim engaged in sexual intercourse beforehand (after having entered into the state of pilgrim sanctity). (3) Most of the Ṭawāf of Visitation (*ṭawāf al-ziyāra*), i.e., four of the seven rounds, accompanied with its intention. This ṭawāf may be performed anytime after the standing at ʿArafāt until the end of one's life, in terms of fulfilling the obligation (*farḍ*).

The central mandatory (*wājib*) requisites of *ḥajj* are five, namely: (1) The Standing (*wuqūf*) at Muzdalifa, i.e., being present even for a moment, after the entrance of fajr on the 10th of Dhū 'l-Ḥijja. (2) The *Saʿy* (seven circuits) between Mount Ṣafā and Mount Marwa (although it is obligatory (*farḍ*) according to the other three schools of thought—*Durr* 2:148). This ceremonial rite must be conjoined with a proper *ṭawāf* beforehand. (3) The Stoning at Minā. (4) Shaving the head, or trimming its hair. This rite must be performed within the sacred precinct (*ḥaram*), even if outside Minā. (5) The Farewell Ṭawāf (*ṭawāf al-ṣadr*), except for women in menstruation or residents of Makka (for whom it is not mandatory, and hence for whom no expiatory sacrifice is necessary for its omission).

The following actions are also mandatory (*wājib*): entering the state of pilgrim sanctity (*iḥrām*)

designated boundaries (*mīqāt*, pl. *mawāqīt*),[574] such as Rābigh,[575] he should [do the following, as they are recommended:] perform *ghusl*[576] or *wuḍū'*; trim his nails [and moustache]; shave [his armpits and pubic region]; put on nice scent [and oil]; and wear an upper and lower garment, both new or washed.[577] The most preferred garments are those that are new and white. He then prays two *rakʿas* [which are *sunna*],[578] and says: O Allāh, verily I desire to perform *ḥajj*, so make it easy for me and accept it from me.

---

before crossing the designated boundaries; remaining for the obligatory Standing at ʿArafāt until maghrib, as well as afterwards for at least a moment; starting every *ṭawāf* at the Black Stone; keeping the Kaʿba on one's left therein; performing it behind the semicircular enclosure (*ḥaṭīm*); for one without a valid excuse, walking for *ṭawāf*; being in a state of ritual purity, and covering one's nakedness, throughout *ṭawāf*; ending each *ṭawāf* with its two-*rakʿa* prayer; starting the *saʿy* at Ṣafā; performing it after an appropriate *ṭawāf* (of at least four rounds); for one without a valid excuse, walking for *saʿy*; delaying maghrib and combining it with ʿishā' in Muzdalifa; sacrificing a sheep for one performing the *qirān* or *tamattuʿ* type of *ḥajj*, and doing so after the stoning yet before shaving the head (or trimming the hair), while the one performing *ifrād* does not need to sacrifice yet must shave *after* the stoning; performing the Ṭawāf of Visitation (*ṭawāf al-ziyāra*) in one of the three Days of Sacrifice—10th, 11th, or before maghrib of the 12th; the last three of the seven rounds of that *ṭawāf*; shaving the head (or trimming the hair) in one of those days as well, and within the Sacred Precinct; and avoiding any penalty that necessitates the sacrifice of a sheep (as delineated below, see p. 162). All other actions of *ḥajj* are either emphasized *sunnas* or etiquette (*Hadiyya* 222–5; *Durr*, *Radd* 2:147–150).

574 The designated boundaries are borders around the Sacred Precinct (*ḥaram*) that the pilgrim—who intends on entering Makka (i.e., the Sacred Precinct), even if for business—may not cross without being in a state of pilgrim sanctity (*iḥrām*). They are the following: Dhāt ʿIrq for the people of Iraq; Juḥfa for the people of the Levant; Dhū 'l-Ḥulayfa for the people of Madīna; Qarn for the people of Najd; and Yalamlam for the people of Yemen. Each boundary is designated for the people of that area, as well as anyone that enters the Sacred Precinct from that vicinity, even if he is not from that area. If, however, he does not intend on entering Makka (i.e., the Sacred Precinct) first—but rather somewhere between the designated boundaries and the Sacred Precinct, like Jeddah (e.g., for business)—then he may cross the designated boundaries without being in the state of pilgrim sanctity. If he performs *ḥajj* or *ʿumra* afterwards, he may enter the state of pilgrim sanctity from *that place* (e.g., Jeddah) and then enter the Sacred Precinct, *without* having to go back outside the designated boundaries (*Mukhtār* 1:202–3; *Hadiyya* 227; *Durr*, *Radd* 2:152–5; *Tabyīn*, *Shalabī* 2:6–7).

575 A valley slightly before Juḥfa, on the left side of someone facing Makka (*Ṭaḥṭāwī* 2:413).

576 The purpose of *ghusl* here is general cleanliness, not ritual purification, and is hence recommended even for a woman in menstruation or postnatal bleeding (*Tabyīn* 2:8).

577 There is one garment for the bottom (*izār*) and one for the top (*ridā'*). He should ensure that the bottom garment covers his nakedness, i.e., from above the navel to below the knees. He should fold it above the waist to keep it secure, yet ideally without using a needle or fastening a knot, as doing so is disliked for either the top or bottom garment. He may place a belt with a pouch in which to keep personal belongings over the bottom garment. The top garment should cover both shoulders. Finally, he may wear a ring as well (*Hadiyya* 230; *Kanz* 2:8, *Tabyīn* 2:14; *Durr*, *Radd* 2:157). Based on the permissibility of wearing a ring, it seems that he may also wear a wristwatch (ʿItr, *Al-Ḥajj wal-ʿUmra* 57) and eyeglasses.

578 Unless it is a time in which prayer is disliked (see p. 71). Also, just as with the two *rakʿas* of

He then says the *talbiya* immediately after the prayer, while making the intention of *ḥajj* alone if performing *ifrād*. If, however, he is performing *qirān*, he intends both *ḥajj* and *ʿumra*, and says: O Allāh, verily I desire to perform *ḥajj* and *ʿumra*, so make the two easy for me and accept them both from me.

If, rather, he is performing *tamattuʿ*, he enters the pilgrim state of *ʿumra* alone, and says: O Allāh, verily I desire to perform *ʿumra*, so make it easy for me and accept it from me.

Afterwards, he is to recite the *talbiya* [ideally three times], and he will have then entered the state of pilgrim sanctity. The *talbiya* is to say: Here I am at Your service, O Allāh, at Your service! [At Your service!][579] You have no partner; here I am at Your service! Indeed, all praise, blessings, and the dominion itself are utterly Yours; You have no partner!

He should not say less than this form of the *talbiya*,[580] yet if he wants to add more [as is recommended], he may say: At Your service! At Your obedience! All good is in Your hands![581]

Hence, once the pilgrim has recited the *talbiya* accompanied with an intention of either *ḥajj* or *ʿumra*, or both, he has entered the state of pilgrim sanctity.[582] This state is a condition for the validity of one's actions on the pilgrimage.

greeting the mosque, praying one of the five prescribed prayers instead fulfills this *sunna*, according to some scholars. Lastly, after the prayer yet before entering into the state of pilgrim sanctity, he should seek forgiveness from Allāh Most High and make sincere repentance for all of his sins (*Hadiyya* 231; *Durr, Radd* 2:157–8; *Tabyīn* 2:9).

579 Some Ḥanafī texts, such as the *Kanz* and *Hidāya*, list this third "At Your service!" (*Labbayk*) for extra emphasis. One would pause shortly before it (*Radd* 2:159). It is also mentioned in the *Mukhtār* (1:205) and the *Hadiyya* (229).

580 As it is mildly disliked (*makrūh tanzīhan*). Also, it is recommended according to some, and an emphasized *sunna* according to others, for men to recite it in a raised voice (*Radd* 2:159–60, 165).

581 For the above supplications, as well as those of the entire ḥajj, see p. 198.

582 Just as one may not begin the *ṣalāt* without its opening *taḥrīma*, one may not begin the *ḥajj* without entering into a state of *iḥrām*. Likewise, just as the *taḥrīma* consists of the intention of *ṣalāt* made in the heart, accompanied by a form of *dhikr* uttered on the tongue—specifically the words *Allāhu akbar*—the *iḥrām* also consists of the intention of *ḥajj* made in the heart, accompanied by a form of *dhikr* uttered on the tongue—specifically the *talbiya*. Finally, just as the intention in the heart alone is not sufficient to fulfill the *taḥrīma* for *ṣalāt*, similarly the intention of *ḥajj* is not enough to fulfill the *iḥrām* of *ḥajj*; rather, each must be accompanied by its respective *dhikr*. Hence, once the person makes the intention (for either *ḥajj*, *ʿumra*, or both) and recites the *talbiya*, he has entered into the state of pilgrim sanctity (*Hadiyya* 229). The *talbiya* may be recited in any language, even for one capable of saying it in Arabic, yet it is better to do so in Arabic. It is valid to recite another *dhikr* in its place when entering *iḥrām*, although the *talbiya* form itself is *sunna*. Regardless of whichever *dhikr* one recites, to do so once is obligatory (*farḍ*) in order to enter into *iḥrām*, while repeating it afterwards is *sunna* (*Durr, Radd* 2:158–9).

At this point, the pilgrim must abstain from the following:[583]

1. Sexual intercourse, or speaking about it in front of women (*rafath*),
2. Vulgar speech,
3. Argumentation (*jidāl*),
4. Acts of disobedience (*maʿāṣī*),
5. Killing land game, including pointing them out or indicating their whereabouts to a hunter,
6. Wearing stitched garments,
7. Covering the head [for men][584] or the face [for both men and women],[585]
8. Applying any sort of scent [to one's body or clothes],
9. Shaving or plucking hair.

If one does commit any of the above, he must pay the appropriate penalty [as delineated below, along with other penalties].

One[586] should recite much *talbiya* when changing states, especially in the early morning hours before fajr, with a raised voice.[587]

583 For details, see section on violations, p. 162.

584 The male pilgrim must also keep the upper protruding cuneiform bone of each foot uncovered, and hence must wear appropriate sandals to do so (*Ikhtiyār* 1:206; *Durr, Radd* 2:163; *Kanz, Tabyīn* 2:12).

585 For both the face and the head, what is prohibited is to cover them with *direct* skin contact; hence, taking shade underneath a covering or umbrella is permissible. For women, the prohibition applies only to the face. Yet as mentioned by many Ḥanafī scholars, a woman may drape a cloth or face-covering over a protruding frame (or nowadays, sun cap) so as to keep her face covered while not having direct skin contact (*Durr, Radd* 2:164; *Tabyīn, Shalabī* 2:14).

586 In the original Arabic text, the author here switches from the third person to the second person and directly addresses the reader. However, the English translation above was kept in the third person for consistency and flow.

587 That is, whenever one changes states, such as after the prayer; when ascending or descending a slope; when encountering another group of pilgrims; upon waking up from sleep; or when mounting or dismounting a vehicle. It should ideally be repeated at least three times in a row. He should not interrupt it with speech. It is permissible for him to respond to another's greeting, yet it is disliked for the other person to interrupt his *talbiya* by that greeting (*Imdād* 688–9; *Durr, Radd* 2:164; *Kanz, Tabyīn* 2:14). The man should recite *talbiya* in a raised voice, yet within his capacity so as not to harm himself by exaggeration. He should not recite it silently as that would entail leaving an emphasized *sunna*, yet as with omission of any *sunna*, there is no resulting expiation (although it could be sinful if habitual). If in a group, no two persons should recite their *talbiya* together; rather, everyone should recite it on his own. In general, one makes *talbiya* in the Sacred Mosque of Makka, in Minā and in ʿArafāt, yet not during *ṭawāf* or *saʿy* (*Durr, Radd* 2:164–5; *Tabyīn, Shalabī* 2:14).

Upon reaching Makka, it is recommended for him to perform *ghusl*[588] and to enter in the daytime, from the Gate of Maʿlā, while reciting the *talbiya*, until he reaches the Gate of Salām. He should then enter the mosque in a state of humility, reciting the *talbiya*, followed by *takbīr*, *tahlīl*, and blessings upon the Prophet ﷺ.

Supplication (*duʿā'*) is accepted upon seeing the Ennobled House [i.e., the Kaʿba].[589] He should then face the Black Stone, while saying *takbīr* and *tahlīl*; raise his hands the way he does in [the beginning of] *ṣalāt*; and place them onto the stone and kiss it, without harming anyone [as harming one's fellow Muslim is unlawful (*ḥarām*)].[590]

He should then perform *ṭawāf* around the House [Kaʿba], moving toward his right [i.e., keeping the Kaʿba on his left side], and [for all seven rounds] placing his upper garment under his right armpit, with both ends over his left shoulder (*iḍṭibāʿ*), weeping. If performing *ḥajj* alone (*ifrād*), he should intend the Ṭawāf of Arrival (*ṭawāf al-qudūm*).[591] The *ṭawāf* should be performed behind the semi-circular enclosure (*ḥaṭīm*), in seven rounds. In the first three rounds alone, he should do *raml*,[592] which is to walk briskly in short steps, while gently shaking the shoulders, like a soldier strutting between ranks. Every time he passes by the Black Stone, he should greet it [by raising his hands and recit-

588 This is recommended even for a woman in menstruation or postnatal bleeding, as its purpose is general cleanliness, not ritual purification (*Durr* 2:165; *Tabyīn* 2:14).

589 One should not, however, raise his hands upon seeing the Sacred House, even while supplicating. Imām Ṭaḥāwī's narration of all three Imāms of the Ḥanafī school—Abū Ḥanīfa, Abū Yūsuf, and Muḥammad—is that doing so is disliked (*Radd* 2:165).

590 Otherwise if it is too crowded, then after having raised his hands like in the prayer, he instead points with the inner palms of both hands toward the Black Stone from afar. He does this as if placing his hands upon it, with the back of his hands directed toward his face and parallel to his ears, while reciting *takbīr*, *tahlīl*, *taḥmīd*, and blessings upon the Prophet ﷺ. He then kisses his hands. This constitutes the greeting of the Black Stone, an emphasized *sunna* performed a total of eight times in *ṭawāf*—once at the beginning, and one after ending each of the seven rounds. The first and last greetings, however, are the most emphasized of the eight (*Hadiyya* 237; *Durr*, *Radd* 2:166, 169). If one is performing *saʿy* afterwards, it is recommended to return for a ninth greeting of the Black Stone after praying the two mandatory *rakʿas* after *ṭawāf* (*Durr*, *Radd* 2:170).

591 Which is an emphasized *sunna* only for one who does not reside in Makka (*Durr*, *Radd* 2:166; *Kanz*, *Tabyīn* 2:19).

592 If it is too crowded before he begins *ṭawāf*, he pauses until he finds an opening, whereupon he assumes the fast pace of *raml*. If it is too crowded for *raml* during *ṭawāf*, then he walks normally until he can resume the fast pace of *raml* (*Imdād* 692; *Durr*, *Radd* 2:169; *Tabyīn* 2:18). Both *iḍṭibāʿ* and *raml* are emphasized *sunnas* for any *ṭawāf* followed by *saʿy*. This includes the Ṭawāf of Arrival; the Ṭawāf of ʿUmra; and the Ṭawāf of Visitation, for one who had not performed *saʿy* beforehand. Otherwise, for any *ṭawāf* not followed by *saʿy*, *iḍṭibāʿ* and *raml* are not to be performed (*Radd* 2:167, 169).

ing the appropriate supplication, as described above]. He should also finish the *ṭawāf* with it [i.e., greeting the Black Stone].

He then performs [the mandatory] two *rakʿas* of prayer[593] behind the Station of Ibrahim ﵇, or anywhere in the mosque.[594]

Next he proceeds to Mount Ṣafā [which he ascends][595] and stands facing the *qibla* [i.e., Kaʿba] while reciting *takbīr*, *tahlīl*, and *talbiya*,[596] supplicating and raising his hands toward the sky.[597] He then descends and calmly walks toward Mount Marwa. Upon reaching the middle of the valley, however, he should rush between the two green lines until he crosses them,[598] after which he resumes his relaxed pace until reaching Mount Marwa. He then climbs onto the hill and performs what he did on Mount Ṣafā; this constitutes one round. He then heads back toward Ṣafā and does the same, finishing another round, and continues until he completes seven, having started at Ṣafā and ending at Marwa [thereby completing the ceremonial rite of *saʿy*].[599]

---

593 He re-covers his right shoulder after *ṭawāf*, since it is disliked in general to pray with the shoulders uncovered, and since there is no *iḍṭibāʿ* in *saʿy* (*Radd* 2:167). The *sunna* is to perform this prayer immediately after the *ṭawāf*, without delay, unless it is a time in which prayer is disliked. In that case, it *must* be delayed until after that time, although the *ṭawaf* itself is valid in that time. (Such times are at sunrise, at midday, at sunset, the entire prayer time of fajr, and after the performance of ʿaṣr; see related section, p. 71.) If one is performing *saʿy* afterwards, it is recommended (*mustaḥabb*) to return to and greet the Black Stone once more—making it the ninth time—before proceeding to Mount Ṣafā (*Durr*, *Radd* 2:170; *Tabyīn*, *Shalabī* 2:19).

594 On a side yet important note, Ibn ʿĀbidīn cites some texts of Ḥanafī law which state that in the presence of the Kaʿba, passing in front of someone praying is permissible (*Radd* 2:172).

595 Ascending both Ṣafā and Marwa is an emphasized *sunna* of the *saʿy*. It is done for a total of eight times for the seven rounds, starting at Ṣafā and ending at Marwa. However, one is to ascend somewhat, such that one is able to see the Kaʿba (although seeing the Kaʿba from Marwa is not possible today due to construction). Climbing all the way to the wall and touching it is a reprehensible innovation (*bidʿa*) that is not the way of *Ahl al-Sunna wal-Jamāʿa*. Finally, there is no *iḍṭibāʿ* in *saʿy* according to our school (*Radd* 2:171).

596 He does so in a raised voice, followed by sending blessings upon the Prophet ﷺ and supplication (*duʿā'*) for his needs (*Durr*, *Radd* 2:171; *Kanz* 2:19).

597 That is, he raises his hands to shoulder level, with both palms directed toward the sky (*Imdād* 692; *Radd* 2:171).

598 This is an emphasized *sunna* for each round of *saʿy*. If he is unable to do so due to the crowd, he waits until he finds an opening, or else if forced to move slowly, at least imitates a fast pace with his movements (*Imdād* 692; *Radd* 2:171).

599 There is a sentence in the text here not translated above, which is "This is a *sunna* for the pilgrim that comes from outside Makka." In the Arabic published edition as well as the manuscript, it would seemingly be referring to the *saʿy*. Yet the *saʿy* is not a *sunna* but rather a mandatory requisite (*wājib*). Hence, the statement in the Arabic text appears to be a mistake—perhaps some words were omitted in its transcription, as it is clearly not the opinion of the author himself. He mentions a similar sentence in *Marāqī 'l-Falāḥ* (2:415) and *Imdād al-Fattāḥ* (692), after describing the Ṭawāf

The pilgrim then resides in Makka, remaining in a state of pilgrim sanctity, while taking advantage of his stay by performing as many *ṭawāfs*[600] as possible.

As for the one performing *qirān*, he is to perform the *ʿumra* first, followed by its accompanying *saʿy*. After that, he also performs the Ṭawāf of Arrival,[601] followed by its accompanying *saʿy*. He too, then, resides in Makka, in his state of pilgrim sanctity, until he completes the rites of *ḥajj* as we shall mention.

As for the one performing *tamattuʿ*, who entered the pilgrim state at the designated boundary with the intention of performing *ʿumra* alone, he performs his *ʿumra*[602] upon entering Makka, accompanied by its *saʿy*, and then shaves his head and completely leaves the state of pilgrim sanctity.[603] He then reenters the state of pilgrim sanctity [from within the Sacred Precinct] on the 8th of Dhū ʾl-Ḥijja in order to perform *ḥajj*.[604]

On that day after having prayed fajr in Makka, he should prepare to leave for Minā, [ideally] after sunrise. It is recommended to stop close to the Mosque at the Mountain of *Khayf* at Minā and to stay there until sunrise[605] of the 9th of

---

of Arrival and before explaining the *saʿy*, and explicitly states, "This is the Ṭawāf of Arrival; it is a *sunna* for the pilgrim that comes from outside Makka," which is the relied-upon position of the school, as confirmed in *Hadiyya* (236), *Durr*, *Radd* (2:166), and other works. To summarize, the Ṭawāf of Arrival is an emphasized *sunna* for one who comes from outside Makka, while the *saʿy* is mandatory (*wājib*) for all pilgrims.

600 These serve as voluntary *ṭawāfs*, and for the pilgrim that comes from outside Makka, are deemed more meritorious than voluntary prayers. Because the *saʿy* was performed with an earlier *ṭawāf*, the mandatory requisite (*wājib*) was already fulfilled. Hence, no *saʿy* may be conjoined with any of these voluntary *ṭawāfs*, as the *saʿy* may not be performed voluntarily. And because no *saʿy* is performed *after* these *ṭawāfs*, there is no *raml* or *iḍṭibāʿ* during these *ṭawāfs*. Of course for each *ṭawāf*, even if voluntary, it is mandatory to pray two *rakʿas* afterwards (*Durr*, *Radd* 2:172; *Tabyīn* 2:22).

601 That is, it is recommended for him to perform the Ṭawāf of Arrival. If he performs it, he does do *raml* in it (as there is a *saʿy* conjoined with the *ṭawāf* afterwards), even though he had already done so in the Ṭawāf of ʿUmra (*Radd* 2:166, 192).

602 He stops reciting *talbiya* when he starts *ṭawāf* (upon greeting the Black Stone), since he will completely leave the state of pilgrim sanctity before reentering it for *ḥajj* (*Imdād* 698; *Kanz* 2:45).

603 Such that everything, including intercourse, becomes permissible for him until he reenters the state of pilgrim sanctity for *ḥajj* (*Imdād* 698).

604 He does not, however, perform the Ṭawāf of Arrival—i.e., it is not a *sunna* for him—since he takes the same ruling as a Makkan resident, which is why he enters the state of pilgrim sanctity for *ḥajj* in Makka as well. Hence, he does the *sunnas* of *raml* and *iḍṭibāʿ* in the Ṭawāf of Visitation, and performs the mandatory (*wājib*) *saʿy* after it, since that is the first *ṭawāf* of his *ḥajj*. Alternatively, he may perform those actions (*raml*, *iḍṭibāʿ*, and *saʿy*) with a voluntary *ṭawāf* after reentering the state of pilgrim sanctity for *ḥajj* and before leaving for Minā, which is also valid (*Durr*, *Radd* 2:196; *Tabyīn* 2:46).

605 That is, it is an emphasized *sunna* to spend the night at Minā, and hence to pray ẓuhr, ʿaṣr, maghrib, ʿishāʾ, and fajr there (*Radd* 2:172–3). Because it is not mandatory, there is no expiation for not doing so, yet it entails doing a wrong (*isāʾa*). It is valid nevertheless to leave Minā early, or to

Dhū 'l-Ḥijja.[606] He then heads out [ideally after sunrise] for ʿArafāt, proceeding to the Mosque of Namira, and prays ẓuhr and then ʿaṣr there with the head of state or his representative, after the sermon. He combines these two prayers, praying them both in the time of ẓuhr, with one *adhān* and two *iqāmas*. He should not separate the two obligatory prayers with voluntary prayers.[607] If he misses[608] the congregation with the head imām, he instead prays ʿaṣr in its normal prayer time, according to Abū Ḥanīfa. This is because according to him, both the congregation with the head imām as well as being in a state of pilgrim sanctity are conditions for the validity of praying ʿaṣr early and combining it with ẓuhr. Abū Yūsuf and Muḥammad, however, maintained that even the pilgrim praying alone may combine the two prayers in the time of ẓuhr, which is the more apparent opinion (*aẓhar*) in terms of strength.[609]

He then proceeds to the standing place in ʿArafāt, close to the Mountain of Mercy[610] [although climbing it is not from the *sunna*]. He performs the [obligatory] rite of Standing (*wuqūf*)[611] there, facing the *qibla*, praising Allāh

---

even spend the night in Makka and go straight to ʿArafāt (*Tabyīn* 2:22–3). The same ruling applies to the *sunna* of spending the nights of the 10th and 11th in Minā.

606 Throughout these ceremonial rites, he should not stop reciting *talbiya* in his various states, except for during *ṭawāf* and *saʿy*, until the first stoning as mentioned below (*Marāqī 'l-Falāḥ* 2:415, *Imdād* 692).

607 That is, even for the emphasized *sunna* of two *rakʿas* after ẓuhr, according to the sound position. It is therefore disliked (*makrūh*) for one to do so. If done, the *adhān* should be repeated, just as if there was an undue delay for any reason, as the *sunna* is to pray ʿaṣr immediately after ẓuhr. If, however, the imām himself delays ʿaṣr for some reason, it is no longer disliked for one to pray the two-*rakʿa sunnas* of ẓuhr in that time. Finally, one does not pray any voluntary prayers after ʿaṣr as well (*Ṭaḥṭāwī* 2:415–16; *Durr*, *Radd* 2:173–4).

608 That is, if he *completely* misses *either* congregation, whether ẓuhr or ʿaṣr, since combining both prayers in the time of ẓuhr is valid as long as he catches *any* part of *each* congregation (*Shalabī* 2:24).

609 Ibn ʿĀbidīn notes that perhaps what is meant here (as Imām Ḥaṣkafī uses the same term in the *Durr*) is that it is the more apparent opinion in terms of strength of *proof*, since the sound and relied-upon position (*ṣaḥīḥ muʿtamad*) of the Ḥanafī school is that of Imām Abū Ḥanīfa (*Radd* 2:174; *Kanz*, *Tabyīn* 2:24; *Badāʾiʿ* 2:351).

610 That is, if possible. Otherwise, one stays anywhere in ʿArafāt, especially due to high traffic today.

611 Although termed "Standing," one may perform this rite while sitting or in any other posture, as what is meant by "Standing" is merely *being present*. Hence, if the pilgrim simply *is* at ʿArafāt, for even a moment within the valid time period for the rite— i.e., from midday (*zawāl*) of the 9th of Dhū 'l-Ḥijja until right before fajr of the 10th (the Day of Sacrifice)—then he would have fulfilled the obligation. This holds even if he were simply passing through, while asleep or without consciousness, completely unaware that the place is ʿArafāt, or even while in a state of major ritual impurity (*Durr*, *Radd* 2:175).

and making *takbīr, tahlīl, talbiya,* sending blessings upon the Prophet ﷺ, and raising his hands, earnestly striving in his supplication until sunset.

The pilgrim then calmly departs[612] for Muzdalifa, where he prays both maghrib and ʿishāʾ [in the time of ʿishāʾ],[613] with one *adhān* and one *iqāma*.[614] One may not pray maghrib on the way [before reaching Muzdalifa].[615] [After spending the night there] the pilgrim prays fajr while it is dark (*ghalas*),[616] after which he performs the [mandatory] rite of Standing (*wuqūf*)[617] at the Sacred Site of Muzdalifa (mashʿar ḥarām), praising Allāh and reciting *takbīr, tahlīl, talbiya,* blessings upon the Prophet ﷺ, and [while raising his hands toward the sky] making supplication for anything he desires.

As sunrise approaches, he departs for Minā. He stones[618] at the Jamrat

---

612 It is mandatory (*wājib*) to leave both after sunset, as well as after the head imām departs. If one leaves beforehand, he must sacrifice a sheep as expiation, unless he returns to ʿArafāt before sunset and then departs afterwards, in which case he is absolved of the expiation. If the imām himself delays his departure and remains in ʿArafāt after sunset, the pilgrim may leave, since the imām failed to follow the *sunna*. Finally, in general there is no harm for a pilgrim to wait in ʿArafāt for some time after sunset and after the imām departs, whether due to high traffic or otherwise. Yet to delay departure (after the imām leaves) for a long time without any excuse is considered wrong (*isāʾa*) (*Durr, Radd* 2:176; *Tabyīn* 2:27).

613 That is, even if praying alone, although praying in congregation is an emphasized *sunna* (*Durr, Radd* 2:176).

614 He does not pray voluntary prayers, even the emphasized *sunna* of maghrib, between the two obligatory prayers. If he does, the *iqāma* is repeated for ʿishāʾ, just as it is if he engages in any unrelated action in between the prayers. Rather, he prays the emphasized *sunnas* of both maghrib and ʿishāʾ, followed by witr, *after* ʿishāʾ (*Radd* 2:176).

615 If he does so, whether in ʿArafāt or on the way to Muzdalifa, he would incur sin for having omitted the mandatory (*wājib*) requisite of delaying maghrib until the time of ʿishāʾ and praying them both in Muzdalifa. Hence, he would have to repeat maghrib upon arriving there, unless he failed to do so by fajr, whereupon the maghrib prayer performed before arrival is deemed valid. If, however, for any reason the pilgrim does not go to Muzdalifa but rather directly to Makka, then he would pray maghrib on time, wherever he may be (*Durr, Radd* 2:177; *Tabyīn* 2:28).

616 That is, as soon as the time enters, as opposed to the normal *sunna* of delaying it until some light begins to appear (*isfār*). Praying fajr in its early darkness (*ghalas*) is a *sunna* only on this day, so as to provide more time for the pilgrim to perform the mandatory (*wājib*) rite of Standing at Muzdalifa, whose time is from true dawn until sunrise. Spending the previous night there until fajr is an emphasized *sunna* (*Durr, Radd* 2:178; *Tabyīn* 2:29).

617 That is, *being present*, for even a moment, at any time from true dawn until sunrise. This requisite is fulfilled if one is present there even if while passing through or while unconscious, just as with the Standing at ʿArafāt. Remaining at Muzdalifa until close to sunrise is an emphasized *sunna*. If one does not perform the Standing at Muzdalifa whatsoever due to a *valid* excuse, such as illness; severe weakness; or for a woman, fear of high traffic; then no expiation is due (*Durr, Radd* 2:178–9).

618 On this day (i.e., the Day of Sacrifice—the 10th), the valid time for stoning begins after true dawn and ends at true dawn the next day. It is recommended to do so between sunrise and midday, permissible and not disliked until sunset, and valid yet disliked afterwards until true dawn on the

al-ᶜAqaba only, from the middle of the valley, casting seven pebbles[619] and saying "[*Bismillāhi*] *Allāhu akbar*" with each throw. With the first throw, he is to stop reciting *talbiya* [for the rest of the *ḥajj*].

He then[620] shaves his head or trims his hair; shaving, however, is more superior for men.[621] At that point he has come out of the minor state of pilgrim sanctity, whereupon everything is permissible except for sexual relations [or foreplay].

After that, the one performing *ifrād* sacrifices if he wishes, while it is mandatory (*wājib*) for the one performing *qirān* or *tamattuᶜ* to sacrifice a sheep, and to do so *before* shaving the head. If unable to sacrifice, he must fast three days from the beginning of the month before the Day of Sacrifice [the 10th], and

---

11th. If done afterwards, the pilgrim is obliged to sacrifice a sheep as expiation for delaying it past its valid time (*Hadiyya* 246; *Durr, Radd* 2:181).

619 It is recommended to collect seven pebbles at Muzdalifa, or forty-nine according to some scholars, yet it is permissible to collect them from anywhere. Each should be approximately the size of a bean or chickpea, according to what is recommended; throwing a larger stone is valid yet disliked. It is mildly disliked to collect one's pebbles at the Stoning Site itself. Also, each pebble must be cast separately; if one casts all seven at once, it counts as only one cast, and six more are due. It is *sunna*, yet not a condition, to cast the seven one after another without breaks; to not cast them consecutively is disliked. Also, one ideally casts the pebble with the tips of his fingers, namely, the index finger and thumb of the right hand. It is disliked yet valid to throw it with force. If, however, one simply *places* it down without casting or throwing, it is not valid (*Hadiyya* 245–6; *Durr, Radd* 2:179–181; *Marāqī 'l-Falāḥ* 2:417).

620 In both of the author's larger works, *Marāqī 'l-Falāḥ* (2:417) and *Imdād al-Fattāḥ* (693), this statement comes *after* the next statement regarding the sacrifice, which reflects the correct order of sacrificing before shaving. The sacrifice is recommended for the one performing *ifrād*, and mandatory (*wājib*) for the one performing *qirān* or *tamattuᶜ* (*Tabyīn* 2:32). Hence, for the one performing *ifrād*, what is mandatory is to do the shaving after the stoning, while it is recommended to sacrifice in between. For the one performing *qirān* or *tamattuᶜ*, it is mandatory to do the stoning, *then* the sacrifice, and *then* the shaving. The author clarifies this order above in the following paragraph.

621 The *sunna* is to shave the entire head, although the minimum requirement is one-fourth of the head. The same ruling applies to trimming the hair, and in that case, the minimum *length* of hair that must be trimmed is that of a fingertip (i.e., one of the three sections of a finger). That is, that length of *every* hair of at least one-fourth of the head *must* be trimmed to fulfill the requisite, and since strands of hair often differ in length, one should actually trim a bit more to ensure the requisite length is trimmed from each strand. This criteria for trimming applies to both men and women (while shaving is for men only). If one is bald, or cannot shave or trim due to a medical condition of the head, then he must run a blade over the scalp if possible; otherwise, he is absolved of the requisite altogether. Finally, the shaving or trimming must be performed within the Sacred Precinct (*ḥaram*), and within the three Days of Sacrifice, i.e., before sunset of the 12th. Otherwise, if performed elsewhere or past its time, a sacrifice of a sheep is due as expiation. Not finding a blade or someone to cut one's hair is not an excuse, as both are normally readily available (*Durr, Radd* 2:181, 184; *Tabyīn* 2:39; *Shalabī* 2:33).

seven days after *ḥajj*, even if in Makka. If he does not fast before the 10th, he must sacrifice a sheep as expiation.

Next, the pilgrim proceeds to [Makka for] the Ṭawāf of Visitation (*ṭawāf al-ziyāra*),[622] which is the second of the two pillars of *ḥajj*. It is superior to perform it on the Day of ʿĪd [the 10th]. If he delays it until after the three Days of Sacrifice [i.e., past sunset on the 12th], he must sacrifice a sheep as expiation.[623] After this ceremonial rite, he has left the major state of pilgrim sanctity, and sexual relations are now permissible.[624]

This *ṭawāf* is valid even if performed while in a state of major ritual impurity, yet [it is sinful, and the sacrifice of] a camel or cow is due as expiation. If performed while in a state of minor ritual impurity, [it is also sinful yet] a sheep is due.

He then returns to Minā.[625] After midday (*zawāl*)[626] on the 11th, he is to perform the stoning at all three sites (*jamarāt*), beginning with the one immediately adjacent to the mosque [of Khayf], followed by the one next to it, and ending at the Jamrat al-ʿAqaba.[627] He does the same ritual on the 12th as well.

---

622 For this *ṭawāf*, *saʿy* and *raml* are not performed if they had been performed with an earlier *ṭawāf*; otherwise, both are performed here. In either case, *iḍṭibāʿ* is not performed here. The valid time period for this *ṭawāf* is from true dawn of the 10th until the end of one's life, yet it is mandatory (*wājib*) to do so before sunset on the 12th, *sunna* to do so after the rites of stoning and shaving (or trimming), and recommended to do so on the 10th itself. Finally, this rite is valid only if performed by oneself, even if while being carried, unless one has lost consciousness; it is mandatory to perform it while walking for one able to walk (*Durr*, *Radd* 2:183).

623 And it is deemed prohibitively disliked (*makrūh taḥrīman*), since performing the *ṭawāf* before sunset on the 12th is mandatory (*wājib*). This ruling, however, applies only to one that is able to perform the rite. Hence, if a menstruating woman delays it past the 12th, being unable to perform it—even if only four of its seven rounds—due to her state of menstruation, then it is not sinful and no sacrifice is due. If, however, she becomes pure before sunset on the 12th with sufficient time to take the *ghusl*, get dressed and perform at least four of the seven rounds, it becomes mandatory to do so, and delaying it would be sinful and necessitate a sacrifice as expiation (*Hadiyya* 248; *Durr*, *Radd* 2:183–4).

624 As with any *ṭawāf*, he prays the mandatory two *rakʿas* afterwards.

625 Spending the night in Mina on each night of the 10th and the 11th is an emphasized *sunna*. If one does not do so, it is disliked (*makrūh*) but no expiation is due (*Durr*, *Radd* 2:184). It is, however, mandatory according to the other three schools of thought (*ʿItr* 126), and should therefore be given due consideration.

626 The stoning at any of the three sites on both the 11th and the 12th is not valid before midday (*zawāl*) (*Radd* 2:185).

627 The above order is an emphasized *sunna*. As before, one casts seven pebbles at each site, in the aforementioned manner (see related note, p. 157). After stoning at each of the first two sites, one stops and stands facing the *qibla* to make supplication (*duʿā'*), which is an emphasized *sunna*, while raising one's hands to shoulder-level with the palms directed toward the *qibla*. After the

At that point if he wishes to depart early for Makka, he may do so before sunset. If, however, he stays in Minā until sunset, it is disliked (*makrūh*) to leave for Makka before stoning, yet no expiation is due.

If he stays in Minā until the entrance of true dawn on the 13th, he must perform the stoning, which on this day is valid even [after true dawn] before midday [as opposed to the 11th and 12th].

Any stoning at a site that is followed by stoning at the next site is [ideally] to be performed while walking [i.e., on foot rather than while riding one's mount], such that one can [stop and stand to] make supplication (*duʿāʾ*) afterwards; other than these, one does so [ideally] while riding on his mount so he can leave afterwards without [stopping for] supplication [but rather supplicates while leaving].

Next, as he approaches Makka it is recommended (*mustaḥabb*)[628] for him to stop briefly at the *Muḥaṣṣab* [an area on the outskirts of Makka, on the road to Minā]. Then he enters Makka and performs the Farewell Ṭawāf[629] (*ṭawāf al-ṣadr* or *ṭawāf al-widāʿ*), which is mandatory (*wājib*)[630] for all pilgrims except those residing in Makka. He performs the two *rakʿas* of *ṭawāf*, and then goes to the area of Zamzam and drinks of its water, for which it is recommended to [stand and] face the *qibla*, swallow in gulps, and breathe into the vessel multiple times while drinking. With each gulp, he should raise his glance toward the [Sacred] House. He should then pour some of it over his body, or wipe his entire body with it. He should take out the Zamzam by himself if he is able to do so and, while drinking it, should pray [for anything he wishes].

---

third site, however, one simply supplicates while leaving (i.e., without stopping) (*Hadiyya* 248; *Durr*, *Radd* 2:185).

628 Some scholars considered this recommendation to be a communal *sunna*, meaning that if some pilgrims stop there, the *sunna* is deemed fulfilled for all pilgrims, as that area cannot encompass everyone on *ḥajj* (*Radd* 2:186).

629 It is recommended to perform it when the pilgrim is ready to depart from Makka, yet fulfills the requisite even if performed in advance. Just as with the Ṭawāf of Visitation, there is no *saʿy* or *raml* in this *ṭawāf* either, unless the pilgrim had not yet done so in a previous one (*Marāqī 'l-Falāḥ* 2:418; *Hadiyya* 250; *Durr*, *Radd* 2:186–7).

630 Hence, if a pilgrim without a valid excuse leaves Makka without performing it, he must return for it unless he crosses one of the designated boundaries. In that case, he may either return in a new state of pilgrim sanctity to perform *ʿumra* and then perform the missed Farewell Ṭawāf afterwards, or instead sacrifice a sheep as expiation, the latter being preferred as it is both easier on him as well as more beneficial for the indigent. A pilgrim with a valid excuse however, such as a child, insane person, or woman in menstruation or postnatal bleeding, is altogether absolved of this rite such that no expiation is due if omitted (*Radd* 2:186).

He then proceeds to the door of the Kaʿba and kisses its threshold (*ʿataba*) [out of veneration], after which he clings to the *multazam*, which lies between the Black Stone and the Door. He should place his face[631] on it and plead wholeheartedly to Allāh Most High for some time, supplicating for whatever he desires, regarding matters of both abodes [i.e., this life and the next]. He then says:

> O Allāh, verily this is Your House, which You have blessed and made a source of guidance for humanity. O Allāh, just as You have guided me to it, accept [my works] from me, and let this not be my last visit to Your House. Bless me with a return to it, such that You are pleased with me, by Your infinite grace, O Most Merciful of those who show mercy.

When the pilgrim intends to return to his family, he should [ideally] leave after his Farewell *Ṭawāf*. He should exit while walking backwards, with his face directed toward the [Sacred] House, crying and full of regret, until he leaves the mosque. He should depart from Makka through the Gate of the Tribe of Shayba (*Banū Shayba*).

In all of the rites of *ḥajj* and *ʿumra*, the woman[632] does the same as the man, except for the following:

- □ She does not uncover her head [as it is unlawful to do so];
- □ [If wearing a face cover,] she should place something on her head to keep the face cover at a distance from her face [such that there is no direct skin contact];
- □ She does not raise her voice when reciting the *talbiya*;[633]

---

631 That is, his right cheek, as well as his chest. He also raises his right arm toward the threshold of the Kaʿba, clinging to its covering like one seeking its intercession, just as a lowly slave grabs on to the garment of his glorious master. If not possible, he instead places both hands onto his head while they are upright, palms outspread onto the wall of the Kaʿba, with his body pressed against the wall as well. In either case, he should cry—or at least pretend to cry, as crying is a sign that the pilgrimage was accepted—while intensely supplicating, glorifying Allāh, and sending blessings upon the Prophet ﷺ (*Hadiyya* 250; *Ikhtiyār* 1:221; *Durr*, *Radd* 2:187).

632 A woman in menstruation or postnatal bleeding may perform all the rites of *ḥajj* and *ʿumra* except for the *ṭawāf* (and hence *saʿy*), which is unlawful for her while in that state. If she performs *ṭawāf* despite the prohibition, it would be valid yet sinful, and would require expiation (*Durr*, *Radd* 2:190).

633 Rather, she recites it only loud enough for herself to hear it (*Durr* 2:189; *Tabyīn* 2:38).

- ☐ She does not do *raml*;
- ☐ She does not rush [between the two green lines] when performing *saʿy*;
- ☐ She does not shave her head, but rather trims her hair;
- ☐ She may wear stitched garments;[634]
- ☐ She should not go in between a crowd of men when greeting the Black Stone [or at any point during the pilgrimage if possible].

This concludes the ceremonial rites of *ḥajj*; the pilgrim then departs from Makka.

Visiting the Prophet ﷺ is an emphasized *sunna*, either before or after the *ḥajj*.[635]

Makka is deemed better [than Madīna], except for the ground that is honored with the blessed body of the Messenger ﷺ.[636]

THE LESSER PILGRIMAGE (*ʿUMRA*)

The *ʿumra* is a *sunna* [that is emphasized], and is valid any time throughout the year,[637] although it is prohibitively disliked (*makrūh taḥrīman*) on five days, namely, the Day of ʿArafa, the Day of Sacrifice, and the three days of Tashrīq [i.e., the 9th through the 13th of Dhū 'l-Ḥijja].[638]

One enters the state of pilgrim sanctity (*iḥrām*)[639] outside the Sacred Precinct. After entering Makka, the pilgrim performs *ṭawāf* around the [Sacred] House in seven rounds and then performs two *rakʿas* of *ṭawāf*, followed by

---

634 As well as shoes (that cover the protruding cuneiform bone, which men must leave uncovered), gloves, and jewelry (*Durr, Radd* 2:190; *Tabyīn* 2:12, 39).

635 See Appendix 2, p. 209.

636 For indeed the very earth that touches his blessed limbs ﷺ is better than the rest of creation, including even the Kaʿba, the Footstool (*kursī*), and the Throne (*ʿarsh*) of Allāh Most High (*Ṭaḥṭāwī* 2:422; *Durr, Radd* 2:257).

637 It is recommended to perform *ʿumra* during Ramaḍān (*Hadiyya* 226).

638 It is also prohibitively disliked (*makrūh taḥrīman*) for a resident of Makka who intends to perform *ḥajj* to perform *ʿumra* during the months of *ḥajj* (*Radd* 2:152).

639 For *ʿumra*, the state of pilgrim sanctity (*iḥrām*) is a condition for its validity. Four rounds of *ṭawāf* are its pillar and hence obligatory (*farḍ*). The remaining three rounds of *ṭawāf*, the *saʿy* between Ṣafā and Marwa, and shaving the head (or trimming the hair) are its three mandatory (*wājib*) elements (*Hadiyya* 226; *Durr, Radd* 2:151).

the *saʿy* of seven rounds between Ṣafā and Marwa. He then shaves his head, or trims his hair, by which he exits the state of pilgrim sanctity.

Important Note

The best of days is the Day of ʿArafa if it falls on a Friday,[640] which is better than 70 *ḥajj* pilgrimages without a Friday, as has been narrated with rigorous authentication from the Prophet ﷺ.[641]

EXPIATION (*FIDYA*) FOR VIOLATIONS (*JINĀYĀT*)

Violations of Pilgrim Sanctity and Ceremonial Rites

The sacrifice of a sheep is mandatory (*wājib*) as expiation[642] for any one of the following violations[643] by the pilgrim:[644]

---

640 If the Day of ʿArafa falls on a Friday, there is agreement that the pilgrims do not pray the Friday prayer but rather still pray ẓuhr (*Shalabī* 2:24).

641 This ḥadīth is mentioned by Razīn ibn Muʿāwiya in *Tajrīd al-Ṣiḥāḥ*. However, Ibn Ḥajar states in *Fatḥ al-Bārī* that it is a ḥadīth of which he is not aware, since Razīn did not mention any Companion or ḥadīth scholar who narrated it, but rather inserted it (*adrajahū*) in another ḥadīth of the *Muwaṭṭa'* related on the authority of Ṭalḥa ibn ʿUbayd Allāh ibn Jarīr, and such insertions are not given any consideration in books like the *Muwaṭṭa'*. However, Ibn al-Fākihānī authored a book called *Al-Lumʿa* in which he discusses the immense merits of the Day of ʿArafa that falls on a Friday, since it occurred as such on the *ḥajj* of the Messenger of Allāh ﷺ, and based on the merits of Friday itself, being the best day of the week (*Tabyīn*, *Shalabī* 2:26).

642 With regard to the expiation for doing something prohibited (as opposed to the expiation for omitting a mandatory requisite—see following note), there is no difference between a pilgrim that commits the violation on purpose, out of forgetfulness, out of ignorance, by accident, out of coercion, while asleep or awake, with or without paying attention, or even having lost consciousness. The difference between such states is only with regard to incurring sin or not. Finally, just because there is expiation for certain prohibited acts does not mean one can *choose* to do such an act and perform expiation instead; this entails pure ignorance, as that would still be sinful (*Durr*, *Radd* 2:200).

643 A general rule for expiation is that omitting a mandatory (*wājib*) requisite is sinful and necessitates the sacrifice of a sheep, unless there was a valid excuse for its omission, whereby there is no sin and no expiation is due. Omitting a *sunna* is disliked, yet there is no expiation. Doing something prohibited, such as wearing a stitched garment, necessitates expiation even with an excuse (see previous note), yet the penalty is less severe than if there was no excuse (*Radd* 2:179). Finally, the two *rakʿas* that are performed after completing any *ṭawāf*, even a voluntary one, are mandatory (*wājib*), yet no expiation is due for missing them. Rather, they remain mandatory and must be performed, even after the pilgrim returns home (*Shalabī* 2:18).

644 Each violation of the state of pilgrim sanctity (*iḥrām*) that necessitates the sacrifice of a sheep or donation of charity applies to the pilgrim performing *ifrād* or *tamattuʿ*, whereas two sheep or two donations are due for each such violation committed by the pilgrim performing *qirān*, as his violation is in effect of *two* states of pilgrim sanctity. This ruling applies only to violations

- ☐ To apply scent on an entire limb;[645]
- ☐ To apply oil[646] on an entire limb;
- ☐ [For a man] to wear a stitched garment[647] for at least an entire day [or entire night];[648]
- ☐ [For a man] to cover [a fourth or more of] one's head for at least an entire day [or entire night];[649]
- ☐ To shave[650] a fourth or more of one's head [or beard];
- ☐ To shave one or both armpits;
- ☐ To shave one's pubic region;
- ☐ To clip all of one's nails [i.e., of both hands and both feet] in one sitting,[651] or [all five of] the nails of one foot or of one hand;

---

of the state of pilgrim sanctity, such as wearing a stitched garment or shaving hair, as opposed to general *ḥajj* violations, such as omitting the *saʿy*, the penalties of which are not doubled for the pilgrim performing *qirān* (*Mukhtār*, *Ikhtiyār* 1:237; *Durr*, *Radd* 2:223–4). Moreover in general, a sheep is sufficient for all violations necessitating sacrifice except for two, each of which requires the sacrifice of a camel or cow instead: (1) if the pilgrim has sexual intercourse after the Standing at ʿArafāt but before shaving or trimming, and (2) if the pilgrim performs the Ṭawaf of Visitation while in a state of major ritual impurity, menstruation, or postnatal bleeding. For the latter violation though, the pilgrim is absolved of the expiation if he or she repeats the Ṭawaf of Visitation within its time while in a state of ritual purity (*Mukhtār*, *Ikhtiyār* 1:232–3; *Ṭaḥṭāwī* 2:423). Finally, if the pilgrim has intercourse before the Standing of ʿArafāt, then the *ḥajj* itself is rendered invalid, yet he must still complete it, sacrifice a sheep as expiation, and then return the following year to make up the *ḥajj* (*Mukhtār* 1:232; *Kanz*, *Tabyīn* 2:57).

645 This ruling applies to an adult but not a child. Within one sitting, the entire body is deemed *one limb.* If done over multiple sittings, multiple expiations are due, one per sitting in which an entire limb or more is scented (*Ṭaḥṭāwī* 2:423; *Durr*, *Radd* 2:201).

646 That is, which is scented, such as olive oil or sesame oil, as opposed to almond oil or the like (*Durr*, *Radd* 2:202).

647 That is, in the normal way the garment is worn, "normal" meaning that if he were to busy himself with some task, he could comfortably do so with the garment remaining on. Therefore, if the pilgrim wraps a stitched garment around his waist or drapes it over his shoulders, or places a jacket over his back and shoulders but *without* placing his arms in the sleeves, then no expiation is due yet it is disliked (*Ṭaḥṭāwī* 2:424; *Durr*, *Radd* 2:203; *Tabyīn*, *Shalabī* 2:54).

648 In this context, an entire day is from fajr until maghrib, while an entire night is from maghrib until fajr. However, what is meant here is for that equivalent length of time, so as to include for example wearing a stitched garment from midday to midnight (*Radd* 2:203).

649 Expiation is due for violations of doing something prohibited even if done out of forgetfulness, ignorance, or coercion. Hence, even if one covers his head while asleep, or his head is covered by someone else, it is still deemed a violation and expiation is due. One does not incur sin, however, unless a violation is done purposefully and willingly (*Durr*, *Radd* 2:200–1).

650 For all violations, shaving refers to removing hair by any means, even if by rubbing one's body, although there is no penalty for hair falling off on its own (*Radd* 2:204).

651 If done over multiple sittings, then one sacrifice is due per limb if *all* of the nails of that limb are clipped (*Lubāb* 202; *Ikhtiyār* 1:230).

- ☐ To omit the *saʿy*;
- ☐ To omit all of the stoning, or that of one day;
- ☐ To delay the act of shaving [or trimming] past its appropriate time;
- ☐ To delay the *Ṭawāf* of Visitation—the second pillar of *ḥajj*—past its appropriate time;[652]
- ☐ To delay the Standing at ʿArafāt past the day, and rather perform it that night [i.e., it is still valid until fajr of the 10th, yet the mandatory (*wājib*) requisite of performing it between ẓuhr and maghrib was omitted].

If the pilgrim applies scent, wears a stitched garment, or shaves [or trims] his hair *with a valid excuse*, he may choose between sacrificing a sheep, donating three *ṣāʿs* [13.2 kg] of wheat [or its equivalent monetary value] to six poor persons, or fasting three days.[653]

Any one of the following violations by the pilgrim requires donation of a half *ṣāʿ* [2.2 kg] of wheat [or its equivalent monetary value]:

- ☐ To apply scent on less than an entire limb;
- ☐ [For a man] to cover one's head for less than an entire day [or night];
- ☐ [For a man] to wear a stitched garment for less than an entire day [or night];
- ☐ To shave less than a fourth of one's head [or beard];
- ☐ To shave someone else's head [or trim his hair, or cut his nails];
- ☐ To perform either the Ṭawāf of Arrival or the Farewell Ṭawāf in a state of minor ritual impurity.

An equivalent donation is also required:

---

652 The time for both shaving (or trimming) as well as the Ṭawāf of Visitation is from fajr of the 10th of Dhū 'l-Ḥijja until maghrib of the 12th of Dhū 'l-Ḥijja (*Tabyīn* 2:62). The sacrifice of a sheep is also due if one performs this *ṭawāf* in a state of minor ritual impurity, or if one performs either the Ṭawāf of Arrival or the Farewell Ṭawāf in a state of major ritual impurity (*Mukhtār* 1:230; *Tanwīr* 2:205).

653 As with all sacrifices on *ḥajj*, this sacrifice must be performed within the Sacred Precinct (*ḥaram*) and is not valid elsewhere, while the donation or fasting are not specific to any place. Also, the fasting of three days does not have to be consecutive (*Ikhtiyār* 1:232; *Durr*, *Radd* 2:210).

- ☐ For each round missed of the Farewell *Ṭawāf*, up to three rounds [whereas one sacrifices a sheep for missing four or more rounds];
- ☐ For each nail clipped from five separate nails [i.e., that are not on one limb];[654]
- ☐ For each pebble omitted if less than an entire day's stoning, [yet with regard to this issue and the one before it] unless the amount due reaches the equivalent value of sacrificing a sheep, whereby he may slightly decrease the amount due by as much as he likes. And Allāh knows best.

Hunting Violations

If the pilgrim [does any one of the following violations:]

- ☐ Kills land game;
- ☐ Points out land game or indicates its whereabouts to a hunter;
- ☐ Cuts off an animal's legs or wings such that it is prevented from running or flight;
- ☐ Or plucks a bird's feathers [such that it is prevented] from flight;

then he must perform expiation, which is based on the animal's value, as estimated by two upright men of the area in which the animal was killed, or the next closest area. [He then has the choice to do one of the following:]

- ☐ He may purchase a sacrificial animal of that value;[655]
- ☐ Or purchase food of that value, which he must donate, a half *ṣāʿ* [2.2 kg] to each poor person;[656]
- ☐ Or [based on that value] fast one day for the equivalent food given to each poor person.

[For the latter two options,] if there is an extra amount of food leftover that

---

654 That is, an equivalent donation is required for each nail clipped from any limb as long as all five nails of one limb are not clipped, as in that case a sacrifice of a sheep is due for that limb (*Lubāb* 202; *Ikhtiyār* 1:231; *Marāqī 'l-Falāḥ*, *Ṭaḥṭāwī* 2:424).

655 And then sacrifice it in the Sacred Precinct (*ḥaram*) (*Marāqī 'l-Falāḥ*, *Ṭaḥṭāwī* 2:425).

656 He may donate this food wherever he wishes. It is the same amount as that of *ṣadaqat al-fiṭr* (*Ṭaḥṭāwī* 2:425; *Durr*, *Radd* 2:215).

is less than the amount given to one poor person, he may either donate that amount of food or fast one day in its stead.

If the pilgrim pulls out the hair of an animal, he must pay the resulting deficiency in that animal's value. If he milks an animal, he pays the equivalent value of that milk. If he breaks an egg, he pays the value of the egg.

If a dead chick comes out of the animal that he harmed or killed, he must additionally pay the value of the chick.

If two or more pilgrims partake in killing game, the penalty is multiplied by the number of pilgrims involved.

The pilgrim that kills game pays the value of what he eats of it in addition to the penalty of killing it, as opposed to a pilgrim that does not kill it.[657]

A nonpilgrim that kills game within the Sacred Precinct must pay the equivalent of one penalty, yet does not have the option of fasting.

It is unlawful to send one's sheep to graze in the grass of the Sacred Precinct.

If one cuts wet grass, or a tree or plant that grows naturally out of the earth, he must pay its equivalent value, except for the *idhkhir* plant.[658] He does not, however, have to pay for cutting a tree or plant planted by people.

There is no penalty[659] for killing a crow, falcon, scorpion, snake, mouse, wild dog, mosquito, ant, or flea.[660]

If one kills one louse [from his body] or one locust, he must donate money, yet he may choose any amount to donate.[661]

For all violations, one may perform the sacrifice on any day, except for the sacrifices of *qirān* and *tamattuʿ*, which must be done on one of the Days of Sacrifice [i.e., the 10th, 11th, or 12th of Dhū 'l-Ḥijja]. All sacrifices pertaining to

657 That is, there is no penalty on another pilgrim that eats from it yet had not participated in its killing, as he would not have violated a "state" of pilgrim sanctity (*iḥrām*). He would, however, have to seek forgiveness, as its meat would be deemed dead flesh and hence unlawful to consume, since the killing was prohibited (*Majmaʿ al-Anhur, Al-Durr al-Muntaqā* 1:300).

658 A kind of sweet rush; juncus odoratus; or *schoenanthum* (Lane's Lexicon 1:956). The Prophet ﷺ made an exception for this plant at the request of his uncle ʿAbbās ؓ. In addition, it is permissible for one to take a small amount of dirt from the Sacred Precinct out of seeking its blessing (*tabarruk*) (*Majmaʿ al-Anhur* 1:301–2).

659 It is likewise permissible for the pilgrim to slaughter sheep, cows, camels, and chickens, as none of them are game (*Majmaʿ al-Anhur* 1:300).

660 This ruling includes all insects and vermin, as well as sea creatures such as fish and turtles. However for all of these creatures, it is impermissible to kill that which does not harm (*Majmaʿ al-Anhur* 1:299–300; *Durr, Radd* 2:219).

661 Yet for more than three, a half *ṣāʿ* (2.2 kg) of wheat or its equivalent value is due (*Majmaʿ al-Anhur* 1:299).

ḥajj [and *ʿumra*], however, must be performed within the Sacred Precinct, as opposed to sacrifices unrelated to pilgrimage.

For *ḥajj*-related sacrifices and *uḍḥiya* sacrifices, no animal is sufficient other than a *thanī* of a camel or cow or goat. A *thanī* of a camel is at least five years old; that of a cow is two years old; and that of a goat is one year old.

If one is to sacrifice a sheep, a younger one is sufficient, i.e., one that is more than six months old.

The sacrificial animal must be free from defect.[662]

For voluntary sacrifices as well as those related to *qirān* or *tamattuʿ*, the meat of the animal may be eaten by a wealthy person or the one who performed the sacrifice.

One camel may be sacrificed on behalf of seven people, with the condition that each of them intends thereby to perform an act of worship. And Allāh knows best.

---

662 The details of both this issue as well as the last issue of this chapter (one camel sufficing seven people) are delineated in the next chapter, Ritual Sacrifice of ʿĪd al-Aḍḥā (*uḍḥiya*).

Ritual Sacrifice of ʿĪd al-Aḍḥā (ʿUḍḥiya)

The *uḍḥiya* is mandatory (*wājib*) on every Muslim[663] that is wealthy based on the criterion for paying *ṣadaqat al-fiṭr*;[664] in the Days of Sacrifice, i.e., the 10th, 11th, and 12th of Dhū 'l-Ḥijja. It must be performed on behalf of the person himself. It is not mandatory on behalf of one's indigent (*faqīr*) child who is a minor according to *ẓāhir al-riwāya*,[665] nor on behalf of one's wealthy child who is a minor from his [the child's] wealth, according to the soundest opinion upon which legal verdict is given (*aṣaḥḥ mā yuftā bihī*).[666]

It is valid only with a sheep or camel or cow, the latter [two] being permissible on behalf of seven people, or less. Co-participation [before purchase] is more preferable.[667]

---

663 That is, with the condition of being a resident; it is not mandatory on a traveller (*Lubāb* 595; *Majmaʿ al-Anhur* 2:516; *Durar* 1:267).

664 That is, possessing *niṣāb ḥirmān al-zakāt* (see related note, p. 139). Hence, it is not mandatory on one who has less (i.e., one who is indigent (*faqīr*)), *unless* he purchased an animal *with* the intention of the *uḍḥiya*, whereby it becomes mandatory on him due to the purchase (*Durr*, *Radd* 5:204; *Durar* 1:268).

665 That is, it is not mandatory on the parent to spend from his own wealth to sacrifice on behalf of his indigent child, yet it is recommended to do so; this is according to *ẓāhir al-riwāya*, and is the position of legal verdict (*fatwā*). This is in contrast to *ṣadaqat al-fiṭr*, which is mandatory on the father on behalf of his indigent child who is a minor (*Durr*, *Radd* 5:200; *Durar*, *Shurunbulāliyya* 1:267).

666 That is, the parent is not obliged to sacrifice on behalf of his wealthy child from the child's wealth (nor from the parent's wealth *a fortiori*) yet may do so from his (the parent's) own wealth if he wishes. This is also the opinion given precedence in *Al-Durr al-Mukhtār* and *Multaqā 'l-Abḥur*, while the author of the *Hidāya* (4:356) mentions that the sounder position (*aṣaḥḥ*) is that it is indeed mandatory on behalf of the wealthy child, to be spent from his (the child's) wealth. Ibn ʿĀbidīn concurs with the former opinion, which is mentioned in the *Durr* as being the relied-upon position (*muʿtamad*) (*Durr*, *Radd* 5:201–2).

667 That is, it is preferable for them to agree on co-participation before the animal is purchased, although if one purchases the animal for himself alone and then sells six of seven equal shares to others to co-participate, it still suffices them all. Furthermore, seven or less may co-participate in

The meat should be divided based on weight rather than by mere conjecture, unless with it are some of its trotters and a part of its hide.

It is not permissible for one residing in a city to sacrifice the animal before the ᶜĪd prayer. The village dweller, however, may sacrifice after the entrance of fajr [of the 10th].[668]

The best day for the *uḍḥiya* is the first [of the three], followed by the next day. If one [who is not indigent] does not sacrifice before the Days of Sacrifice are over, he must donate the equivalent value of a sheep, even if he still has possession of the sheep.[669]

One who becomes indigent (*faqīr*) before the Days of Sacrifice have passed[670] no longer has to sacrifice.

It is preferred for the one who must sacrifice to do the following: to eat from a third of the meat, to donate a third, and to set aside a third; to donate the hide or to make an apparatus out of it, such as a bag, leather mat, or sieve; and to slaughter the animal himself.[671] If he has someone else perform the sacrifice, he should [preferably] witness it himself.

It is disliked for a Jew or Christian to perform the sacrifice [on behalf of a Muslim]. It is also disliked to milk the animal or cut off its wool before the sacrifice.[672]

---

the sacrifice of one cow or camel, with the following conditions: (a) they are no more than seven, (b) all being Muslims, (c) each intending thereby an act of worship, and (d) each receiving no less than one-seventh of a share. Hence, if there are eight or more participants; or if one non-Muslim participates; or if one of the seven Muslims participates only to obtain meat, without intending a specific act of worship; then (in either case) the animal will not count for the *uḍḥiya* of *any* participant (*Ikhtiyār* 2:437).

668 However, the place where the actual sacrifice takes place is what is considered for this ruling rather than the location of the one upon whom it is mandatory. Hence, if a city resident has his sacrifice performed outside the city, it is valid after fajr (*Durr*, *Radd* 5:202).

669 That is, according to the text above, even if he had purchased a sheep and it remains in his possession, he must donate the market price of the sheep in charity. He may not give the sheep itself in charity, unless he is indigent and had purchased it for the *uḍḥiya*. This is also mentioned in *Durar al-Ḥukkām* (1:268–9), the *Hidāya* (4:358), and other works. However, Ibn ᶜĀbidīn cites other reliable sources stating that the sound position of the school is that even a wealthy person who purchased a sheep for the *uḍḥiya* may donate the sheep itself despite the expiration of the valid time (*Radd* 5:204).

670 That is, just before maghrib of the 12th (*Durr* 5:202; *Durar* 1:268).

671 That is, if he is able to do so properly. Otherwise, it is preferable for him to appoint another to slaughter on his behalf, and in that case, it is recommended for him to witness the slaughtering (*Ikhtiyār* 2:440).

672 Because the animal was purchased for an act of worship, all of its parts are deemed reserved for that act of worship, i.e., the sacrifice. Hence, it is disliked in general to derive any personal ben-

The *uḍḥiya* is not valid with the following:[673]

- ☐ An animal with only one eye [or missing both],
- ☐ An emaciated animal,
- ☐ An animal that was born without an ear,
- ☐ An animal that is missing most of an ear or [most of] its tail,
- ☐ An animal with a paralyzed leg such that it cannot walk to the place of sacrifice,
- ☐ An animal missing most of its teeth such that it cannot eat properly.[674]

efit from the animal beforehand, such as riding it, using it to carry items, or taking from it milk or wool. If any benefit is derived, an equivalent value of money should be donated to the poor. After the sacrifice, however, one may benefit from its parts (*Durr*, *Radd* 5:209).

673 The following, however, are valid: an animal without a horn; an animal without testicles; or an animal gone mad, as long as it still grazes freely (*Durar*, *Shurunbulāliyya* 1:269).

674 In the Arabic published edition as well as the manuscript, there is one more sentence here that appears to be incomplete and was therefore not translated.

Ritually-Slaughtered Animals (Dhabā'iḥ)

Slaughtering[675] is a condition for the permissibility of eating the meat of any animal except fish and locusts. The condition of its validity is that the one who performs it not be a Magian, apostate, or idol worshipper; and that he not intentionally omit the *basmala* [when slaughtering].[676]

The slaughtering must take place at the throat, cutting any three of the following four vessels: the trachea, the esophagus, and the two carotid arteries. If less than three of the four are severed, it is unlawful to eat the meat.

It is also unlawful to eat the meat of [an animal slaughtered by] one who intentionally omits the *basmala*,[677] or who mentions any other name alongside the Name of Allāh, connected by a conjunction.[678] If no conjunction is used, it is lawful yet disliked.[679]

---

675 Legally, there are two types of slaughtering: (1) *voluntary slaughtering* (*dhabḥ*), which is to actually sacrifice the animal by cutting its neck between the larynx and the chest and severing at least three of the four vessels mentioned above; and (2) *forced slaughtering* (*ṣayd*), which is to wound the animal in any part of its body with a hunting animal or a sharp weapon, thereby spilling its blood (see related chapter, p. 179). The general principle for killing animals for their meat is that one may not resort to *forced slaughtering* (i.e., hunting) unless one is *forced* to do so, that is, when one is unable to legally sacrifice the animal by *voluntary slaughtering*. Hence, if one hunted an animal that could have been ritually sacrificed, its meat would be unlawful (*Durr*, *Radd* 5:186; *Ikhtiyār* 2:426).

676 If he forgetfully omits the *basmala*, however, it is permissible to eat the meat (*Tanwīr* 5:190).

677 The phrase to be uttered when slaughtering that has been transmitted and passed down over successive generations is *Bismillāhi Allāhu akbar* ("In the Name of Allāh; Allāh is the Greatest"). However, any praise of Allāh suffices as long as it is uttered with the intention of sacrifice and not in the form of a supplication, such as *Allāhumma 'ghfirlī* ("O Allāh Forgive me!"), which would be invalid and therefore render the meat unlawful (*Ikhtiyār* 2:428).

678 Such as if one says "In the Name of Allāh, *and* so-and-so," as the phrase entails associating a partner with Allāh (*shirk*), making it unlawful (*Majmaᶜ al-Anhur*, *Al-Durr al-Muntaqā* 2:509; *Ikhtiyār* 2:427).

679 Such as if one says *Bismillāhi Muḥammadu 'r-Rasūlu 'Llāh* ﷺ ("In the Name of Allāh; Muḥammad is the Messenger of Allāh ﷺ"), since without the conjunction "and" there is no

It is also disliked to say the following during the cutting, after having laid the animal on its side and reciting the *basmala*: "O Allāh, accept [this work] from so-and-so."[680]

It is recommended to sharpen the blade[681] before laying the animal down on its side, yet it is disliked to let the animal know of the slaughtering [such as by sharpening the blade in front of it].

It is also disliked[682] to cut the throat all the way to the spinal cord; to completely sever the head; or to slaughter the animal from the back of the neck forwards—if it remains alive—until reaching [three of] the [aforementioned four] vessels.[683]

Slaughtering is valid with anything that cuts and causes blood to spill, such as the following:

- ☐ A butcher's knife,
- ☐ A sharp, white stone,
- ☐ The peel of a cane,
- ☐ A bone or tooth pulled out of an animal, although using either one is disliked.[684]

---

ascription of a partner to Allāh (*shirk*), and the meat is therefore lawful. It is disliked, however, as it *appears* to do so due to the connecting of the two phrases (*Majmaʿ al-Anhur* 2:508–9; *Ikhtiyār* 2:427–8). If the two phrases are not connected, such as if they are separated by an action like laying the animal down or like the actual sacrifice, or if the second phrase is mentioned before the *basmala*, then it is not even disliked as there is no resemblance to ascription of partnership with Allāh (*Majmaʿ al-Anhur* 2:509; *Ikhtiyār* 2:427).

680 That is, it is disliked to conjoin such a phrase (i.e., one of supplication) to the *basmala*, yet the meat is still lawful. It is not disliked to utter the supplication before laying the animal down, before the *basmala*, or after the slaughtering, as the *basmala* then would be completely independent from any other speech, which is the prescribed manner of slaughtering (*Durr*, *Radd* 5:191).

681 Using a dull blade is disliked (*Durr* 5:188).

682 In general, any type of unnecessary harm or torture done to the animal is disliked, such as sharpening the blade in front it, dragging it to the slaughter area by its leg, using a dull blade for the slaughter, or skinning it or breaking its neck while it remains moving after having been slaughtered. Skinning it or breaking a bone after it stops moving is not disliked as it would no longer feel any pain (*Durr*, *Radd* 5:188; *Ikhtiyār* 2:429).

683 That is, if it dies before three of the four vessels are cut, then the meat is unlawful. If it is alive by the time the blade cuts three of the four vessels, then it is valid yet disliked, just as if one wounded the animal first before severing three of the four vessels, due to the additional yet unnecessary pain caused thereby (*Radd* 5:188; *Ikhtiyār* 2:429–30).

684 Due to the extra pain it would cause to the animal (*Tabyīn* 5:291); the same would apply to a horn. Nevertheless, the meat would still be lawful (*Shurunbulāliyya* 1:277). The general principle is that in all cases where the slaughtering is disliked, the meat is still lawful since the permissibility

It is prohibited to use a bone [i.e., nail, claw, horn] or tooth that is still connected to an animal [and if used, the meat is unlawful].[685]

After a pregnant animal is slaughtered, the fetus must also be slaughtered if still alive [in order to be lawful to eat]; if dead, it is unlawful to eat [as it was not slaughtered].

It is *sunna* to sacrifice the camel by cutting the blood vessels at the bottom of its neck while it is upright (*naḥr*); the cow or sheep, however, should be slaughtered while lying on its side [as described above (*dhabḥ*)]. To do the opposite is disliked.[686]

A wild animal that becomes tame and poses no danger must be slaughtered [rather than hunted].[687]

A normally domesticated animal [such as a cow or goat] that becomes violent or falls into a well [yet remains alive], whereby it cannot be slaughtered, may be wounded [i.e., hunted] instead.[688]

According to *ẓāhir al-riwāya*, it is still permissible to slaughter an animal that has been choked; that has been struck [by a staff or stone, for example]; that has fallen from an elevated place; that has been rammed by another animal's head or horn; or one whose abdomen has been pierced by a wolf—yet

---

of meat is based on only two factors: the proper severing of vessels as the cause of death, and the conjoined *basmala* (*Shalabī* 5:292).

685 This is because while still connected, the claw or tooth will not kill by severing and spilling blood, but rather by the pressure and strength of the person holding it. This resembles strangling, which is not a permissible form of sacrifice and therefore renders the animal's meat dead flesh (*Ikhtiyār* 2:429; *Tabyīn* 5:291). This ruling would therefore apply to any object that kills the animal by the pressure or force of the person holding it rather than by its *own* function of severing and spilling blood (*Tabyīn* 6:59).

686 The *sunna* method of sacrificing the camel is to pierce its lower neck, immediately above the chest, and cut the vessels therein (*naḥr*) while it is standing. The cow or sheep, however, should be slaughtered (*dhabḥ*), which is to cut the vessels at the top of the neck, underneath the jaw and the protruding larynx, while it is made to lie on the ground. The opposite is disliked, and should be deemed *makrūh tanzīhan* (*Radd* 5:192). Finally, when laying the animal down for *dhabḥ*, it is disliked for one without a valid excuse to not direct it toward the *qibla*, as doing so is an emphasized *sunna* (*Durr*, *Radd* 5:188; *Tabyīn*, *Shalabī* 5:292).

687 As one may resort to *forced slaughtering* (i.e., hunting) only when unable to perform *voluntary slaughtering* (*Durr* 5:192).

688 This is the exact opposite scenario of the previous case: *voluntary slaughtering* proves impossible or very difficult, whereby *forced slaughtering* (i.e., hunting) becomes permissible (*Ikhtiyār* 2:430; *Radd* 5:192). For the case of falling into the well, the permissibility of eating its meat applies if one knows that the wound inflicted from the hunt caused the death. If, however, one knows that the fall caused the animal's death, it's meat is rendered dead flesh and is hence unlawful. If one is unsure, the meat is still lawful, as the apparent cause of death would seem to have been by the wound (*Shurunbulāliyya* 1:280; *Tabyīn* 5:292; *Radd* 5:192).

in each case, with the condition that it still has some life in it.[689] Its remaining life is estimated to be [enough to live] a complete day according to one narration, while Abū Yūsuf maintained that most of a day is sufficient. Imām Muḥammad, however, stipulated that its remaining life be [merely] more than that of a slaughtered animal.

If one knows that the animal is alive when sacrificing it, its meat is lawful, even if it was not moving or if blood was not exiting from it; otherwise, one of the two indications must be present at the time of sacrifice.[690]

ANIMALS THAT ARE LAWFUL OR UNLAWFUL TO EAT

It is unlawful to eat any of the following:

- Any predatory land animal or predatory bird that possesses fangs or claws;[691]
- All vermin, such as hedgehogs, jerboas, or hornets;[692]
- Domesticated donkeys and mules born from female donkeys. The meat of horses is prohibitively disliked (*makrūh taḥrīman*) according to Imām Abū Ḥanīfa, or mildly disliked (*makrūh tanzīhan*), as the two companions maintained;[693]

---

689 That is, if any of those actions causes the animal's death, it's meat is rendered dead flesh and is hence unlawful.

690 That is, if he was not originally certain that there was some remaining life in the animal, one of the above two indications must be present. This is because movement or exit of blood are signs of life, which is a condition for the validity of ritual sacrifice, as dead flesh is unlawful. Yet if he did originally know that it was alive at the time of sacrificing it, no indication is necessary (*Majmaʿ al-Anhur, Al-Durr al-Muntaqā* 2:515; *Kanz, Tabyīn* 5:297). This issue would apply to, for example, one finding an animal wounded by any means (see previous paragraph)—he may still slaughter it based on these criteria (*Durr, Radd* 5:196).

691 Such as lions, tigers, cheetahs, wolves, foxes, bears, elephants, apes, monkeys, weasels, dogs or cats, whether domesticated or wild; or eagles, falcons, hawks or kites (*Ikhtiyār* 2:431; *Majmaʿ al-Anhur* 2:512–3). This ruling, however, applies to animals or birds that kill using fangs or claws, as opposed to for example camels or pigeons, both of which are permissible (*Majmaʿ al-Anhur, Al-Durr al-Muntaqā* 2:512).

692 Including rats, mice, geckos, snakes, frogs, or turtles; as well as insects, such as flies, mosquitoes, lice, or fleas (*Ikhtiyār* 2:431–2; *Majmaʿ al-Anhur* 2:513).

693 Although it is narrated that Imām Abū Ḥanīfa himself changed his mind three days before his demise. Hence, it is deemed mildly disliked (*makrūh tanzīhan*) according to *ẓāhir al-riwāya*, which is the sound position (*ṣaḥīḥ*) (*Majmaʿ al-Anhur* 2:513).

- ☐ Lizards;
- ☐ Hyenas;
- ☐ Foxes.

Rabbits and farm crows[694] are lawful to eat, as opposed to crows that eat dead corpses; vultures; or foxes.

It is impermissible to eat water-born animals, except for fish and eel, although it is [prohibitively] disliked (*makrūh taḥrīman*) to eat them if they are found floating on the surface of water.[695]

It is disliked to eat any of the following body parts of a slaughtered animal:

- ☐ Testicles,
- ☐ Penis [or Vagina],
- ☐ Glands,
- ☐ Urinary bladder,
- ☐ Gall bladder.

It is unlawful to consume spilled blood [or anything mixed with it, as it is filth].

---

694 That is, since they eat seeds, and are neither predatory birds nor filthy creatures (*Tabyīn* 5:295).

695 That is, by an unknown cause of death (*ḥatfa anfihī*). If, however, it dies by a known cause (*āfa*), such as heat, cold, or being caught in a net, then the fish is lawful (*Tabyīn* 5:297; *Durr*, *Radd* 5:194–5). This would, of course, not apply if the fish were rendered unlawful for another reason, despite the cause being known, such as if it died by toxins or poison in the water.

Hunting (Ṣayd)

It is permissible for the Muslim who is not in a state of pilgrim sanctity (*iḥrām*) to hunt game outside of the Sacred Precinct (*ḥaram*), both animals that are permissible to eat as well as those impermissible to eat.[696]

After being hunted, an animal whose meat is permissible to eat may be eaten, as long as the hunter was not a Magian, a Muslim who purposefully left out the *basmala* at the time of releasing the hunting animal or throwing the weapon, or a Muslim in a state of pilgrim sanctity; and as long as it was wounded and subsequently died before the hunter caught up to it. Hence, its meat may be eaten, regardless of whether it was wounded by a sharp weapon, or by a trained hunting dog, trained wildcat or trained falcon.[697]

---

696 For the sake of its hide or fur, for example (*Mukhtār* 2:420; *Multaqā* 2:574), or to ward off its harm, such as with wild animals (*Al-Durr al-Muntaqā* 2:575).

697 Hunting is legally permissible if its 15 requisite conditions are fulfilled. Hunting is not permissible if done for sport, or according to some, as a profession; other Ḥanafī scholars deemed it permissible as a profession (see *Hidāya* 4:410). The following comprises the 15 general conditions for game that is permissible to eat, in order to eat its meat (taken from *Durr*, *Radd* 5:297):

5 conditions for the hunter

- That he be among those who can ritually slaughter (i.e., Muslim, Jew or Christian, as opposed to Magian, idolator, or apostate);
- That he *sends out* the hunting animal, or *casts out* the weapon (accompanied with the *basmala*);
- That someone whose game is impermissible does not participate in his sending;
- That he not intentionally omit the *basmala*;
- That he not engage in another unrelated action between the sending and the capturing.

5 conditions for the hunting animal

- That it be trained;
- That it proceed in the direction it was sent out;
- That another animal that is not a valid hunting animal not participate with it in the taking (of its prey);

If after being hunted, the animal has more life remaining in it than that of a slaughtered animal, the hunter must slaughter it. If he is unable to do so, its meat is unlawful according to *ẓāhir al-riwāya*.[698]

A hunting dog or wildcat is legally considered trained by its abstaining from eating the game, after having killed it, three consecutive times; while a falcon or the like by its returning to the hunter after being summoned.[699]

In the following situations, the hunting game may not be eaten:

- ☐ If the hunting animal chokes or suffocates it;
- ☐ If another dog, whose game is not permissible,[700] takes part in killing it;
- ☐ If it were killed by the dull side of a featherless arrow [and hence died due to the blow, rather than by being pierced with its sharp end];

- That it kill the game by wounding it, rather than by suffocating or by a severe blow that does not puncture its skin (*Ikhtiyār* 2:420). The wound may be anywhere on the body, yet it must die by that wound (*Tanwīr* 5:299; *Majmaʿ al-Anhur* 2:575);
- That it not eat of its meat (as opposed to drinking of its blood, which is allowed) (*Mukhtār* 2:423; *Durr* 5:299).

5 conditions for the game

- That it not be of vermin;
- That it not be a sea creature, except for fish;
- That it is able to escape predation by its wings or legs, and that it be wild such that ritual slaughtering is not possible. Otherwise if slaughtering is possible without harm to the hunter, then it may not be hunted (*Durr, Radd* 5:300);
- That it not be empowered by fangs or claws (as such an animal is unlawful to eat; yet it may be hunted for other benefits, such as for its hide or bone);
- That it be killed by the hunting animal or weapon before the hunter reaches it, since otherwise he would have to ritually slaughter the animal in order for its meat to be lawful.

698 That is, if the hunter catches up to the game while it is still alive, then he must ritually slaughter it in order for its meat to be lawful to eat, as *voluntary slaughtering* is in that case possible, whereby *forced slaughtering* is deemed insufficient (see related note, p. 173) (*Ikhtiyār* 2:423).

699 The hunting animal may be any creature that possesses fangs or claws, such as a dog or eagle, with the condition that it be trained. It cannot be that which is innately filthy, namely, pig. It may also not be a lion, wolf, or bear (nor a kite according to some) as neither of them can be trained; if they supposedly could be trained, however, then it would be permissible (*Ikhtiyār* 2:420; *Shurunbulāliyya* 1:272; *Tabyīn* 6:50–1; *Durr, Radd* 5:298).

700 Such as a dog released without the pronouncement of the *basmala*, or that of a Magian, or an untrained dog; since when a cause of impermissibility and one of permissibility are conjoined, that of impermissibility takes precedence out of precaution (*iḥtiyāṭ*), which is the basis of legal rulings dealing with meat (*Ikhtiyār* 2:423–4).

- ☐ If it were killed by a rounded clay stone [since it would die due to the blow];
- ☐ If it fell into water;
- ☐ If it fell onto an elevated place such as a roof or mountain, and *then* onto the earth;[701]
- ☐ If the hunter sufficiently wounds the game,[702] followed by another hunter sending his dog or shooting his arrow at it and actually killing it. In this case [the meat may not be eaten, and] the second hunter must pay the first one the equivalent value of that animal in its wounded state from the first wound;[703]
- ☐ If the arrow hits the game, which bears it and continues running, and then disappears from the sight of the hunter, who then pauses from the chase, only to find the animal dead;[704]
- ☐ If the trained hunting dog or trained wildcat eats from the game, as opposed to the falcon;[705]
- ☐ If a Magian releases the hunting animal, which then gets incited toward game by the shout of a Muslim hunter. In the opposite case

---

701 Since it most likely died from the fall rather than the wound, as opposed to game that falls straight onto the ground, since that is almost inevitable in hunting and is hence overlooked (*Ikhtiyār* 2:424; *Multaqā, Majmaʿ al-Anhur* 2:580).

702 Sufficiently wounding the game is to weaken it such that it is unable to escape from predation. In that case, its meat is lawful only by voluntary slaughtering. Therefore, the second hunter's lethal wound renders the meat dead flesh and hence unlawful. If on the other hand the game is not sufficiently wounded by the first wound, it remains game that may be hunted. Hence when it is killed by the second wound, it belongs to the second hunter and its meat is lawful to consume (*Ikhtiyār* 2:425).

703 Since the first hunter came to own it by wounding it in a manner by which it could no longer escape predation (*Ikhtiyār* 2:425).

704 Since if it disappears from his sight, there is a possibility that the animal died from another cause, which is given due consideration as lawfulness of meat is based on precaution. However if he does not pause from the chase, then that possibility is deemed negligible, as otherwise there would be undue difficulty in hunting since game frequently disappears from the hunter's sight (*Ikhtiyār* 2:421). If, however, he actually finds another wound on the animal, then the possibility of it being the cause of death is given precedence and the meat is rendered unlawful, despite his not having paused from the chase (*Multaqā, Majmaʿ al-Anhur* 2:578–9).

705 As that is an indication that the dog or wildcat is not trained, and hence all meat from its hunting, even previous hunts, is deemed unlawful. This differs from the falcon, whose training is based on responding to being summoned. However, if the dog or wildcat does not eat from the game but drinks from its blood, it is still deemed trained and the meat is lawful (*Ikhtiyār* 2:422–3). Likewise, the game may not be eaten if the hunting animal engaged in another act, such as eating or urination, after being released yet before killing or wounding the game, since the attack must be ascribed directly to the release (*Durr, Radd* 5:300).

however, it would be permissible to eat the meat, namely, if a Muslim hunter released the hunting animal, which was then incited toward game by the shout of a Magian hunter;[706]

- ☐ The severed limb of hunted game [while it was still alive] may not be eaten, unless the animal was split in half or in thirds [i.e., into two parts, one part two-thirds and the other one-third] *if* the larger part included the rear of the animal [while the head was in the smaller part].[707]

In the following scenarios, the hunted game may be eaten:

- ☐ If the hunting animal were released onto game, and it wounded it as well as other animals in its path;
- ☐ If the hunting animal were released onto multiple animals with one pronouncement of the *basmala*, and it killed each animal immediately, one after another;
- ☐ If the hunting dog threw down the game with a severe blow and then killed it by wounding it;
- ☐ If the hunter releases two dogs simultaneously and one dog throws down the game with a severe blow, followed by the other dog killing it by wounding it;
- ☐ If the hunter aimed for a wolf but rather struck a deer; it may be eaten, although Imām Zufar disagreed;

If a bird gives birth to a chick or lays an egg on a piece of land not designated for that, it is permissible for anyone to take. The same ruling applies if a deer peacefully enters such an area.[708]

---

706 The basis of this ruling is that the state of *release* is given consideration, regardless of incitement afterwards—if the initial release is valid, it does not later become invalid by incitement, and if originally invalid, it is not later made valid by incitement (*Ikhtiyār* 2:422). Also, the wording of this issue is a bit unclear in the original Arabic text, yet its meaning as translated above is sound and accurate, as confirmed from other Ḥanafī works (see *Durr, Radd* 5:303; *Ikhtiyār* 2:422).

707 Since in that case it is assumed that the wound itself killed the game, as opposed to if the larger of the two parts had its head, in which case it could have still been alive and hence would have to be voluntary slaughtered (*Ikhtiyār* 2:425).

708 If, however, the owner had designated his land with a net, ditch or the like to collect the chick or egg, or to capture the deer—or if he were close enough to it so as to take it for himself—then it is thereby automatically deemed his property (*Durr, Radd* 4:218).

And Allāh Glorified and Exalted knows best.

The primer of the most erudite scholar, the exemplar, the astute thinker of sound understanding, the Shaykh, Ḥasan al-Shurunbulālī al-Wafā'ī al-Miṣrī (the Egyptian), has been completed. May Allāh Most High immerse him in His divine mercy, and give him residence in His expansive Garden. The primer is called "Ascent to Felicity in the Sciences of Theology and Jurisprudence of Worship" (*Marāqī 'l-Saʿādāt fī ʿIlmayi 'l-Tawḥīd wa 'l-ʿIbādāt*).

Its transcription was completed by the hand of the weakest of servants, the most needy of the divine mercy of his Ever-Generous Lord, Aḥmad ibn Burhān, the one who is ever hopeful of the Overwhelming Judge (*al-Dayyān*) [Most High] to pardon his sins and acts of disobedience. May Allāh forgive him and all the Muslims. All praise is due to Allāh, the Lord of all the worlds. Its transcription was completed in the month of Shawwāl, in the year 1114 AH.

Appendix 1
Supplications

SUPPLICATIONS OF *WUḌŪ'*

With each limb, one does the following: pronounces the *tasmiya*, followed by its corresponding supplication (as listed below), and then sends blessings upon the Prophet ﷺ.

While rinsing the mouth (after the opening *tasmiya*):

اَللّٰهُمَّ أَعِنِّيْ عَلٰى تِلَاوَةِ الْقُرْاٰنِ وَذِكْرِكَ وَشُكْرِكَ وَحُسْنِ عِبَادَتِكَ.

Allāhumma aʿinnī ʿalā tilāwati 'l-Qur'ān(i) wa dhikrika wa shukrika wa ḥusni ʿibādatik(a).

O Allāh! Help me in recitation of the Qur'ān, remembrance of You, showing gratitude to You, and perfection of Your worship.

While rinsing the nose:

بِسْمِ اللهِ، اَللّٰهُمَّ أَرِحْنِيْ رَائِحَةَ الْجَنَّةِ، وَلَا تُرِحْنِيْ رَائِحَةَ النَّارِ.

Bismi 'Llāh(i), Allāhumma ariḥnī rā'iḥata 'l-janna(ti), wa lā turiḥnī rā'iḥata 'n-nār(i).

In the Name of Allāh. O Allāh! Let me smell the scent of Paradise, and do not let me smell the scent of the Fire.

While washing the face:

بِسْمِ اللهِ، اَللّٰهُمَّ بَيِّضْ وَجْهِيْ يَوْمَ تَبْيَضُّ وُجُوْهٌ وَّتَسْوَدُّ وُجُوْهٌ.

Bismi 'Llāh(i), Allāhumma bayyiḍ wajhī yawma tabyaḍḍu wujūh(uw) wa tas-waddu wujūh(un).

In the Name of Allāh. O Allāh! Illuminate my face the day when some faces are illuminated and other faces are darkened.

While washing the right arm:

بِسْمِ اللهِ، اَللّٰهُمَّ أَعْطِنِيْ كِتَابِيْ بِيَمِيْنِيْ، وَحَاسِبْنِيْ حِسَابًا يَّسِيْرًا.

Bismi 'Llāh(i), Allāhumma aʿṭinī kitābī bi yamīnī, wa ḥāsibnī ḥisābay yasīran.

In the Name of Allāh. O Allāh! Give me my book [of deeds] in my right hand, and make my reckoning easy.

While washing the left arm:

بِسْمِ اللهِ، اَللّٰهُمَّ لَا تُعْطِنِيْ كِتَابِيْ بِشِمَالِيْ، وَلَا مِن وَّرَاءِ ظَهْرِيْ.

Bismi 'Llāh(i), Allāhumma lā tuʿṭinī kitābī bi shimālī, wa lā miw warā'i ẓahrī.

In the Name of Allāh. O Allāh! Do not give me my book [of deeds] in my left hand, nor from behind my back.

While wiping the head:

بِسْمِ اللهِ، اَللّٰهُمَّ أَظِلَّنِيْ تَحْتَ ظِلِّ عَرْشِكَ يَوْمَ لَا ظِلَّ إِلَّا ظِلُّ عَرْشِكَ.

Bismi 'Llāh(i), Allāhumma aẓillanī taḥta ẓilli ʿarshika yawma lā ẓilla illā ẓillu ʿarshik(a).

In the Name of Allāh. O Allāh! Cover me under the shade of Your throne on the Day there is no shade except the shade of Your throne.

While wiping the ears:

بِسْمِ اللهِ، اَللّٰهُمَّ اجْعَلْنِيْ مِنَ الَّذِيْنَ يَسْتَمِعُوْنَ الْقَوْلَ فَيَتَّبِعُوْنَ أَحْسَنَهُ.

Bismi 'Llāh(i), Allāhumma 'jʿalnī mina 'lladhīna yastamiʿūna 'l-qawla fa yattabiʿūna aḥsanah(ū).

In the Name of Allāh. O Allāh! Make me among those who listen attentively to speech and then follow the best of it.

While wiping the back of the neck:

بِسْمِ اللهِ، اَللّٰهُمَّ أَعْتِقْ رَقَبَتِيْ مِنَ النَّارِ.

Bismi ’Llāh(i), Allāhumma aʿtiq raqabatī mina ’n-nār(i).

In the Name of Allāh. O Allāh! Save my neck from the Fire.

While washing the right foot:

بِسْمِ اللهِ، اَللّٰهُمَّ ثَبِّتْ قَدَمِيْ عَلَى الصِّرَاطِ يَوْمَ تَزِلُّ الْأَقْدَامُ.

Bismi ’Llāh(i), Allāhumma thabbit qadamī ʿala ’ṣ-ṣirāṭi yawma tazillu ’l-aqdām(u).

In the Name of Allāh. O Allāh! Make firm my foot upon the bridge on the Day that feet trip up.

While washing the left foot:

بِسْمِ اللهِ، اَللّٰهُمَّ اجْعَلْ ذَنْبِيْ مَغْفُوْرًا وَّسَعْيِيْ مَشْكُوْرًا وَّتِجَارَتِيْ لَنْ تَبُوْرَ.

Bismi ’Llāh(i), Allāhumma ’jʿal dhambī maghfūraw wa saʿyī mashkūranw wa tijāratī lan tabūr(a).

In the Name of Allāh. O Allāh! Make my sins forgiven, my efforts appreciated [i.e., rewarded], and my trade ever-successful.

Finally upon completion of *wuḍū’*, one says the following:

أَشْهَدُ أَنْ لَّا إِلٰهَ إِلَّا اللهُ وَحْدَهٗ لَا شَرِيْكَ لَهٗ، وَأَشْهَدُ أَنَّ مُحَمَّدًا عَبْدُهٗ وَرَسُوْلُهٗ.

Ashhadu al lā ilāha illa ’Llāhu waḥdahū lā sharīka lah(ū), wa ashhadu anna Muḥammadan ʿabduhū wa rasūluh(ū).

I testify that there is no deity except Allāh, alone, without partner; and I testify that Muḥammad is His servant and His Messenger.

اَللّٰهُمَّ اجْعَلْنِيْ مِنَ التَّوَّابِيْنَ وَاجْعَلْنِيْ مِنَ الْمُتَطَهِّرِيْنَ.

Allāhumma ’jʿalnī mina ’t-tawwābīna wa ’jʿalnī mina ’l-mutaṭahhirīn(a).

O Allāh! Make me among the oft-repenting, and make me among those who maintain utmost purity. (*Imdād* 75–6; *Marāqī ’l-Falāḥ*, *Ṭaḥṭāwī* 1:117–8.)

Imām Ṭaḥṭāwī mentions the following regarding these supplications and their authenticity:

Ibn Amīr al-Ḥājj said, “Our Shaykh, the Ḥadīth Master (*Ḥāfiẓ*) of his age, Shihāb al-Dīn Ibn Ḥajar al-ʿAsqalānī, was asked about the ḥadīths that are mentioned in *Muqaddima Abū 'l-Layth* regarding the supplications of the limbs, and he responded that they are weak, yet scholars have given leeway in mentioning weak ḥadīths and in acting upon them in virtuous acts. None of them is established to be from the Messenger of Allāh ﷺ, neither from his statements nor from his actions."

None of their chains of transmission is divest of someone accused of fabrication, so ascribing these supplications to the pious predecessors (*salaf ṣāliḥ*) is more appropriate than ascribing them to the Messenger of Allāh ﷺ, out of precaution from falling into the category of [the well-known ḥadīth], "Whoever purposely lies regarding me should prepare his seat in the Fire."

Hence, regarding this, they [scholars] have said, as mentioned in [Nawawī's] *Taqrīb* and its commentary [by Suyūṭī], "If you want to narrate a weak ḥadīth without its chain of transmission, then do not say, 'The Messenger of Allāh ﷺ said,' or a similar statement of certainty [in ascription], but rather say, 'It is narrated on him,' or 'It has reached us,' or 'It has come,' or 'It has been transmitted,' or a similar statement indicating weakness or uncertainty [in ascription]. The same applies to that which you doubt concerning its authenticity or weakness. As for a rigorously authenticated narration, mention it with certainty [of ascription], for using a phrase of weakness or uncertainty [of ascription] for it is problematic, just as using a phrase of certainty [of ascription] is problematic for a weak ḥadīth."

Hindī and others said, "Nothing has been established [as authentic to the Messenger ﷺ] except the two testifications of faith after finishing *wuḍū'*." Sayyid mentioned this quoting *Nahr* (*Ṭaḥṭāwī* 1:117).

Before entering the lavatory:

اَللّٰهُمَّ إِنِّيْ أَعُوْذُ بِكَ مِنَ الْخُبْثِ وَالْخَبَائِثِ.

Allāhumma innī aʿūdhu bika mina 'l-khubthi wa 'l-khabā'ith.

O Allāh! I seek refuge in You from male and female devils [and filth in general]" (*Bukhārī, Muslim*).[709]

When exiting the lavatory:

[غُفْرَانَكَ:] اَلْحَمْدُ لله الَّذِيْ أَذْهَبَ عَنِّيْ الْأَذٰى وَعَافَانِيْ.

709 In his commentary on *Ṣaḥīḥ Muslim*, Qāḍī ʿIyāḍ mentions that if one does not say this supplication, devils collectively laugh at the person while he exposes his nakedness to relieve himself (*Ikmāl al-Muʿlim* 2:229).

[Ghufrānak(a),] al-ḥamdu li 'Llāhi 'lladhī adhhaba ʿanni 'l-adhā wa ʿāfānī.

[(O Allāh, I seek) Your forgiveness!] Praise be to Allāh, Who removed harm from my body and granted me well-being.

THE CALL TO PRAYER, ITS COMMENCEMENT, AND RELATED SUPPLICATIONS

The Call to Prayer (*adhān*):

اَللهُ أَكْبَرْ، اَللهُ أَكْبَرْ.

Allāhu akbar, Allāhu akbar. Allāh is the greatest. Allāh is the greatest.

اَللهُ أَكْبَرْ، اَللهُ أَكْبَرْ.

Allāhu akbar, Allāhu akbar. Allāh is the greatest. Allāh is the greatest.

أَشْهَدُ أَن لَّا إِلٰهَ إِلَّا اللهْ، أَشْهَدُ أَن لَّا إِلٰهَ إِلَّا اللهْ.

Ashhadu al lā ilāha illa 'Llāh, Ashhadu al lā ilāha illa 'Llāh. I testify that there is no deity except Allāh. I testify that there is no deity except Allāh.

أَشْهَدُ أَنَّ مُحَمَّدًا رَّسُوْلُ اللهْ، أَشْهَدُ أَنَّ مُحَمَّدًا رَّسُوْلُ اللهْ.

Ashhadu anna Muḥammadar rasūlu 'Llāh, Ashhadu anna Muḥammadar rasūlu 'Llāh. I testify that Muḥammad is the Messenger of Allāh. I testify that Muḥammad is the Messenger of Allāh.

حَيَّ عَلَى الصَّلَاة، حَيَّ عَلَى الصَّلَاة.

Ḥayya ʿala 'ṣ-ṣalāh, Ḥayya ʿala 'ṣ-ṣalāh. Come to the prayer. Come to the prayer.

حَيَّ عَلَى الْفَلَاحْ، حَيَّ عَلَى الْفَلَاحْ.

Ḥayya ʿala 'l-falāḥ, Ḥayya ʿala 'l-falāḥ. Come to success. Come to success.

اَللهُ أَكْبَرْ، اَللهُ أَكْبَرْ.

Allāhu akbar, Allāhu akbar. Allāh is the greatest. Allāh is the greatest.

لَا إِلٰهَ إِلَّا اللهْ.

Lā ilāha illa 'Llāh. There is no deity except Allāh.

For the Call to Prayer of fajr, one adds the following after *Ḥayya ʿala ʾl-falāḥ*:

اَلصَّلَاةُ خَيْرٌ مِّنَ النَّوْمْ، اَلصَّلَاةُ خَيْرٌ مِّنَ النَّوْمْ.

Aṣ-ṣalātu khayrum mina ʾn-nawm, Aṣ-ṣalātu khayrum mina ʾn-nawm.

Prayer is better than sleep. Prayer is better than sleep.

For the Call to Commencement (*iqāma*), one adds the following after *Ḥayya ʿala ʾl-falāḥ*:

قَدْ قَامَتِ الصَّلَاة، قَدْ قَامَتِ الصَّلَاة.

Qad qāmati ʾṣ-ṣalāh, Qad qāmati ʾṣ-ṣalāh.

The prayer has commenced. The prayer has commenced.

Supplication After the Call to Prayer:

اَللّٰهُمَّ رَبَّ هٰذِهِ الدَّعْوَةِ التَّامَّةِ وَالصَّلَاةِ الْقَائِمَةِ، أٰتِ سَيِّدَنَا مُحَمَّدًا الْوَسِيْلَةَ وَالْفَضِيْلَةَ وَالدَّرَجَةَ الرَّفِيْعَةَ، وَابْعَثْهُ اللّٰهُمَّ الْمَقَامَ الْمَحْمُوْدَ الَّذِيْ وَعَدتَّهُ.

Allāhumma Rabba hādhihī ʾd-daʿwati ʾt-tāmmāti wa ʾṣ-ṣalāti ʾl-qāʾima(ti), āti Sayyidanā Muḥammadani ʾl-wasīlata wa ʾl-faḍīlata wa ʾd-darajata ʾr-rafīʿa(ta), wa ʾbʿathhū ʾLlāhumma ʾl-maqāma ʾl-maḥmūda ʾlladhī waʿattah(ū).

O Allāh, Lord of this perfect call and established prayer! Give our Master Muḥammad the Station of Mediation, the Greatest Rank, and the Highest Degree; and resurrect him, O Allāh, upon the Praiseworthy Station that You promised him.

Then one sends blessings and peace upon the Messenger ﷺ, and makes general supplication for one's needs or desires.

SUPPLICATIONS OF THE RITUAL PRAYER (*ṢALĀT*)

The Opening Supplication (*thanāʾ*):

سُبْحَانَكَ اللّٰهُمَّ وَبِحَمْدِكَ وَتَبَارَكَ اسْمُكَ وَتَعَالٰى جَدُّكَ وَلَا إِلٰهَ غَيْرُكَ.

Subḥānakka ʾLlāhumma wa biḥamdik(a) wa tabāraka ʾsmuka wa taʿālā jadduka wa lā ilāha ghayruk(a).

Glory be to You, O Allāh, with Your praise. Blessed is Your Name; Exalted is Your Honor. There is no deity besides You.

Testification of faith said in the sitting position (*tashahhud*):

اَلتَّحِيَّاتُ لِلّٰهِ وَالصَّلَوَاتُ وَالطَّيِّبَاتُ، السَّلَامُ عَلَيْكَ أَيُّهَا النَّبِيُّ وَرَحْمَةُ اللهِ وَبَرَكَاتُهُ، السَّلَامُ عَلَيْنَا وَعَلٰى عِبَادِ اللهِ الصَّالِحِيْنَ، أَشْهَدُ أَنْ لَّا إِلٰهَ إِلَّا اللهُ وَأَشْهَدُ أَنَّ مُحَمَّدًا عَبْدُهُ وَرَسُوْلُهُ.

At-Taḥiyyātu li 'Llāhi wa 'ṣ-ṣalawātu wa 'ṭ-ṭayyibāt(u), as-salāmu ʿalayka ayyuha 'n-nabiyyu wa raḥmatu 'Llāhi wa barakātuh(ū), as-salāmu ʿalaynā wa ʿalā ʿibādi 'Llāhi 'ṣ-ṣāliḥīn(a). Ashhadu al lā ilāha illa 'Llāh(u) wa ashhadu anna Muḥammadan ʿabduhū wa rasūluh(ū).

Greetings are for Allāh, as well as prayers and all things pure. Peace be upon you, O Prophet, as well as the mercy of Allāh and His blessings. Peace be upon us, and upon all the righteous servants of Allāh. I testify that there is no deity except Allāh, and I testify that Muḥammad is His servant and messenger.

Blessings sent upon the Messenger ﷺ in the final sitting position, after the above supplication:

اَللّٰهُمَّ صَلِّ عَلٰى مُحَمَّدٍ وَّعَلٰى اٰلِ مُحَمَّدٍ كَمَا صَلَّيْتَ عَلٰى إِبْرَاهِيْمَ وَعَلٰى اٰلِ إِبْرَاهِيْمَ [إِنَّكَ حَمِيْدٌ مَّجِيْدٌ]، وَبَارِكْ عَلٰى مُحَمَّدٍ وَّعَلٰى اٰلِ مُحَمَّدٍ كَمَا بَارَكْتَ عَلٰى إِبْرَاهِيْمَ وَعَلٰى اٰلِ إِبْرَاهِيْمَ فِي الْعَالَمِيْنَ، إِنَّكَ حَمِيْدٌ مَّجِيْدٌ.

Allāhumma ṣalli ʿalā Muḥammadiw wa ʿalā āli Muḥammadin kamā ṣallayta ʿalā Ibrāhīma wa ʿalā āli Ibrāhīm(a), [innaka Ḥamīdum Majīd(un),] wa bārik ʿalā Muḥammadiw wa ʿalā āli Muḥammadin kamā bārakta ʿalā Ibrāhīma wa ʿalā āli Ibrāhīma fi 'l-ʿālamīn(a), innaka Ḥamīdum Majīd(un).

O Allāh! Send mercy upon Muḥammad and upon the family of Muḥammad, just as You sent mercy upon Ibrāhīm and upon the family of Ibrāhīm; [indeed, You are Praiseworthy and Majestic;] and send blessings upon Muḥammad and upon the family of Muḥammad, just as You sent blessings upon Ibrāhīm and upon the family of Ibrāhīm; indeed, You are Praiseworthy and Majestic.

Final supplication of the prayer:

رَبَّنَا اٰتِنَا فِي الدُّنْيَا حَسَنَةً وَّفِي الْاٰخِرَةِ حَسَنَةً وَّقِنَا عَذَابَ النَّارِ.

Rabbanā ātinā fi 'd-dunyā ḥasanataw wa fi 'l-ākhirati ḥasanataw wa qinā ʿadhāba 'n-nār[i].

Our Lord! Grant us much good in this life and much good in the next life, and protect us from the punishment of the Fire.

Supplication of the Witr Prayer (*qunūt*):

اَللّٰهُمَّ إِنَّا نَسْتَعِيْنُكَ وَنَسْتَهْدِيْكَ، وَنَسْتَغْفِرُكَ وَنَتُوْبُ إِلَيْكَ، وَنُؤْمِنُ بِكَ وَنَتَوَكَّلُ عَلَيْكَ، وَنُثْنِيْ عَلَيْكَ الْخَيْرَ كُلَّهُ، نَشْكُرُكَ وَلَا نَكْفُرُكَ، وَنَخْلَعُ وَنَتْرُكُ مَن يَّفْجُرُكَ. اَللّٰهُمَّ إِيَّاكَ نَعْبُدُ، وَلَكَ نُصَلِّيْ وَنَسْجُدُ، وَإِلَيْكَ نَسْعٰى وَنَحْفِدُ، نَرْجُوْ رَحْمَتَكَ وَنَخْشٰى عَذَابَكَ، إِنَّ عَذَابَكَ الْجِدَّ بِالْكُفَّارِ مُلْحِقٌ، وَصَلَّى اللهُ عَلٰى سَيِّدِنَا مُحَمَّدِ النَّبِيِّ الْأُمِّيِّ، وَعَلٰى أٰلِهِ وَصَحْبِهِ وَسَلَّمَ.

Allāhumma innā nastaʿīnuka wa nastahdīk(a), wa nastaghfiruka wa natūbu ilayk(a), wa nuʾminu bika wa natawakkalu ʿalayk(a), wa nuthnī ʿalayka ʾl-khayra kullah(ū), nashkuruka wa lā nakfuruk(a), wa nakhlaʿu wa natruku may yafjuruk(a). Allāhumma iyyāka naʿbudu, wa laka nuṣallī wa nasjud(u), wa ilayka nasʿā wa naḥfid(u), narjū raḥmataka wa nakhshā ʿadhābak(a), inna ʿadhābaka ʾl-jidda bi ʾl-kuffāri mulḥiq(un). Wa ṣallā ʾLlāhu ʿalā Sayyidinā Muḥammadini ʾn-Nabiyyi ʾl-ummiyy(i), wa ʿalā ālihī wa ṣaḥbihī wa sallam(a).

O Allāh! Verily, we seek Your help and Your guidance. We ask for Your forgiveness and turn to You in repentance. We believe in You and place our trust in You. We praise You with every good praise; we thank You, and we do not reject You. We cast out and abandon anyone who disobeys You. O Allāh, You alone do we worship, and for Your sake alone do we pray and prostrate. To You alone do we earnestly strive and hasten. We hope for Your mercy and fear Your punishment; verily, Your true punishment will be meted out to the disbelievers. May Allāh send blessings and peace upon our Master Muḥammad, the unlettered Prophet, and upon his family and Companions.

The Prayer of Making a Decision (*ṣalāt al-istikhāra*)

After performing two voluntary *rakʿas* of prayer, one praises Allāh, sends blessings and peace upon the Messenger 🕌, and then makes the following supplication:

اَللّٰهُمَّ إِنِّيْ أَسْتَخِيْرُكَ بِعِلْمِكَ وَأَسْتَقْدِرُكَ بِقُدْرَتِكَ وَأَسْأَلُكَ مِنْ فَضْلِكَ الْعَظِيمِ، فَإِنَّكَ تَقْدِرُ وَلَا أَقْدِرُ، وَتَعْلَمُ وَلَا أَعْلَمُ، وَأَنْتَ عَلَّامُ الْغُيُوْبِ. اَللّٰهُمَّ إِنْ كُنْتَ تَعْلَمُ أَنَّ [هٰذَا الْأَمْرَ] خَيْرٌ لِّيْ فِيْ دِيْنِيْ وَمَعَاشِيْ وَعَاقِبَةِ أَمْرِيْ، فَاقْدُرْهُ لِيْ وَيَسِّرْهُ لِيْ ثُمَّ بَارِكْ لِيْ فِيْهِ، وَإِنْ كُنْتَ تَعْلَمُ أَنَّ [هٰذَا الْأَمْرَ] شَرٌّ لِّيْ فِيْ دِيْنِيْ وَمَعَاشِيْ وَعَاقِبَةِ أَمْرِيْ، فَاصْرِفْهُ عَنِّيْ وَاصْرِفْنِيْ عَنْهُ وَاقْدُرْ لِيَ الْخَيْرَ حَيْثُ كَانَ، ثُمَّ رَضِّنِيْ بِهِ.

Allāhumma innī astakhīruka bi ʿilmika wa astaqdiruka bi qudratika wa asʾaluka min faḍlika 'l-ʿaẓīm(i), fa innaka taqdiru wa lā aqdir(u), wa taʿlamu wa lā aʿlam(u), wa Anta ʿAllāmu 'l-ghuyūb(i). Allāhumma in kunta taʿlamu anna [hādhā 'l-amr] khayrul lī fī dīnī wa maʿāshī wa ʿāqibati amrī, fa 'qdurhu lī wa yassirhu lī thumma bārik lī fīh(i), wa in kunta taʿlamu anna [hādhā 'l-amr] sharrul lī fī dīnī wa maʿāshī wa ʿāqibati amrī, fa 'ṣrifhu ʿannī wa 'ṣrifnī ʿanhu wa 'qdur līya 'l-khayra ḥaythu kān(a), thumma raḍḍinī bih(ī).

O Allāh, verily I seek the better [of either choice] from You, by Your knowledge, and I seek ability from You, by Your power, and I ask You from Your immense bounty. For indeed You have power, and I am powerless; You have knowledge, and I know not; You are the Knower of the unseen realms. O Allāh, if You know that *this matter* is good for me, with regard to my religion, my livelihood, and the end of my affair, then decree it for me, facilitate it for me, and grant me blessing in it. And if You know that *this matter* is bad for me, with regard to my religion, my livelihood, and the end of my affair, then turn it away from me and me from it; and decree for me better than it, wherever it may be, and make me content with it.

The Prayer of Need (*ṣalāt al-ḥāja*)

One performs *wuḍū'*, perfects it, and performs two voluntary *rakʿas* of prayer. One then praises Allāh, sends blessings and peace upon the Messenger ﷺ, and makes the following supplication:

لَا إِلٰهَ إِلَّا اللهُ الْحَلِيْمُ الْكَرِيْمُ، سُبْحَانَ اللهِ رَبِّ الْعَرْشِ الْعَظِيْمِ، اَلْحَمْدُ لله رَبِّ الْعَالَمِيْنَ. أَسْأَلُكَ مُوْجِبَاتِ رَحْمَتِكَ، وَعَزَائِمَ مَغْفِرَتِكَ، وَالْغَنِيْمَةَ مِنْ كُلِّ بِرٍّ، وَّالسَّلَامَةَ مِنْ كُلِّ إِثْمٍ. لَّا تَدَعْ لِيْ ذَنْبًا إِلَّا غَفَرْتَهُ، وَلَا هَمًّا إِلَّا فَرَّجْتَهُ، وَلَا حَاجَةً هِيَ لَكَ رِضًا إِلَّا قَضَيْتَهَا، يَا أَرْحَمَ الرَّاحِمِيْنَ.

Lā ilāha illa 'Llāhu 'l-Ḥalīmu 'l-Karīm(u), subḥāna 'Llāhi Rabbi 'l-ʿarshi 'l-ʿaẓīm(i), al-ḥamdu li 'Llāhi Rabbi 'l-ʿālamīn(a). As'aluka mūjibāti raḥmatik(a), wa ʿazā'ima maghfiratik(a), wa 'l-ghanīmata min kulli birr(iw), wa 's-salāmata min kulli ithm(in). Lā tadaʿ lī dhamban illā ghafartah(ū), wa lā hamman illā farrajtah(ū), wa lā ḥājatan hiya laka riḍan illā qaḍaytahā, yā Arḥama 'r-rāḥimīn(a).

There is no deity but Allāh, the Most Forbearing, the Ever-Generous. Glory be unto Allāh, Lord of the Great Throne. Praise be to Allāh, Lord of all the worlds. I ask you for those things that bring about Your mercy and Your complete forgiveness; [for] a full portion of every righteous act, and safety from every vice. Do not leave any sin of mine except that You forgive it; any anxiety except that You relieve it; nor any need of mine that pleases You except that You fulfill it, O Most Merciful of those who show mercy.

He then asks for his worldly or spiritual need(s) (*Marāqi 'l-Falāḥ*, *Ṭaḥṭāwī* 1:540–3).

The Fourteen Verses of Prostration:[710]

١. ﴿إِنَّ الَّذِيْنَ عِنْدَ رَبِّكَ لَا يَسْتَكْبِرُوْنَ عَنْ عِبَادَتِهٖ وَيُسَبِّحُوْنَهٗ وَلَهٗ يَسْجُدُوْنَ﴾ (الْأَعْرَاف ٢٠٦)

٢. ﴿وَلِلّٰهِ يَسْجُدُ مَنْ فِي السَّمَاوَاتِ وَالْأَرْضِ طَوْعًا وَّكَرْهًا وَّظِلَالُهُمْ بِالْغُدُوِّ وَالْأٰصَالِ﴾ (الرَّعْد ١٥)

٣. ﴿وَلِلّٰهِ يَسْجُدُ مَا فِي السَّمَاوَاتِ وَمَا فِي الْأَرْضِ مِنْ دَابَّةٍ وَّالْمَلَائِكَةُ وَهُمْ لَا يَسْتَكْبِرُوْنَ ۞ يَخَافُوْنَ رَبَّهُمْ مِنْ فَوْقِهِمْ وَيَفْعَلُوْنَ مَا يُؤْمَرُوْنَ﴾ (النَّحْل ٤٩–٥٠)

٤. ﴿قُلْ اٰمِنُوْا بِهٖ أَوْ لَا تُؤْمِنُوْا، إِنَّ الَّذِيْنَ أُوْتُوا الْعِلْمَ مِنْ قَبْلِهٖ إِذَا يُتْلٰى عَلَيْهِمْ يَخِرُّوْنَ لِلْأَذْقَانِ سُجَّدًا ۞ وَّيَقُوْلُوْنَ سُبْحَانَ رَبِّنَا إِنْ كَانَ وَعْدُ رَبِّنَا لَمَفْعُوْلًا ۞ وَّيَخِرُّوْنَ لِلْأَذْقَانِ يَبْكُوْنَ وَيَزِيْدُهُمْ خُشُوْعًا﴾ (الإِسْرَاء ١٠٧–١٠٩)

٥. ﴿أُولٰئِكَ الَّذِيْنَ أَنْعَمَ اللهُ عَلَيْهِمْ مِنَ النَّبِيِّيْنَ مِنْ ذُرِّيَّةِ اٰدَمَ وَمِمَّنْ حَمَلْنَا مَعَ نُوْحٍ وَّمِنْ ذُرِّيَّةِ إِبْرَاهِيْمَ وَإِسْرَائِيْلَ وَمِمَّنْ هَدَيْنَا وَاجْتَبَيْنَا إِذَا تُتْلٰى عَلَيْهِمْ اٰيَاتُ الرَّحْمٰنِ خَرُّوْا سُجَّدًا وَّبُكِيًّا﴾ (مَرْيَم ٥٨)

---

710 These verses are listed here for two reasons: (a) to indicate the verses according to the Ḥanafī school, as there is difference of opinion with the Shāfiʿī school regarding 22:77, which is not of the verses of prostration according to the Ḥanafīs (and hence not listed above) yet is according to the Shāfiʿīs. There is also disagreement regarding 38:24–5; according to the stronger position of the Ḥanafī school, the obligation of prostration lies after the recitation of verse 25, as listed above, yet after verse 24 according to others in the school, while neither is a verse of prostration according to the Shāfiʿīs. Many modern-day copies of the Qur'ān are based on the Shāfiʿī school, so Ḥanafīs should take note of the above list; and (b) to facilitate for the reader the recommendation of Imām Nasafī and others, mentioned by Imām Shurunbulālī on page 111 of this work, namely, "If one recites all [fourteen] verses of prostration in one sitting, and performs a separate prostration for each verse, then Allāh Most High will take care of all his worries [in both this life and the next]." Imāms Shurunbulālī and Ibn ʿĀbidīn state that one should take heed and have fervent aspiration to learn and teach this practice. Many imāms, including Kamāl ibn al-Humām, have transmitted this advice in their commentaries. Imām Ṭaḥṭāwī maintains that it is more preferable to prostrate for each verse immediately after its recitation, although one could also perform all fourteen prostrations after having recited all fourteen verses, which seems closer to Imām Nasafī's statement; in any case, neither way is deemed disliked (*Marāqi 'l-Falāḥ*, *Ṭaḥṭāwī* 2:110–11; *Hadiyya* 135; *Durr*, *Radd* 1:523–4).

٦. ﴿أَلَمْ تَرَ أَنَّ اللهَ يَسْجُدُ لَهُ مَنْ فِي السَّمَاوَاتِ وَمَنْ فِي الْأَرْضِ وَالشَّمْسُ وَالْقَمَرُ وَالنُّجُومُ وَالْجِبَالُ وَالشَّجَرُ وَالدَّوَابُّ وَكَثِيرٌ مِّنَ النَّاسِ وَكَثِيرٌ حَقَّ عَلَيْهِ الْعَذَابُ وَمَن يُّهِنِ اللهُ فَمَا لَهُ مِن مُّكْرِمٍ إِنَّ اللهَ يَفْعَلُ مَا يَشَاءُ﴾ (الْحَجّ ١٨)

٧. ﴿وَإِذَا قِيلَ لَهُمُ اسْجُدُوْا لِلرَّحْمٰنِ قَالُوْا وَمَا الرَّحْمٰنُ أَنَسْجُدُ لِمَا تَأْمُرُنَا وَزَادَهُمْ نُفُوْرًا﴾ (الفُرْقَان ٦٠)

٨. ﴿أَلَّا يَسْجُدُوْا لِلهِ الَّذِي يُخْرِجُ الْخَبْءَ فِي السَّمَاوَاتِ وَالْأَرْضِ وَيَعْلَمُ مَا تُخْفُوْنَ وَمَا تُعْلِنُوْنَ ۞ اَللهُ لَا إِلٰهَ إِلَّا هُوَ رَبُّ الْعَرْشِ الْعَظِيْمِ﴾ (النَّمْل ٢٥–٢٦)

٩. ﴿إِنَّمَا يُؤْمِنُ بِأٰيَاتِنَا الَّذِيْنَ إِذَا ذُكِّرُوْا بِهَا خَرُّوْا سُجَّدًا وَّسَبَّحُوْا بِحَمْدِ رَبِّهِمْ وَهُمْ لَا يَسْتَكْبِرُوْنَ﴾ (السَّجْدَة ١٥)

١٠. ﴿وَظَنَّ دَاوُودُ أَنَّمَا فَتَنَّاهُ فَاسْتَغْفَرَ رَبَّهُ وَخَرَّ رَاكِعًا وَّأَنَابَ ۞ فَغَفَرْنَا لَهُ ذٰلِكَ وَإِنَّ لَهُ عِنْدَنَا لَزُلْفٰى وَحُسْنَ مَاٰبٍ﴾ (ص ٢٤–٢٥)

١١. ﴿وَمِنْ أٰيَاتِهِ اللَّيْلُ وَالنَّهَارُ وَالشَّمْسُ وَالْقَمَرُ لَا تَسْجُدُوْا لِلشَّمْسِ وَلَا لِلْقَمَرِ وَاسْجُدُوْا لِلهِ الَّذِيْ خَلَقَهُنَّ إِنْ كُنْتُمْ إِيَّاهُ تَعْبُدُوْنَ ۞ فَإِنِ اسْتَكْبَرُوْا فَالَّذِيْنَ عِنْدَ رَبِّكَ يُسَبِّحُوْنَ لَهُ بِاللَّيْلِ وَالنَّهَارِ وَهُمْ لَا يَسْأَمُوْنَ﴾ (فُصِّلَتْ ٣٧–٣٨)

١٢. ﴿فَاسْجُدُوْا لِلهِ وَاعْبُدُوْا﴾ (النَّجْم ٦٢)

١٣. ﴿فَمَا لَهُمْ لَا يُؤْمِنُوْنَ ۞ وَإِذَا قُرِئَ عَلَيْهِمُ الْقُرْأٰنُ لَا يَسْجُدُوْنَ﴾ (الاِنْشِقَاق ٢٠–٢١)

١٤. ﴿كَلَّا لَا تُطِعْهُ وَاسْجُدْ وَاقْتَرِبْ﴾ (الْعَلَق ١٩)

The ʿĪd al-Aḍḥā prayer

The *takbīrs* of *tashrīq* are to say:

اَللهُ أَكْبَرْ اَللهُ أَكْبَرْ، لَا إِلٰهَ اِلَّا اللهُ. وَاللهُ أَكْبَرْ اَللهُ أَكْبَرْ، وَلِلهِ الْحَمْدُ.

Allāhu akbar Allāhu akbar, lā ilāha illa 'Llāh. Wa 'Llāhu akbar Allāhu akbar, wa li 'Llāhi 'l-ḥamd.

Allāh is the greatest, Allāh is the greatest; There is no deity except Allāh. Indeed, Allāh is the greatest, Allāh is the greatest; For Allāh is all praise.

It is recommended to add:

اَللهُ أَكْبَرُ كَبِيْرًا، وَّالْحَمْدُ لِلهِ كَثِيْرًا، وَّسُبْحَانَ اللهِ وَبِحَمْدِهٖ بُكْرَةً وَّأَصِيْلًا. لَّآ إِلٰهَ إِلَّا اللهُ وَحْدَهٗ، صَدَقَ وَعْدَهٗ، وَنَصَرَ عَبْدَهٗ، وَأَعَزَّ جُنْدَهٗ وَهَزَمَ الْأَحْزَابَ وَحْدَهٗ. لَا إِلٰهَ إِلَّا اللهُ، وَلَا نَعْبُدُ إِلَّا إِيَّاهُ، مُخْلِصِيْنَ لَهُ الدِّيْنَ وَلَوْ كَرِهَ الْكَافِرُوْنَ. اَللّٰهُمَّ صَلِّ عَلٰى سَيِّدِنَا مُحَمَّدٍ، وَّعَلٰى اٰلِ سَيِّدِنَا مُحَمَّدٍ، وَّعَلٰى أَصْحَابِ سَيِّدِنَا مُحَمَّدٍ، وَّعَلٰى أَزْوَاجِ سَيِّدِنَا مُحَمَّدٍ، وَّسَلِّمْ تَسْلِيْمًا كَثِيْرًا.

Allāhu akbar kabīraw, wa 'l-ḥamdu li 'Llāhi kathīraw, wa subḥāna 'Llāhi wa bi ḥamdihī bukrataw wa aṣīlan. Lā ilāha illā 'Llāhu waḥdah(ū), ṣadaqa waʿdah(ū), wa naṣara ʿabdah(ū), wa aʿazza jundahū wa hazama 'l-aḥzāba waḥdah(ū). Lā ilāha illā 'Llāh(u), wa lā naʿbudu illā iyyāh(u), mukhliṣīna lahu 'd-dīna wa law kariha 'l-kāfirūn(a). Allāhumma ṣalli ʿalā Sayyidinā Muḥammad(iw), wa ʿalā āli Sayyidinā Muḥammad(iw), wa ʿalā aṣḥābi Sayyidinā Muḥammad(iw), wa ʿalā azwāji Sayyidinā Muḥammad(iw), wa sallim taslīman kathīran.

Allāh is indeed the Greatest; Much Praise is for Him; Glory be to Him, with much praise, morning and evening. There is no deity except Him alone; He fulfilled His promise, gave victory to His servant, strengthened His soldiers, and [He] alone defeated the confederates. There is no deity except Him. We worship none but Him, practicing the religion solely for His sake, even if the disbelievers hate it. O Allāh, send blessings upon our Master Muḥammad, and on the family of our Master Muḥammad, and on the Companions of our Master Muḥammad, and on the wives of our Master Muḥammad; and send abundant peace on them all.

Supplication after the Prayer for Rain (*istisqā'*):

اَللّٰهُمَّ اسْقِنَا غَيْثًا مُّغِيْثًا هَنِيْئًا غَدَقًا عَاجِلًا غَيْرَ أٰجِلٍ مُّجَلِّلًا سَحًّا طَبَقًا دَائِمًا.

Allāhumma 'sqinā ghaytham mughīthan hanī'an ghadaqan ʿājilan ghayra ājilim mujallilan saḥḥan ṭabaqan dā'iman.

O Allāh! Bless us with abundant and pleasant rainwater that will deliver us [from this calamity], immediately rather than delayed; one that fills the entire horizon and pounds hard on the earth, completely covering our lands, lasting as long as is needed.

SUPPLICATIONS RELATED TO THE DECEASED

When closing the deceased's eyes, one says:

بِسْمِ اللهِ وَعَلٰى مِلَّةِ رَسُوْلِ اللهِ. اَللّٰهُمَّ يَسِّرْ عَلَيْهِ أَمْرَهُ، وَسَهِّلْ عَلَيْهِ مَا بَعْدَهُ، وَأَسْعِدْهُ بِلِقَائِكَ، وَاجْعَلْ مَا خَرَجَ إِلَيْهِ خَيْرًا مِمَّا خَرَجَ عَنْهُ.

Bismi 'Llāhi wa ʿalā millati rasūli 'Llāh(i). Allāhumma yassir ʿalayhi amrah(ū), wa sahhil ʿalayhi mā baʿdah(ū), wa asʿidhū bi liqā'ik(a), wa 'jʿal mā kharaja ilayhi khayram mimmā kharaja ʿanh(ū).

In the Name of Allāh, and on the way of the Messenger of Allāh ﷺ. O Allāh, make his affair smooth for him; ease for him that which is to follow; make him felicitous by his meeting You; and make that which he has gone off to better than that which he has left.

In the Funeral Prayer (*janāza*) for an adult, after the third *takbīr*, one says:

اَللّٰهُمَّ اغْفِرْ لَهُ وَارْحَمْهُ، وَعَافِهِ وَاعْفُ عَنْهُ، وَأَكْرِمْ مَنْزِلَهُ، وَوَسِّعْ مَدْخَلَهُ، وَاغْسِلْهُ بِالْمَاءِ وَالثَّلْجِ وَالْبَرَدِ، وَنَقِّهِ مِنَ الْخَطَايَا كَمَا يُنَقَّى الثَّوْبُ الْأَبْيَضُ مِنَ الدَّنَسِ، وَأَبْدِلْهُ دَارًا خَيْرًا مِنْ دَارِهِ وَأَهْلًا خَيْرًا مِنْ أَهْلِهِ وَزَوْجًا خَيْرًا مِنْ زَوْجِهِ، وَأَدْخِلْهُ الْجَنَّةَ وَأَعِذْهُ مِنْ عَذَابِ الْقَبْرِ وَعَذَابِ النَّارِ.

Allāhumma 'ghfir lahū wa 'rḥamh(ū), wa ʿāfihī waʿfu ʿanh(ū), wa akrim manzilah(ū), wa wassiʿ madkhalah(ū), wa 'ghsilhu bi 'l-mā'i wa 'th-thalji wa 'l-barad(i), wa naqqihī mina 'l-khaṭāyā kamā yunaqqa 'th-thawbu 'l-abyaḍu mina 'd-danas(i), wa abdilhū dāran khayram min dārihī wa ahlan khayram min ahlihī wa zawjan khayram min zawjih(ī), wa adkhilhu 'l-janna(ta) wa aʿidhhū min ʿadhābi 'l-qabri wa ʿadhābi 'n-nār(i).

O Allāh, forgive him and have mercy on him. Give him well-being, and pardon him. Honor his place of residence, and make his entrance expansive. Wash him with water, ice, and snow. Purify him from sins just as a white garment is purified from filth. Replace his abode with a better one, his family with a better one, and his spouse with a better one. Enter him into Paradise, and save him from the punishment of the grave and that of the Fire.

In the Funeral Prayer (*janāza*) for a child, after the third *takbīr*, one says:

اَللّٰهُمَّ اجْعَلْهُ لَنَا فَرَطًا، وَّاجْعَلْهُ لَنَا أَجْرًا وَّذُخْرًا، وَّاجْعَلْهُ لَنَا شَافِعًا وَّمُشَفَّعًا.

Allāhumma 'jʿalhu lanā faraṭaw, wa 'jʿalhu lanā ajraw wa dhukhraw, wa 'jʿalhu lanā shāfiʿaw wa mushaffaʿan.

O Allāh, make him one who is sent forth on our behalf, as well as a reward and a stored treasure for us. Make him an intercessor for us, and accept his intercession.

SUPPLICATIONS OF THE PILGRIMAGE (*ḤAJJ*)

From Marāqi 'l-Saʿādāt
Supplication after performing the two *rakʿas* when entering the state of pilgrim sanctity (*iḥrām*)

For *ḥajj* alone (*ifrād*):

اَللّٰهُمَّ إِنِّيْ أُرِيْدُ الْحَجَّ، فَيَسِّرْهُ لِيْ وَتَقَبَّلْهُ مِنِّيْ.

Allāhumma innī urīdu 'l-ḥajj(a), fa yassirhū lī wa taqabbalhū minnī.

O Allāh, verily I desire to perform *ḥajj*, so make it easy for me and accept it from me.

For both *ḥajj* and *ʿumra* (*qirān*):

اَللّٰهُمَّ إِنِّيْ أُرِيْدُ الْعُمْرَةَ وَالْحَجَّ، فَيَسِّرْهُمَا لِيْ وَتَقَبَّلْهُمَا مِنِّيْ.

Allāhumma innī urīdu 'l-ʿumrata wa 'l-ḥajj(a), fa yassirhumā lī wa taqabbalhumā minnī.

O Allāh, verily I desire to perform *ḥajj* and *ʿumra*, so make the two easy for me and accept them both from me.

For *ʿumra* alone (*ḥajj tamattuʿ* or *ʿumra*):

اَللّٰهُمَّ إِنِّيْ أُرِيْدُ الْعُمْرَةَ، فَيَسِّرْهَا لِيْ وَتَقَبَّلْهَا مِنِّيْ.

Allāhumma innī urīdu 'l-ʿumra(ta), fa yassirhā lī wa taqabbalhā minnī.

O Allāh, verily I desire to perform *ʿumra*, so make it easy for me and accept it from me.

The *talbiya*, which immediately follows either one of the above supplications:

لَبَّيْكَ اللّٰهُمَّ لَبَّيْكَ، [لَبَّيْكَ] لَا شَرِيْكَ لَكَ لَبَّيْكَ، إِنَّ الْحَمْدَ وَالنِّعْمَةَ لَكَ وَالْمُلْكَ، لَا شَرِيْكَ لَكَ.

Labbayka 'Llāhumma labbayk(a), [labbayka] lā sharīka laka labbayk(a), inna 'l-ḥamda wa 'n-niʿmata laka wa 'l-mulk(a), lā sharīka lak(a).

Here I am at Your service, O Allāh, at Your service! [At Your service!] You have no partner; here I am at Your service! Indeed, all praise, blessings, and the dominion itself are utterly Yours; You have no partner!

One may add if he wishes:

لَبَّيْكَ وَسَعْدَيْكَ، وَالْخَيْرُ كُلُّهُ بِيَدَيْكَ.

Labbayka wa saʿdayk(a), wa 'l-khayru kulluhū bi yadayk(a).

At Your service! At Your obedience! All good is in Your hands!

From Imām Mawṣilī's Ikhtiyār (1:208–21)
It is recommended (*mustaḥābb*) to say when entering Makka:

اَللّٰهُمَّ هٰذَا حَرَمُكَ وَمَأْمَنُكَ. اَللّٰهُمَّ إِنَّكَ قُلْتَ وَقَوْلُكَ الْحَقُّ ﴿وَمَنْ دَخَلَهُ كَانَ اٰمِنًا﴾. اَللّٰهُمَّ حَرِّمْ لَحْمِيْ وَدَمِيْ عَلَى النَّارِ، وَقِنِيْ عَذَابَكَ يَوْمَ تَبْعَثُ عِبَادَكَ.

Allāhumma hādhā ḥaramuka wa ma'manuk(a). Allāhumma innaka qulta wa qawluka 'l-ḥaqq(u), "Wa man dakhalahū kāna āminan." Allāhumma ḥarrim laḥmī wa damī ʿalā 'n-nār(i), wa qinī ʿadhābaka yawma tabʿathu ʿibādak(a).

O Allāh, this is Your sacred precinct and Your sanctuary. O Allāh, verily You have said, and Your statements are true, "Whoever enters it will be protected." O Allāh, safeguard my flesh and my blood from the Fire, and protect me from Your punishment on the day that You resurrect Your servants.

When entering the Sacred Mosque, one says:

بِسْمِ اللهِ وَعَلٰى مِلَّةِ رَسُوْلِ اللهِ. اَلْحَمْدُ لِلّٰهِ الَّذِيْ بَلَّغَنِيْ بَيْتَهُ الْحَرَامَ. اَللّٰهُمَّ افْتَحْ لِيْ أَبْوَابَ رَحْمَتِكَ وَمَغْفِرَتِكَ، وَأَدْخِلْنِيْ فِيْهَا، وَأَغْلِقْ عَنِّيْ أَبْوَابَ مَعَاصِيْكَ، وَجَنِّبْنِي الْعَمَلَ بِهَا.

Bismi 'Llāhi wa ʿalā millati rasūli 'Llāh(i). Al-ḥamdu li 'Llāhi 'lladhī ballaghanī baytahu 'l-ḥarām(a). Allāhumma 'ftaḥ lī abwāba raḥmatika wa maghfiratik(a), wa adkhilnī fīhā, wa aghliq ʿannī abwāba maʿāṣīk(a), wa jannibni 'l-ʿamala bihā.

In the name of Allāh, and upon the way of the Messenger of Allāh ﷺ. All praise is due to Allāh, who caused me to arrive at His sacred house. O Allāh, open for me the doors of Your mercy and forgiveness, and let me enter them; and close upon me the doors of disobedience to You, and keep me away from engaging in such acts.

It is recommended (*mustaḥābb*) to say:

اَللهُ أَكْبَرُ اللهُ أَكْبَرُ. اَللّٰهُمَّ أَنْتَ السَّلَامُ وَمِنْكَ السَّلَامُ، حَيِّنَا رَبَّنَا بِالسَّلَامِ، وَأَدْخِلْنَا دَارَ السَّلَامِ. اَللّٰهُمَّ زِدْ بَيْتَكَ هٰذَا تَشْرِيْفًا وَّمَهَابَةً وَّتَعْظِيْمًا. اَللّٰهُمَّ تَقَبَّلْ تَوْبَتِيْ وَأَقِلْنِيْ عَثْرَتِيْ، وَاغْفِرْ لِيْ خَطِيْئَتِيْ، يَا حَنَّانُ يَا مَنَّانُ.

Allāhu akbar Allāhu akbar(u). Allāhumma Anta 's-Salāmu wa minka 's-salām(u), ḥayyinā Rabbanā bi 's-salām(i), wa adkhilnā dāra 's-salām(i). Allāhumma zid baytaka hādhā tashrīfaw wa mahābataw wa taʿẓīman. Allāhumma taqabbal tawbatī wa aqilnī ʿathratī, wa 'ghfir lī khaṭī'atī, yā Ḥannānu yā Mannān(u).

Allāh is the greatest, Allāh is the greatest. O Allāh, You are peace, and from You is peace; cause us to live in peace, our Lord, and let us enter the abode of peace. O Allāh, increase this house of Yours in honor, majesty, and veneration. O Allāh, accept my repentance, and regard my offense as undone; forgive me for my error, O Compassionate, O Benefactor.

When greeting the black stone, it is recommended (*mustaḥābb*) to say:

اَللهُ أَكْبَرُ اللهُ أَكْبَرُ. اَللّٰهُمَّ إِيْمَانًا بِكَ وَتَصْدِيْقًا بِكِتَابِكَ وَوَفَاءً بِعَهْدِكَ وَاتِّبَاعًا لِّنَبِيِّكَ. أَشْهَدُ أَنْ لَّا إِلٰهَ إِلَّا اللهُ وَحْدَهُ لَا شَرِيْكَ لَهُ، وَأَشْهَدُ أَنَّ مُحَمَّدًا عَبْدُهُ وَرَسُوْلُهُ. أٰمَنْتُ بِاللهِ وَكَفَرْتُ بِالْجِبْتِ وَالطَّاغُوْتِ.

Allāhu akbaru Allāhu akbar(u). Allāhumma īmānam bika wa taṣdīqam bikitābika wa wafā'am bi ʿahdika wa 'ttibāʿal li nabiyyik(a). Ashhadu al lā ilāha illa 'Llāhu waḥdahū lā sharīka lah(ū), wa ashhadu anna Muḥammadan ʿabduhū wa rasūluh(ū). Āmantu bi 'Llāhi wa kafartu bi 'l-jibti wa 'ṭ-ṭāghūt(i).

Allāh is the greatest, Allāh is the greatest. O Allāh, out of faith in You, conviction in Your book, maintaining Your covenant, and in accordance with Your Prophet ﷺ. I testify that there is no deity except Allāh, alone, without partner, and I testify that Muḥammad ﷺ is His servant and His Messenger; I believe in Allāh, and I reject idols and false deities.

When beginning *ṭawāf*, one says:

سُبْحَانَ اللهِ وَالْحَمْدُ لِلهِ وَلَا إِلٰهَ إِلَّا اللهُ وَاللهُ أَكْبَرُ. اَللّٰهُمَّ أَعِذْنِيْ مِنْ أَهْوَالِ يَوْمِ الْقِيَامَةِ.

Subḥāna 'Llāhī wa 'l-ḥamdu li 'Llāhī wa lā ilāha illa 'Llāhu wa 'Llāhu akbar(u). Allāhumma aʿidhnī min ahwāli yawmi 'l-qiyāma(ti).

Glory be to Allāh; all praise is due to Allāh; there is no deity except Allāh; Allāh is the greatest. O Allāh, give me refuge from the terrors of the Day of Resurrection.

It is recommended (*mustaḥābb*) to say the following at the Iraqi corner:

اَللّٰهُمَّ إِنِّيْ أَعُوْذُ بِكَ مِنَ الشِّرْكِ وَالْكُفْرِ وَالنِّفَاقِ وَسُوْءِ الْأَخْلَاقِ.

Allāhumma innī aʿūdhu bika mina 'sh-shirki wa 'l-kufri wa 'n-nifāqi wa sū'i 'l-akhlāq(i).

O Allāh, verily I seek refuge in You from polytheism, disbelief, hypocrisy, and bad character.

At the water sprout (*mīzāb*):

اَللّٰهُمَّ اسْقِنِيْ بِكَأْسِ نَبِيِّكَ مُحَمَّدٍ ﷺ شَرْبَةً لَّا أَظْمَأُ بَعْدَهَا.

Allāhumma 'sqinī bi ka'si nabiyyika Muḥammadin ﷺ shurbatal lā aẓma'u baʿdahā.

O Allāh, let me drink from the cup of Your Prophet Muḥammad ﷺ one sip, after which I am never thirsty again.

At the Syrian (Shāmī) corner:

اَللّٰهُمَّ اجْعَلْهُ حَجًّا مَّبْرُوْرًا وَّسَعْيًا مَّشْكُوْرًا وَّذَنْبًا مَّغْفُوْرًا وَّتِجَارَةً لَّنْ تَبُوْرَ، بِرَحْمَتِكَ يَا عَزِيْزُ يَا غَفُوْرُ.

Allāhumma 'jʿalhū ḥajjam mabrūraw wa saʿyam mashkūraw wa dhambam maghfūraw wa tijāratal lan tabūr(a), bi raḥmatika yā ʿAzīzu yā Ghafūr(u).

O Allāh, make it an accepted pilgrimage, a rewarded effort; [make] my sins forgiven, and [make it] a trade that is not failing; by Your mercy, O Most Merciful of those who show mercy.

At the Yemeni corner:

اَللّٰهُمَّ إِنِّيْ أَعُوْذُ بِكَ مِنْ عَذَابِ الْقَبْرِ وَفِتْنَةِ الْمَحْيَا وَالْمَمَاتِ.

Allāhumma innī aʿūdhu bika min ʿadhābi 'l-qabri wa fitnati 'l-maḥyā wa 'l-mamāt(i).

O Allāh, verily I seek refuge in You from the punishment of the grave, and [from] tribulation in life and [in] death.

Immediately after the two *rakʿas* of *ṭawāf*, one says:

اَللّٰهُمَّ هٰذَا مَقَامُ الْعَائِذِ بِكَ مِنَ النَّارِ، فَاغْفِرْ لِيْ ذُنُوْبِيْ، إِنَّكَ أَنْتَ الْغَفُوْرُ الرَّحِيْمُ.

Allāhumma hādhā maqāmu ’l-ʿā’idhi bika mina ’n-nār(i), fa ’ghfir lī dhunūbī, innaka Anta ’l-Ghafūru ’r-Raḥīm(u).

O Allāh, this is the station of the one who seeks refuge in You from the Fire, so forgive me for my sins; verily, You are All-Forgiving, Ever-Merciful.

It is recommended to say when heading for Ṣafā:

بِسْمِ اللهِ وَالصَّلَاةُ عَلٰى رَسُوْلِ اللهِ ﷺ. اَللّٰهُمَّ افْتَحْ لِيْ أَبْوَابَ رَحْمَتِكَ وَأَدْخِلْنِيْ فِيْهَا.

Bismillāhi wa ’ṣ-ṣalātu ʿalā rasūli ’Llāh(ī) ﷺ. Allāhumma ’ftaḥ lī abwāba raḥmatika wa adkhilnī fīhā.

In the Name of Allāh, and may blessings be upon the Messenger of Allāh ﷺ. O Allāh, open for me doors of Your mercy, and let me enter them.

On Ṣafā, one says:

اَللهُ أَكْبَرُ اَللهُ أَكْبَرُ، لَا إِلٰهَ إِلَّا اللهُ وَحْدَهُ لَا شَرِيْكَ لَهُ، لَهُ الْمُلْكُ وَلَهُ الْحَمْدُ، يُحْيِيْ وَيُمِيْتُ وَهُوَ حَيٌّ لَّا يَمُوْتُ، بِيَدِهِ الْخَيْرُ وَهُوَ عَلٰى كُلِّ شَيْءٍ قَدِيْرٌ. لَا إِلٰهَ إِلَّا اللهُ، وَلَا نَعْبُدُ إِلَّا إِيَّاهُ، مُخْلِصِيْنَ لَهُ الدِّيْنَ وَلَوْ كَرِهَ الْكَافِرُوْنَ. لَا إِلٰهَ إِلَّا اللهُ أَهْلُ التَّكْبِيْرِ وَالتَّحْمِيْدِ وَالتَّهْلِيْلِ. لَا إِلٰهَ إِلَّا اللهُ وَحْدَهُ، أَنْجَزَ وَعْدَهُ، وَنَصَرَ عَبْدَهُ، وَهَزَمَ الْأَحْزَابَ وَحْدَهُ، فَلَهُ الْمُلْكُ وَلَهُ الْحَمْدُ.

Allāhu akbar Allāhu akbar, lā ilāha illa ’Llāhu waḥdahū lā sharīka lah(ū), lahu ’l-mulku wa lahu ’l-ḥamd(u), yuḥyī wa yumīt(u), wa Huwa ḥayyul lā yamūt(u), bi yadihi ’l-khayru wa Huwa ʿalā kulli shay’in qadīr(un). Lā ilāha illa ’Llāh(u), wa lā naʿbudu illā iyyāh(u), mukhliṣīna lahu ’d-dīna wa law kariha ’l-kāfirūn(a). Lā ilāha illa ’Llāhu Ahlu ’t-takbīri wa ’t-taḥmīdi wa ’t-tahlīl(i). Lā ilāha illa ’Llāhu waḥdah(ū), anjaza waʿdah(ū), wa naṣara ʿabdah(ū), wa hazama ’l-aḥzāba waḥdah(ū), fa lahu ’l-mulku wa lahu ’l-ḥamd(u).

Allāh is the greatest, Allāh is the greatest. There is no deity except Allāh, alone, without partner; for Him [alone] is the dominion, and for Him [alone] is all praise; He gives life and He give death, while He is Ever-Living and never dies; in His hand is all good, and He is able to do all things. There is no deity except Allāh; we do not worship other than Him, practicing the religion in full sincerity, even if the disbelievers despise it. There is no deity except Allāh, who is worthy of magnification, praise, and declaring His oneness. There is no deity except Allāh, alone; He fulfilled His promise, gave victory to His servant, destroyed the confederates alone; so for Him is the dominion, and for Him is all praise.

Then one asks for all of his needs to be fulfilled.

When descending from Ṣafā, one says:

اَللّٰهُمَّ يَسِّرْ لِيْ الْيُسْرٰى، وَجَنِّبْنِي الْعُسْرٰى، وَاغْفِرْ لِيْ فِي الْأٰخِرَةِ وَالْأُوْلٰى.

Allāhumma yassir li 'l-yusrā, wa jannibni 'l-ʿusrā, wa 'ghfir lī fi 'l-ākhirati wa 'l-ūlā.

O Allāh, make good easy for me, and keep me away from evil; forgive me in the next life and in this life.

During the *saʿy*, one says:

رَبِّ اغْفِرْ وَارْحَمْ، وَتَجَاوَزْ عَمَّا تَعْلَمُ، إِنَّكَ أَنْتَ الْأَعَزُّ الْأَكْرَمُ.

Rabbi 'ghfir wa 'rḥam, wa tajāwaz ʿammā taʿlam(u), innaka Anta 'l-Aʿazzu 'l-Akram(u).

My Lord! Forgive and have mercy, and overlook that which You know; verily, You are mightier and more generous.

One does the same on Marwā as on Ṣafā.

Then make much remembrance with the phrases:

سُبْحَانَ اللهِ وَالْحَمْدُ لِلّٰهِ وَلَا إِلٰهَ إِلَّا اللهُ وَاللهُ أَكْبَرُ.

Subḥāna 'Llāhi wa 'l-ḥamdu li 'Llāhi wa lā ilāha illa 'Llāhu wa 'Llāhu akbar(u).

Glory be to Allāh; all praise is due to Allāh; there is no deity except Allāh; Allāh is the greatest.

Upon arriving in Minā, one says:

اَللّٰهُمَّ هٰذِهِ مِنًى، وَهِيَ مِمَّا مَنَنْتَ بِهَا عَلَيْنَا مِنَ الْمَنَاسِكِ، فَامْنُنْ عَلَيَّ بِمَا مَنَنْتَ بِهِ عَلٰى عِبَادِكَ الصَّالِحِيْنَ.

Allāhumma hādhihī Minā, wa hiya mimmā mananta bihā ʿalaynā mina 'l-manāsik(i), fa 'mnun ʿalayya bimā mananta bihī ʿalā ʿibādika 'ṣ-ṣāliḥīn(a).

O Allāh, this is Minā, and she is of the rites that You have bestowed upon us; so bestow upon me that which You bestowed upon Your righteous servants.

At ʿArafāt, it is recommended that one recite Sūrat al-Fātiḥa and al-Ikhlāṣ ten times after the prayers (ẓuhr and ʿaṣr), and then say:

لَا إِلٰهَ إِلَّا اللهُ وَحْدَهٗ لَا شَرِيْكَ لَهٗ، لَهُ الْمُلْكُ وَلَهُ الْحَمْدُ، يُحْيِي وَيُمِيْتُ، وَهُوَ حَيٌّ لَّا يَمُوْتُ، بِيَدِهِ الْخَيْرُ وَهُوَ عَلٰى كُلِّ شَيْءٍ قَدِيْرٌ. سُبْحَانَ اللهِ وَالْحَمْدُ للهِ وَلَا إِلٰهَ إِلَّا اللهُ وَاللهُ أَكْبَرُ، وَلَا حَوْلَ وَلَا قُوَّةَ إِلَّا بِاللهِ الْعَلِيِّ الْعَظِيْمِ. يَا رَفِيْعَ الدَّرَجَاتِ، يَا مُنَزِّلَ الْبَرَكَاتِ، يَا فَاطِرَ الْأَرَضِيْنَ وَالسَّمٰوَاتِ، ضَجَّتْ لَكَ الْأَصْوَاتُ بِصُنُوْفِ اللُّغَاتِ تَسْأَلُكَ الْحَاجَاتِ، وَحَاجَتِيْ أَنْ تَرْحَمَنِيْ فِيْ دَارِ الْبَلَاءِ إِذَا نَسِيَنِيْ أَهْلُ الدُّنْيَا. أَسْأَلُكَ أَنْ تُوَفِّقَنِيْ لِمَا افْتَرَضْتَ عَلَيَّ، وَتُعِيْنَنِيْ عَلٰى طَاعَتِكَ وَأَدَاءِ حَقِّكَ وَقَضَاءِ الْمَنَاسِكِ الَّتِيْ أَرَيْتَهَا خَلِيْلَكَ إِبْرَاهِيْمَ عَلَيْهِ الصَّلَاةُ وَالسَّلَامُ، وَدَلَلْتَ عَلَيْهَا مُحَمَّدًا حَبِيْبَكَ ﷺ. اَللّٰهُمَّ لِكُلِّ مُتَضَرِّعٍ إِلَيْكَ إِجَابَةٌ وَّلِكُلِّ مِسْكِيْنٍ لَّدَيْكَ رَأْفَةٌ، وَّقَدْ جِئْتُكَ مُتَضَرِّعًا إِلَيْكَ مِسْكِيْنًا لَّدَيْكَ، فَاقْضِ حَاجَتِيْ وَاغْفِرْ ذُنُوْبِيْ، وَلَا تَجْعَلْنِيْ مِنْ أَخْيَبِ وَفْدِكَ، وَقَدْ قُلْتَ وَأَنْتَ لَا تُخْلِفُ الْمِيْعَادَ ﴿ادْعُوْنِيْ أَسْتَجِبْ لَكُمْ﴾، وَقَدْ دَعَوْتُكَ مُتَضَرِّعًا سَائِلًا، فَأَجِبْ دُعَائِيْ وَأَعْتِقْنِيْ مِنَ النَّارِ وَلِوَالِدَيَّ وَلِجَمِيْعِ الْمُسْلِمِيْنَ وَالْمُسْلِمَاتِ، بِرَحْمَتِكَ يَا أَرْحَمَ الرَّاحِمِيْنَ.

Lā ilāha illa ’Llāhu waḥdahū lā sharīka lah(ū), lahu ’l-mulku wa lahu ’l-ḥamd(u), yuḥyī wa yumīt(u), wa Huwa ḥayyul lā yamūt(u), bi yadihi ’l-khayru wa Huwa ʿalā kulli shay’in qadīr(un). Subḥāna ’Llāhi wa ’l-ḥamdu li ’Llāhi wa lā ilāha illa ’Llāhu wa ’Llāhu akbar(u), wa lā ḥawla wa lā quwwata illā bi ’Llāhi ’l-ʿAlīyyi ’l-ʿAẓīm(i). Yā Rafīʿa ’d-darajāt(i), yā Munazzila ’l-barakāt(i), yā Fāṭira ’l-araḍīna wa ’s-samāwāt(i), ḍajjat laka ’l-aṣwātu bi ṣunūfi ’l-lughāti tas’aluka ’l-ḥājāt(i), wa ḥājatī an tarḥamanī fī dāri ’l-balā’i idhā nasiyanī ahlu ’d-dunyā. As’aluka an tuwaffiqanī lima ’ftaraḍta ʿalayy(a), wa tuʿīnanī ʿalā ṭāʿatika wa adā’i ḥaqqika wa qaḍā’i ’l-manāsiki ’llatī araytahā Khalīlaka Ibrāhīma ʿalayhi ’ṣ-ṣalātu wa ’s-salām(u), wa dalalta ʿalayhā Muḥammadan ḥabībaka ﷺ. Allāhumma li kulli mutaḍarriʿin ilayka ijābatuw wa li kulli miskīnil ladayka raʿfatun, wa qad ji’tuka mutaḍarriʿan ilayka miskīnal ladayk(a), fa ’qḍi ḥājatī wa ’ghfir dhunūbī, wa lā tajʿalnī min akhyabi wafdik(a), wa qad qulta wa Anta lā tukhlifu ’l-mīʿād(a), “Udʿūnī astajiblakum,” wa qad daʿawtuka mutaḍarriʿan sā’ilan, fa ajib duʿā’ī wa aʿtiqnī mina ’n-nār(i), wa li wālidayya wa li jamīʿi ’l-muslimīna wa ’l-muslimāt(i), bi raḥmatika yā Arḥama ’r-rāḥimīn(a).

There is no deity except Allāh, alone, without partner; for Him alone is the dominion, and for Him alone is all praise; He gives life and He give death, while He is Ever-Living and never dies; in His hand is all good, and He is able to do all things. Glory be to Allāh; all praise is due to Allāh; there is no deity except Allāh; Allāh is the greatest; there is no might nor power except with Allāh, the Most High, thc Greatest. O Raiser of degrees; O One who sends down blessings; O Originator of the earths and the heavens! Voices in all languages are crying out, asking You for all needs, and my need is that You show me mercy in the abode of trials, when the people of this life forget me. I ask You to enable me to perform what You made obligatory on me, and to help me obey You and fulfill Your rights, and to carry out the rites that You showed to Your Intimate Friend Ibrāhīm, upon whom be blessings and peace, and that You indicated to Your Beloved Muḥammad ﷺ. O Allāh, for everyone who pleads to You is an answer, and for every poor person with You is kindness, and I have come to You pleading to You and poor in Your presence, so fulfill my need and forgive my sins, and do not make me from the most unsuccessful of Your delegation. You have indeed said, and You do not break promises, "Call on me—I will answer you," and I have called on You, pleading and asking, so answer my call, and save me from the Fire, as well as my parents, and all Muslim men and women. By Your mercy, O Most Merciful of those who show mercy.

It is recommended to say the following at sunset before leaving ʿArafāt:

اَللّٰهُمَّ لَا تَجْعَلْهُ أٰخِرَ الْعَهْدِ بِهٰذَا الْمَوْقِفِ، وَارْزُقْنِيْهِ مَا أَبْقَيْتَنِيْ، وَاجْعَلِ الْيَوْمَ مُفْلِحًا مَّرْحُوْمًا مُّسْتَجَابًا دُعَائِيْ مَغْفُوْرًا ذُنُوْبِيْ، يَا أَرْحَمَ الرَّاحِمِيْنَ.

Allāhumma lā tajʿalhū ākhira 'l-ʿahdi bi hādha 'l-mawqif(i), wa 'rzuqnīhi mā abqaytanī, wa 'jʿali 'l-yawma mufliḥam marḥūmam mustajāban duʿā'ī maghfūran dhunūbī, yā Arḥama 'r-rāḥimīn(a).

O Allāh, do not make this the last appointment at this place; bestow it upon me as long as You give me life. Make today successful, full of mercy; my call answered and my sins forgiven, O Most Merciful of those who show mercy.

One should seek much forgiveness.

It is recommended to say the following when arriving at Muzdalifa:

اَللّٰهُمَّ هٰذِهِ مُزْدَلِفَةٌ وَجَمْعٌ، أَسْأَلُكَ أَنْ تَرْزُقَنِيْ جَوَامِعَ الْخَيْرِ، وَاجْعَلْنِيْ مِمَّنْ سَأَلَكَ فَأَعْطَيْتَهٗ، وَدَعَاكَ فَأَجَبْتَهٗ، وَتَوَكَّلَ عَلَيْكَ فَكَفَيْتَهٗ، وَأٰمَنَ بِكَ فَهَدَيْتَهٗ.

Allāhumma hādhihī Muzdalifatuw wa jamʿ(un), as'aluka an tarzuqanī jawāmiʿa 'l-khayr(i), wa 'jʿalnī mimman sa'alaka fa aʿṭaytah(ū), wa da'āka fa ajabtah(ū), wa tawakkala ʿalayka fa kafaytah(ū), wa āmana bika fa hadaytah(ū).

O Allāh, this is Muzdalifa and a gathering place. I ask You to provide me with collective forms of goodness. Make me of those who ask You and You grant them; who call upon You and You answer them; who rely on You and You suffice them; who believe in You and You guide them.

After completing maghrib and ʿishā' there, one says:

اَللّٰهُمَّ حَرِّمْ لَحْمِيْ وَشَعْرِيْ وَدَمِيْ وَعَظْمِيْ وَجَمِيْعَ جَوَارِحِيْ عَلَى النَّارِ، يَا أَرْحَمَ الرَّاحِمِيْنَ.

Allāhumma ḥarrim laḥmī wa shaʿrī wa damī wa ʿaẓmī wa jamīʿa jawāriḥī ʿala 'n-nār(i), yā Arḥama 'r-rāḥimīn(a).

O Allāh, make my flesh, my hair, my blood, my bones, and all of my limbs forbidden for the Fire; O Most Merciful of those who show mercy.

One should specifically ask Allāh Most High to make his enemies pleased with him, for verily Allāh has promised that for one who asks it in this night.

It is recommended to stop after fajr with the imām and supplicate. It is recommended that one recite *takbīr*, *tahlīl*, *talbiya*, and say:

اَللّٰهُمَّ أَنْتَ خَيْرُ مَطْلُوْبٍ وَّخَيْرُ مَرْغُوْبٍ إِلَيْهِ، إِلٰهِيْ لِكُلِّ وَفْدٍ جَائِزَةٌ وَّقِرًى، فَاجْعَلِ اللّٰهُمَّ جَائِزَتِيْ وَقِرَايَ فِيْ هٰذَا الْمَقَامِ أَنْ تَتَقَبَّلَ تَوْبَتِيْ، وَتَتَجَاوَزَ عَنْ خَطِيْئَتِيْ، وَتَجْمَعَ عَلَى الْهُدٰى أَمْرِيْ، وَتَجْعَلَ الْيَقِيْنَ مِنَ الدُّنْيَا هَمِّيْ. اَللّٰهُمَّ ارْحَمْنِيْ وَأَجِرْنِيْ مِنَ النَّارِ، وَأَوْسِعْ عَلَيَّ الرِّزْقَ الْحَلَالَ. اَللّٰهُمَّ لَا تَجْعَلْهُ أٰخِرَ الْعَهْدِ بِهٰذَا الْمَوْقِفِ، وَارْزُقْنِيْهِ أَبَدًا مَّا أَحْيَيْتَنِيْ، بِرَحْمَتِكَ يَا أَرْحَمَ الرَّاحِمِيْنَ.

Allāhumma Anta khayru maṭlūbiw wa khayru marghūbin ilayh(ī), Ilāhī li kulli wafdin jā'izatuw wa qiran, fa 'jʿali 'Llāhumma jā'izatī wa qirāya fī hādha 'l-maqāmi an tataqabbala tawbatī, wa tatajāwaza ʿan khaṭī'atī, wa tajmaʿa ʿala 'l-hudā amrī, wa tajʿala 'l-yaqīna mina 'd-dunyā hammī. Allāhumma 'rḥamnī wa ajirnī mina 'n-nār(i), wa awsiʿ ʿalayya 'r-rizqa 'l-ḥalāl(a). Allāhumma lā tajʿalhū ākhira 'l-ʿahdi bi hādha 'l-mawqif(i), wa 'rzuqnīhi abadam mā aḥyaytanī, bi raḥmatika yā Arḥama 'r-rāḥimīn(a).

O Allāh, You are the best of those sought, and the best of those desired. My Lord, for every delegation is a prize and a hospitable reception; so make my prize and my hospitable reception, O Allāh, in this station, that You accept my repentance, overlook my faults, gather my affair upon guidance, make my concern having certitude in this life. O Allāh, have mercy on me and save me from the Fire, and make lawful provisions expansive for me. O Allāh, do not make it the last appointment in this place, and bestow it upon me as long as You give me life. By Your mercy, O Most Merciful of those who show mercy.

When stoning, one says (with each throw):

بِسْمِ اللهِ وَاللهُ أَكْبَرُ.

Bismi 'Llāhi wa 'Llāhu akbar(u). In the Name of Allāh; Allāh is the greatest.

This is to spite the devil and his followers.

It is recommended to say when shaving (or trimming):

اَللّٰهُمَّ هٰذِهِ نَاصِيَتِيْ بِيَدِكَ، فَاجْعَلْ لِّيْ بِكُلِّ شَعْرَةٍ نُّوْرًا يَّوْمَ الْقِيَامَةِ، يَا أَرْحَمَ الرَّاحِمِيْنَ.

Allāhumma hādhihī nāṣiyatī biyadik(a), fa 'jʿal lī bikulli shaʿratin nūray yawma 'l-qiyāma(ti), yā Arḥama 'r-rāḥimīn(a).

O Allāh, this is my forelock, in Your hand; so make for me, for every strand of hair, a light on the Day of Resurrection. O Most Merciful of those who show mercy.

It is narrated on Abū Yūsuf that one should also say:

اَللّٰهُمَّ اجْعَلْهُ حَجًّا مَّبْرُوْرًا وَّذَنْبًا مَّغْفُوْرًا. اَللّٰهُمَّ إِلَيْكَ أَفَضْتُ، وَمِنْ عَذَابِكَ أَشْفَقْتُ، وَإِلَيْكَ رَغِبْتُ، وَمِنْكَ رَهِبْتُ، فَاقْبَلْ نُسُكِيْ، وَعَظِّمْ أَجْرِيْ، وَارْحَمْ تَضَرُّعِيْ، وَاقْبَلْ تَوْبَتِيْ، وَاسْتَجِبْ دَعْوَتِيْ، وَأَعْطِنِيْ سُؤْلِيْ.

Allāhumma 'jʿalhu ḥajjam mabrūraw wa dhambam maghfūra(n). Allāhumma ilayka afaḍt(u), wa min ʿadhābika ashfaqt(u), wa ilayka raghibt(u), wa minka rahibt(u), fa 'qbal nusukī, wa ʿaẓẓim ajrī, wa 'rḥam taḍarruʿī, wa 'qbal tawbatī, wa 'stajib daʿwatī, wa aʿṭinī su'lī.

O Allāh, make it an accepted pilgrimage, sins forgiven. O Allāh, to You do I journey; Your punishment do I fear; You alone do I desire; and You alone do I have awe of. So accept my rites; make my reward immense; have mercy on my pleading; accept my repentance; answer my call; and grant me my request.

When drinking zamzam, it is recommended that one breathe in the vessel three times, and with each sip look upon the Sacred House and say:

بِسْمِ اللهِ وَالْحَمْدُ لِلّٰهِ وَالصَّلَاةُ عَلٰى رَسُوْلِ اللهِ.

Bismi 'Llāhi wa 'l-ḥamdu li 'Llāhi wa 'ṣ-ṣalātu ʿalā rasūli 'Llāh(i).

In the Name of Allāh; all praise is due to Allāh, and may blessings be upon the Messenger of Allāh.

And then with the last sip, one says:

اَللّٰهُمَّ إِنِّي أَسْأَلُكَ رِزْقًا وَّاسِعًا وَّعِلْمًا نَّافِعًا وَّشِفَاءً مِّنْ كُلِّ دَاءٍ وَّسَقَمٍ، يَا أَرْحَمَ الرَّاحِمِيْنَ.

Allāhumma innī as'aluka rizqaw wāsiʿaw wa ʿilman nāfiʿaw wa shifā'am min kulli dā'iw wa saqam(iy), yā Arḥama 'r-rāḥimīn(a).

O Allāh, verily I ask You for expansive provisions, beneficial knowledge, and a cure for every illness and disease; O Most Merciful of those who show mercy.

One also cries, or at least pretends to cry, as that is a sign of acceptance.

It is recommended to say at the final departure:

اَللّٰهُمَّ هٰذَا بَيْتُكَ الَّذِيْ جَعَلْتَهُ مُبَارَكًا وَّهُدًى لِّلْعَالَمِيْنَ، فِيْهِ اٰيَاتٌ بَيِّنَاتٌ مَّقَامُ إِبْرَاهِيْمَ، وَمَنْ دَخَلَهُ كَانَ اٰمِنًا. اَلْحَمْدُ لِلّٰهِ الَّذِيْ هَدَانَا لِهٰذَا وَمَا كُنَّا لِنَهْتَدِيَ لَوْلَا أَنْ هَدَانَا اللّٰهُ. اَللّٰهُمَّ فَكَمَا هَدَيْتَنَا لِذٰلِكَ فَتَقَبَّلْهُ مِنَّا، وَلَا تَجْعَلْهُ اٰخِرَ الْعَهْدِ مِنْ بَيْتِكَ الْحَرَامِ، وَارْزُقْنِيْ الْعَوْدَ إِلَيْهِ حَتّٰى تَرْضٰى عَنِّيْ، بِرَحْمَتِكَ يَا أَرْحَمَ الرَّاحِمِيْنَ.

Allāhumma hādhā baytuka 'lladhī jaʿaltahū mubārakaw wa hudal li 'l-ʿālamīn(a), fīhi āyātum bayyinātum maqāmu Ibrāhīm(a), wa man dakhalahū kāna āminan. Al-ḥamdu li 'Llāhi 'lladhī hadānā li hādhā wa mā kunnā li nahtadiya lawlā an hadāna 'Llāh(u). Allāhumma fakamā hadaytanā li dhālika fa taqabbalhū minnā, wa lā tajʿalhū ākhira 'l-ʿahdi mim baytika 'l-ḥarām(i), wa 'rzuqni 'l-ʿawda ilayhi ḥattā tarḍā ʿannī, bi raḥmatika yā Arḥama 'r-rāḥimīn(a).

O Allāh, this is Your house that You have made blessed and a guidance for all the worlds; in it are clear signs, and the station of Ibrāhīm ﵇; whoever enters it is protected. All praise is due to Allāh, who guided us to this, and we would not have been guided had Allāh not guided us. O Allāh, just as You guided us to this, accept it from us, and do not make it the last appointment at Your sacred house. Provide me with a return to it, such that You are pleased with me; by Your mercy, O Most Merciful of those who show mercy.

Appendix 2

Visiting the Messenger ﷺ

From Imām Mawṣilī's *Ikhtiyār* (1:247–51)

Because according to traditional custom, pilgrims, after having completed their ceremonial rites and departed from the sacred precinct, set off to Madīna to visit the Prophet's grave ﷺ[711]—as it is of the best recommended acts, indeed, it approximates the level of mandatory acts, for he ﷺ strongly encouraged it and emphasized the recommendation to perform it, saying, "Whoever has the ability yet does not visit me has indeed turned away from me," as well as, "Whoever visits my grave, my intercession is incumbent for him," and "Whoever visits me after my death, it is as if he has visited me during my life," and other ḥadīths—and [because] I found most people to be unaware of its etiquette and recommendations, ignorant of its legal issues and particulars—I desired to devote a section to it in this book, after the [section on] ceremonial rites, to mention therein a portion of its etiquette. So I note:

Whoever departs to visit the grave of our liegelord, the Prophet ﷺ, should send abundant blessings upon him ﷺ, as it is narrated in a ḥadīth that they are sent forth to him and reach him. When he sees the wall of Madīna, he should send blessings upon him ﷺ and say:

اَللّٰهُمَّ هٰذَا حَرَمُ نَبِيِّكَ، فَاجْعَلْهُ وِقَايَةً لِّيْ مِنَ النَّارِ، وَأَمَانًا مِّنَ الْعَذَابِ وَسُوْءِ الْحِسَابِ.

Allāhumma hādhā ḥaramu nabiyyik(a), fa 'jʿalhū wiqāyatal lī mina 'n-nār(i), wa amānam mina 'l-ʿadhābi wa sū'i 'l-ḥisāb(i).

---

711 One also intends visiting his mosque ﷺ (*Durr* 2:257). This ruling—that visiting the Prophet's grave ﷺ is recommended—is established by scholarly consensus (*ijmāʿ*) of the Muslims. Moreover, the sound position (*ṣaḥīḥ*) regarding women visiting his grave ﷺ is that it is also recommended, not being disliked at all (*Radd* 2:257).

O Allāh, this is the sanctuary of Your Prophet, so make it a protection for me from the Fire, and a safety from punishment and a bad reckoning.

He should perform a purificatory bath (*ghusl*) before entering [the city], or afterwards, if possible; apply scent; and wear his finest clothes, for that is greater in veneration. He should enter it [the city] in a state of humility, tranquility and stillness, and say:

بِسْمِ اللهِ وَعَلٰى مِلَّةِ رَسُوْلِ اللهِ، ﴿رَّبِّ أَدْخِلْنِي مُدْخَلَ صِدْقٍ وَّأَخْرِجْنِي مُخْرَجَ صِدْقٍ وَّاجْعَل لِّي مِن لَّدُنْكَ سُلْطَانًا نَّصِيْرًا﴾، اَللّٰهُمَّ صَلِّ عَلٰى سَيِّدِنَا مُحَمَّدٍ وَّعَلٰى اٰلِ سَيِّدِنَا مُحَمَّدٍ، وَّاغْفِرْ لِيْ ذُنُوْبِيْ، وَافْتَحْ لِيْ أَبْوَابَ رَحْمَتِكَ وَفَضْلِكَ.

Bismi 'Llāhi wa ʿalā millati rasūli 'Llāh(i). "Rabbi adkhilnī mudkhala ṣidqiw wa akhrijnī mukhraja ṣidqiw wa 'jʿal lī mil ladunka sulṭānan naṣīran." Allāhumma ṣalli ʿalā Sayyidinā Muḥammadiw wa ʿalā āli Sayyidinā Muḥammadiw, wa 'ghfirlī dhunūbī, wa 'ftaḥ lī abwāba raḥmatika wa faḍlik(a).

In the Name of Allāh, and on the way of the Messenger of Allāh. "My Lord, let me enter with sincerity, and exit with sincerity, and give me from Thy presence an authority of victory." O Allāh, send blessings upon our Master Muḥammad, and upon the family of our Master Muḥammad; forgive me for my sins; and open for me the doors of Your mercy and grace.

He then enters the mosque and prays two *rakʿas* at his pulpit (*minbar*) ﷺ, standing such that the column of the pulpit is parallel to his [the person's] right shoulder, as that is his [the Prophet's] standing place ﷺ; it is between his grave and his pulpit. He ﷺ said, "Between my grave and my pulpit is a meadow (*rawḍa*) of the meadows of Paradise, and my pulpit is upon my Watering Pool." He then prostrates out of gratitude to Allāh Most High for having enabled him [to come there], and supplicates for whatever he desires.

He then rises and directs himself to his grave ﷺ, stands across his head ﷺ, facing the *qibla*,[712] at a distance of about 1.5–2 meters from him ﷺ, but not closer. He should not place his hand upon the gate in the dirt, as that entails more

712 According to our teacher, Shaykh Aḥmad al-Jammāl, this is incorrect and entails poor etiquette, as the person's back would be toward the Messenger ﷺ. Rather, the person should directly face the Messenger ﷺ, with his back toward the *qibla*. This is supported by the following discussion in Kamāl ibn al-Humām's *Fatḥ al-Qadīr*, "He [the visitor] then comes to the noble grave and faces its wall, with his back toward the *qibla*, approximately two meters from the pillar at the head of the grave, in the corner of the wall. And what is related from Abū 'l-Layth, that one should stand facing the *qibla*, is rejected by what Abū Ḥanīfa ؓ narrates in his *Musnad*, on the authority of Ibn ʿUmar ؓ, that he said, 'It is from the sunna to approach the grave of the Messenger of Allāh

veneration and reverence of [his ﷺ] sanctity. He should stand as he does in the ritual prayer, and should imagine his noble and beautiful form ﷺ, as if he were sleeping in his grave, aware of the visitor and hearing his words. He ﷺ said, "If one sends blessings upon me at my grave, I hear it," and in another narration, "An angel is appointed at his grave ﷺ to relay to him the greetings of one who greets him of his Umma." He should say:

اَلسَّلَامُ عَلَيْكَ يَا رَسُوْلَ اللهِ، اَلسَّلَامُ عَلَيْكَ يَا نَبِيَّ اللهِ، اَلسَّلَامُ عَلَيْكَ يَا صَفِيَّ اللهِ، اَلسَّلَامُ عَلَيْكَ يَا حَبِيْبَ اللهِ، اَلسَّلَامُ عَلَيْكَ يَا نَبِيَّ الرَّحْمَةِ، اَلسَّلَامُ عَلَيْكَ يَا شَفِيْعَ الأُمَّةِ، اَلسَّلَامُ عَلَيْكَ يَا سَيِّدَ الْمُرْسَلِيْنَ، اَلسَّلَامُ عَلَيْكَ يَا خَاتَمَ النَّبِيِّيْنَ، اَلسَّلَامُ عَلَيْكَ يَا مُزَّمِّلُ، اَلسَّلَامُ عَلَيْكَ يَا مُدَّثِّرُ، اَلسَّلَامُ عَلَيْكَ يَا مُحَمَّدُ، اَلسَّلَامُ عَلَيْكَ يَا أَحْمَدُ، اَلسَّلَامُ عَلَيْكَ وَعَلٰى أَهْلِ بَيْتِكَ الطَّيِّبِيْنَ الطَّاهِرِيْنَ الَّذِيْنَ أَذْهَبَ اللهُ عَنْهُمُ الرِّجْسَ وَطَهَّرَهُمْ تَطْهِيْرًا. جَزَاكَ اللهُ عَنَّا أَفْضَلَ مَا جَزٰى نَبِيًّا عَنْ قَوْمِهِ، وَرَسُوْلًا عَنْ أُمَّتِهِ. أَشْهَدُ أَنَّكَ قَدْ بَلَّغْتَ الرِّسَالَةَ، وَأَدَّيْتَ الْأَمَانَةَ، وَنَصَحْتَ الأُمَّةَ، وَأَوْضَحْتَ الْحُجَّةَ، وَجَاهَدْتَ فِيْ سَبِيْلِ اللهِ، وَقَاتَلْتَ عَلٰى دِيْنِ اللهِ حَتّٰى أَتَاكَ الْيَقِيْنُ. فَصَلَّى اللهُ عَلٰى رُوْحِكَ وَجَسَدِكَ وَقَبْرِكَ صَلَاةً دَائِمَةً إِلٰى يَوْمِ الدِّيْنِ. يَا رَسُوْلَ اللهِ، نَحْنُ وَفْدُكَ وَزُوَّارُ قَبْرِكَ، جِئْنَاكَ مِنْ بِلَادٍ شَاسِعَةٍ، وَنَوَاحٍ بَعِيْدَةٍ، قَاصِدِيْنَ قَضَاءَ حَقِّكَ، وَالنَّظَرَ إِلٰى مَأْثِرِكَ، وَالتَّيَامُنَ بِزِيَارَتِكَ، وَالْاِسْتِشْفَاعَ بِكَ إِلٰى رَبِّنَا، فَإِنَّ الْخَطَايَا قَدْ قَصَمَتْ ظُهُوْرَنَا، وَالْأَوْزَارَ قَدْ أَثْقَلَتْ كَوَاهِلَنَا، وَأَنْتَ الشَّافِعُ وَالْمُشَفَّعُ الْمَوْعُوْدُ بِالشَّفَاعَةِ وَالْمَقَامِ الْمَحْمُوْدِ. وَقَدْ قَالَ اللهُ تَعَالَى ﴿وَلَوْ أَنَّهُمْ إِذْ ظَلَمُوْا أَنْفُسَهُمْ جَاءُوْكَ فَاسْتَغْفَرُوْا اللهَ وَاسْتَغْفَرَ لَهُمُ الرَّسُوْلُ لَوَجَدُوا اللهَ تَوَّابًا رَّحِيمًا﴾. وَقَدْ جِئْنَاكَ ظَالِمِيْنَ لِأَنْفُسِنَا، مُسْتَغْفِرِيْنَ لِذُنُوْبِنَا، فَاشْفَعْ لَنَا إِلٰى رَبِّكَ، وَاسْأَلْهُ أَنْ يُمِيْتَنَا عَلٰى سُنَّتِكَ، وَأَنْ يَحْشُرَنَا فِيْ زُمْرَتِكَ، وَأَنْ يُوْرِدَنَا حَوْضَكَ، وَأَنْ يَسْقِيَنَا بِكَأْسِكَ، غَيْرَ خَزَايَا وَلَا نَادِمِيْنَ. اَلشَّفَاعَةَ الشَّفَاعَةَ الشَّفَاعَةَ يَا رَسُوْلَ اللهِ! ﴿رَبَّنَا اغْفِرْ لَنَا وَلِإِخْوَانِنَا الَّذِيْنَ سَبَقُوْنَا بِالْإِيْمَانِ وَلَا تَجْعَلْ فِيْ قُلُوْبِنَا غِلًّا لِّلَّذِيْنَ اٰمَنُوْا رَبَّنَا إِنَّكَ رَؤُوْفٌ رَّحِيمٌ﴾.

As-salāmu ʿalayka yā rasūla ʾLlāh(i), as-salāmu ʿalayka yā nabiyya ʾLlāh(i), as-salāmu ʿalayka yā ṣafiyya ʾLlāh(i), as-salāmu ʿalayka yā ḥabība ʾLlāh(i), as-salāmu ʿalayka yā nabiyya ʾr-raḥma(ti), as-salāmu ʿalayka yā shafīʿa ʾl-umma(ti), as-salāmu

ﷺ from the direction of the *qibla*, and to direct your back toward the *qibla* and your face toward the grave, and to then say: Peace be unto you, O Prophet, and Allāh's mercy and blessings'" (3:95).

ʿalayka yā sayyida 'l-mursalīn(a), as-salāmu ʿalayka yā khātama 'n-nabiyyīn(a), as-salāmu ʿalayka yā muzzammil(u), as-salāmu ʿalayka yā muddaththir(u), as-salāmu ʿalayka yā Muḥammad(u), as-salāmu ʿalayka yā Aḥmad(u), as-salāmu ʿalayka wa ʿalā ahli baytika 'ṭ-ṭayyibīna 'ṭ-ṭāhirīna 'l-ladhīna adhhaba 'Llāhu ʿanhumu 'r-rijsa wa ṭahharahum taṭhīran. Jazāka 'Llāhu ʿannā afḍala mā jazā nabiyyan ʿan qawmih(ī), wa rasūlan ʿan ummatih(ī). Ashhadu annaka qad ballaghta 'r-risāla(ta), wa addayta 'l-amāna(ta), wa naṣaḥta 'l-umma(ta), wa awḍaḥta 'l-ḥujja(ta), wa jāhadta fī sabīli 'Llāh(i), wa qātalta ʿalā dīni 'Llāhi ḥattā atāka 'l-yaqīn(u). Fa ṣalla 'Llāhu ʿalā rūḥika wa jasadika wa qabrika ṣalātan dā'imatan ilā yawmi 'd-dīn(i). Yā rasūla 'Llāh(i), naḥnu wafduka wa zuwwāru qabrik(a), ji'nāka min bilādin shāsiʿa(tin), wa nawāḥin baʿīda(tin), qāṣidīna qaḍā'a ḥaqqik(a), wa 'n-naẓara ilā ma'āthirik(a), wa 't-tayāmuna bi ziyāratik(a), wa 'l-istishfāʿa bika ilā Rabbinā, fa inna 'l-khaṭāyā qad qaṣamat ẓuhūranā, wa 'l-awzāra qad athqalat kawāhilanā, wa anta 'sh-shāfiʿu wa 'l-mushaffaʿu 'l-mawʿūdu bi 'sh-shafāʿati wa 'l-maqāmi 'l-maḥmūd(i). Wa qad qāla 'Llāhu taʿālā "Wa law annahum iẓ ẓalamū anfusahum jā'ūka fa 'staghfaru 'Llāha wa 'staghfara lahumu 'r-rasūlu lawajadu 'Llāha Tawwābar Raḥiman." Wa qad ji'nāka ẓālimīna li anfusinā, mustaghfirīna li dhunūbinā, fa 'shfaʿ lanā ilā Rabbik(a), wa 's'alhu ay yumītanā ʿalā sunnatik(a), wa ay yaḥshuranā fī zumratik(a), wa ay yūridanā ḥawḍak(a), wa ay yasqiyanā bi ka'sik(a), ghayra khazāyā wa lā nādimīn(a). Ash-shafāʿata 'sh-shafāʿata 'sh-shafāʿata yā rasūla 'Llāh(i)! "Rabbana 'ghfirlanā wa li ikhwānina 'l-ladhīna sabaqūnā bi 'l-īmāni wa lā tajʿal fī qulūbinā ghilal li 'l-ladhīna āmanū Rabbanā innaka Ra'ūfur Raḥīm(un)."

Peace be upon you, O Messenger of Allāh. Peace be upon you, O Prophet of Allāh. Peace be upon you, O Pure Selection of Allāh. Peace be upon you, O Beloved of Allāh. Peace be upon you, O Prophet of mercy. Peace be upon you, O Intercessor of the nation. Peace be upon you, O Master of all messengers. Peace be upon you, O Seal of the prophets. Peace be upon you, O Wrapped One. Peace be upon you, O Cloaked One. Peace be upon you, O Muḥammad. Peace be upon you, O Aḥmad. Peace be upon you and upon your family, the wholesome and chaste, those from whom Allāh removed indecency, and made absolutely pure. May Allāh reward you, on our behalf, the best recompense that He rewarded a prophet on behalf of his people, or a messenger on behalf of his nation. I testify that you indeed conveyed the message; fulfilled the trust; gave sincere counsel to the nation; clarified the proof; struggled in the way of Allāh; and fought for the religion of Allāh, until death came to you. So may Allāh send blessings upon your soul, your body, and your grave, forever until the Day of Judgment. O Messenger of Allāh, we are your delegation, and the visitors of your grave. We came to you from far lands and distant corners [of the earth], seeking to fulfill your right, to look upon your traces, to take blessings by

> visiting you, and to seek your intercession with your Lord; for verily sins have broken our backs, and evil has overwhelmed our shoulders, and you are the intercessor, the one granted intercession, the one promised intercession and the praiseworthy station. Allāh has indeed said, "And if only, after having oppressed themselves, they had come to you and sought Allāh's forgiveness, and you had sought forgiveness of their behalf, they would certainly have found Allāh to be Ever-Returning, All-Merciful." And we have come to you having oppressed ourselves, seeking forgiveness for our sins, so intercede with your Lord on our behalf, and ask Him to cause us to die on your sunna, to resurrect us in your company, to let us take water from your Watering Pool, and to let us drink from your cup, without disgrace or remorse. Intercession! Intercession! Intercession! O Messenger of Allāh! "Our Lord, forgive us, and our brethren that preceded us in faith; and place not in our hearts rancor for those who believed. Our Lord! Verily, You are All-Kind, Most-Merciful."

And if someone had requested to convey greetings to the Prophet ﷺ on his behalf, one says:

اَلسَّلَامُ عَلَيْكَ يَا رَسُوْلَ اللهِ مِنْ [فُلَانِ بْنِ فُلَانٍ]، يَّسْتَشْفِعُ بِكَ إِلٰى رَبِّكَ، فَاشْفَعْ لَهٗ وَلِجَمِيْعِ الْمُسْلِمِيْنَ.

As-salāmu ʿalayka yā rasūla 'Llāhi min [fulāni 'bni fulān], yastashfiʿu bika ilā Rabbik(a), fa 'shfaʿ lahū wa li jamīʿi 'l-muslimīn(a).

Peace be upon you, O Messenger of Allāh, from [so-and-so], who seeks your intercession with Your Lord; so intercede on his behalf and on behalf of all Muslims.

He then stands directed toward his face ﷺ, with his back toward the *qibla*,[713] and sends as many blessings upon him ﷺ as he wishes. He then moves a half-meter [to the right] until he is parallel with the head of our master, Abū Bakr (al-Ṣiddīq) رضي الله عنه, and says:

اَلسَّلَامُ عَلَيْكَ يَا خَلِيْفَةَ رَسُوْلِ اللهِ، اَلسَّلَامُ عَلَيْكَ يَا صَاحِبَ رَسُوْلِ اللهِ فِي الْغَارِ، اَلسَّلَامُ عَلَيْكَ يَا رَفِيْقَهٗ فِي الْأَسْفَارِ، اَلسَّلَامُ عَلَيْكَ يَا أَمِيْنَهٗ عَلَى الْأَسْرَارِ. جَزَاكَ اللهُ عَنَّا أَفْضَلَ مَا جَازٰى إِمَامًا عَنْ أُمَّةِ نَبِيِّهٖ. وَلَقَدْ خَلَّفْتَهٗ بِأَحْسَنِ خَلَفٍ، وَّسَلَكْتَ طَرِيْقَهٗ وَمِنْهَاجَهٗ أَحْسَنَ مَسْلَكٍ، وَّقَاتَلْتَ أَهْلَ الرِّدَّةِ وَالْبِدَعِ، وَمَهَّدْتَ الْإِسْلَامَ، وَوَصَلْتَ الْأَرْحَامَ، وَلَمْ

713 See previous note—he should have already been facing the Prophet ﷺ, with his back toward the *qibla*.

تَزَلْ قَائِلًا الْحَقَّ، نَاصِرًا لِأَهْلِهِ، حَتَّى أَتَاكَ الْيَقِيْنُ. فَالسَّلَامُ عَلَيْكَ وَرَحْمَةُ اللهِ وَبَرَكَاتُهُ.
اَللّٰهُمَّ أَمِتْنَا عَلَى حُبِّهِ، وَلَا تُخَيِّبْ سَعْيَنَا فِيْ زِيَارَتِهِ، بِرَحْمَتِكَ يَا كَرِيْمُ.

As-salāmu ʿalayka yā khalīfata rasūli 'Llāh(i), as-salāmu ʿalayka yā ṣāḥiba rasūli 'Llāhi fi 'l-ghār(i), as-salāmu ʿalayka yā rafīqahū fi 'l-asfār(i), as-salāmu ʿalayka yā amīnahū ʿala 'l-asrār(i). Jazāka 'Llāhu ʿannā afḍala mā jāzā imāman ʿan ummati nabiyyih(ī). Wa laqad khallaftahū bi aḥsani khalaf(in), wa salakta ṭarīqahū wa minhājahū aḥsana maslak(in), wa qātalta ahla 'r-riddati wa 'l-bidaʿ(i), wa mahhadta 'l-islām(a), wa waṣalta 'l-arḥām(a), wa lam tazal qā'ilani 'l-ḥaqq(a), nāṣiral li ahlih(ī), ḥattā atāka 'l-yaqīn(u). Fa 's-salāmu ʿalayka wa raḥmatu 'Llāhi wa barakātuh(ū). Allāhumma amitnā ʿalā ḥubbih(ī), wa lā tukhayyib saʿyanā fī ziyāratih(ī), bi raḥmatika yā Karīm(u).

Peace be upon you, O caliph of the Messenger of Allāh. Peace be upon you, O companion of the Messenger of Allāh in the cave. Peace be upon you, O friend of his on journeys. Peace be upon you, O one entrusted by him with secrets. May Allāh reward you, on our behalf, the best recompense He has given to a leader of the nation of his prophet! You have indeed succeeded him in the best manner, and have trodden his path and way in the most excellent approach. You fought the people of apostasy and reprehensible innovation; established the cradle of Islam; maintained kinship ties; and remained speaking the truth and giving victory to its people until death came to you. So peace be upon you, and Allāh's mercy and blessings. O Allāh, let us die on his love, and do not let our efforts in visiting him go to waste; by Your mercy, O Generous One.

He then moves over until he is parallel to the grave of our master ʿUmar ﵁, and says:

اَلسَّلَامُ عَلَيْكَ يَا أَمِيْرَ الْمُؤْمِنِيْنَ، اَلسَّلَامُ عَلَيْكَ يَا مُظْهِرَ الْإِسْلَامِ، اَلسَّلَامُ عَلَيْكَ يَا مُكَسِّرَ الْأَصْنَامِ. جَزَاكَ اللهُ عَنَّا أَفْضَلَ الْجَزَاءِ، وَرَضِيَ عَمَّنِ اسْتَخْلَفَكَ. فَلَقَدْ نَصَرْتَ الْإِسْلَامَ وَالْمُسْلِمِيْنَ حَيًّا وَّمَيِّتًا، فَكَفَلْتَ الْأَيْتَامَ، وَوَصَلْتَ الْأَرْحَامَ، وَقَوِيَ بِكَ الْإِسْلَامُ، وَكُنْتَ لِلْمُسْلِمِيْنَ إِمَامًا مَّرْضِيًّا، وَّهَادِيًا مَّهْدِيًّا. جَمَعْتَ شَمْلَهُمْ، وَأَغْنَيْتَ فَقِيْرَهُمْ، وَجَبَرْتَ كَسْرَهُمْ، فَالسَّلَامُ عَلَيْكَ وَرَحْمَةُ اللهِ وَبَرَكَاتُهُ.

As-salāmu ʿalayka yā amīra 'l-mu'minīn(a), as-salāmu ʿalayka yā muẓhira 'l-islām(i), as-salāmu ʿalayka yā mukassira 'l-aṣnām(i). Jazāka 'Llāhu ʿannā afḍala 'l-jazā'(i), wa raḍiya ʿammani 'stakhlafak(a). Fa laqad naṣarta 'l-islāma wa 'l-muslimīna ḥayyaw wa mayyitan, fa kafalta 'l-aytām(a), wa waṣalta 'l-arḥam(a), wa qawiya bika 'l-islām(u), wa kunta li 'l-muslimīna imāmam marḍiyyaw, wa hādiyam mahdiyyan. Jamaʿta shamlahum, wa aghnayta faqīrahum, wa jabarta kasrahum, fa 's-salāmu ʿalayka wa raḥmatu 'Llāhi wa barakātuh(ū).

Peace be upon you, O leader of the believers. Peace be upon you, O one who gave victory to Islam. Peace be upon you, O breaker of idols. May Allāh reward you, on our behalf, with the best recompense; and may He be pleased with your successor. For indeed you gave victory to Islam and the Muslims, in life and after death; for you took care of orphans, maintained kinship ties, and Islam was strengthened by you. You were, for the Muslims, a well-pleasing imām, a guide, and one who was guided. You joined their ranks in unity; enriched their indigent; and fixed their broken elements. So peace be upon you, and Allāh's mercy and blessings.

He then *returns* a quarter-meter and says:

اَلسَّلَامُ عَلَيْكُمَا يَا ضَجِيْعَيْ رَسُوْلِ اللهِ، وَرَفِيْقَيْهِ، وَوَزِيْرَيْهِ، وَمُشِيْرَيْهِ، وَالْمُعَاوِنَيْنِ لَهُ عَلَى الْقِيَامِ فِي الدِّيْنِ، وَالْقَائِمَيْنِ بَعْدَهُ بِمَصَالِحِ الْمُسْلِمِيْنَ. جَزَاكُمَا اللهُ أَحْسَنَ جَزَاءٍ. جِئْنَاكُمَا نَتَوَسَّلُ بِكُمَا إِلَى رَسُوْلِ اللهِ لِيَشْفَعَ لَنَا، وَيَسْأَلَ رَبَّنَا أَن يَّقْبَلَ سَعْيَنَا، وَيُحْيِيَنَا عَلَى مِلَّتِهِ، وَيُمِيْتَنَا عَلَيْهَا، وَيَحْشُرَنَا فِيْ زُمْرَتِهِ.

As-salāmu ʿalaykumā yā ḍajīʿay rasūli 'Llāh(i), wa rafīqayh(i), wa wazīrayh(i), wa mushīrayh(i), wa 'l-muʿāwinayni lahū ʿala 'l-qiyāmi fi 'd-dīn(i), wa 'l-qā'imayni baʿdahū bi maṣāliḥi 'l-muslimīn(a). Jazākuma 'Llāhu aḥsana jazā'in. Ji'nākumā natawassalu bikumā ilā rasūli 'Llāhi li yashfaʿa lanā, wa yas'ala Rabbanā ay yaqbala saʿyanā, wa yuḥyiyanā ʿalā millatih(ī), wa yumītanā ʿalayhā, wa yaḥshuranā fī zumratih(ī).

Peace be upon you both, O two who lie next to the Messenger of Allāh; his two friends; his two ministers; his two consultants; the two who helped him in establishing the religion; who after him took care of the affairs of the Muslims. May Allāh reward you both the best recompense. We have come to you both, seeking mediation by you both to the Messenger of Allāh, so that he may intercede on our behalf, and ask his Lord to accept our efforts; to resurrect us on his way; to cause us to die upon it; and to gather us in his company.

He then prays for himself, his parents, anyone who requested prayers from him, and all Muslims. He then stands facing his head ﷺ like the beginning, and says:

اَللّٰهُمَّ إِنَّكَ قُلْتَ وَقَوْلُكَ الْحَقُّ ﴿وَلَوْ أَنَّهُمْ إِذْ ظَلَمُوْا أَنْفُسَهُمْ جَاءُوْكَ فَاسْتَغْفَرُوا اللهَ وَاسْتَغْفَرَ لَهُمُ الرَّسُوْلُ لَوَجَدُوا اللهَ تَوَّابًا رَّحِيمًا﴾. وَقَدْ جِئْنَاكَ سَامِعِيْنَ قَوْلَكَ، طَائِعِيْنَ

أَمْرَكَ، مُسْتَشْفِعِيْنَ بِنَبِيِّكَ إِلَيْكَ. رَبَّنَا اغْفِرْ لَنَا وَلِآبَائِنَا وَلِأُمَّهَاتِنَا وَلِإِخْوَانِنَا الَّذِيْنَ سَبَقُوْنَا بِالْإِيْمَانِ. ﴿رَبَّنَا آتِنَا فِي الدُّنْيَا حَسَنَةً وَّفِي الْآخِرَةِ حَسَنَةً وَّقِنَا عَذَابَ النَّارِ﴾. ﴿سُبْحَانَ رَبِّكَ رَبِّ الْعِزَّةِ عَمَّا يَصِفُوْنَ ۞ وَسَلَامٌ عَلَى الْمُرْسَلِيْنَ ۞ وَالْحَمْدُ للهِ رَبِّ الْعَالَمِيْنَ﴾.

Allāhumma innaka qulta wa qawluka 'l-ḥaqq[u] "Wa law annahum iẓ ẓalamū anfusahum jā'ūka fa 'staghfaru 'Llāha wa 'staghfara lahumu 'r-rasūlu lawajadu 'Llāha Tawwābar Raḥīman." Wa qad ji'nāka sāmiᶜīna qawlak(a), ṭā'iᶜīna amrak(a), mustashfiᶜīna bi nabiyyika ilayk(a). Rabbanā 'ghfir lanā wa li ābā'inā wa ummahātinā wa li ikhwānina 'lladhīna sabaqūnā bi 'l-īmān(i). "Rabbanā ātinā fi 'd-dunyā ḥasanataw wa fi 'l-ākhirati ḥasanataw, wa qinā ᶜadhāba 'n-nār(i)." "Subḥāna Rabbika Rabbi 'l-ᶜizzati ᶜammā yaṣifūn(a), wa salāmun ᶜala 'l-mursalīn(a), wa 'l-ḥamdu li 'Llāhi Rabbi 'l-ᶜālamīn(a)."

O Allāh! Verily You have said, and Your statement is truth, "And if only, after having oppressed themselves, they had come to you and sought Allāh's forgiveness, and you had sought forgiveness of their behalf, they would certainly have found Allāh to be Ever-Returning, All-Merciful." And we have come to You, hearing Your speech; obeying Your commands; and seeking the intercession of Your Prophet to You. Our Lord, forgive us, our fathers, our mothers, and our brethren who preceded us in faith. "Our Lord, grant us good in this life, and good in the next life; and protect us from the punishment of the Fire." "Glory be to your Lord, the Lord of Honor, above that which they describe. May His peace be upon the messengers. And all praise is due to Allāh, the Lord of all the worlds."

He adds to or subtracts from that as he wishes, and asks for whatever comes to him, for whatever Allāh enables him to, if Allāh Most High wills.

He then goes to the column of Abū Lubāba ﷺ, to which he tied himself until Allāh forgave him in repentance; it is between the grave and the pulpit. He performs two *rakᶜas* there, repents to Allāh Most High, and asks for whatever he wishes.

He then goes to the meadow (*rawḍa*), which is like a square pool . . . he prays as much as he is able to, supplicates, makes abundant glorification (*tasbīḥ*) and praise (*thanā'*), and seeks much forgiveness.

He then goes to the pulpit (*minbar*) and places his hand on the pommel[714] upon which the Prophet ﷺ used to place his hand when delivering the sermon, such that the blessing (*baraka*) of the Messenger ﷺ may reach him. He prays there, asks Allāh for whatever he wishes, and seeks refuge in His mercy from His displeasure and anger.

He then goes to the column that ached, which is the remnant of the palm

714 Unfortunately, this blessed part of the pulpit, among other parts, is no longer there today.

trunk that longed for the Prophet ﷺ when he left it to deliver the sermon from the pulpit, so the Prophet ﷺ descended and embraced it, and it became still and fell silent.

He should strive to stay awake at night during his stay, reciting Qur'ān, making remembrance of Allāh Most High, praying at the pulpit and the grave and between the two, silently and out loud.

After the visitation, it is recommended (*mustaḥabb*) for him to go out to the graveyard (*baqīʿ*), and visit the graves of the martyrs and other notable figures, especially the grave of the master of all martyrs, Ḥamza ﵁. In the graveyard, he should visit the dome[715] of ʿAbbās ﵁; with him therein also lies al-Ḥasan ibn ʿAlī, Zayn al-ʿĀbidīn, his son Muḥammad al-Bāqir, his son Jaʿfar al-Ṣādiq, the commander of the faithful ʿUthmān, Ibrāhīm the son of the Prophet ﷺ, a group of the Prophet's wives ﷺ, his paternal aunt Ṣafiyya, and many other Companions and Followers.

He should pray in the mosque of Fāṭima in the graveyard.

It is recommended (*mustaḥabb*) for him to visit the martyrs at Uḥud on Thursday, and say:

سَلَامٌ عَلَيْكُمْ بِمَا صَبَرْتُمْ فَنِعْمَ عُقْبَى الدَّارِ. سَلَامٌ عَلَيْكُمْ دَارَ قَوْمٍ مُّؤْمِنِيْنَ، وَإِنَّا إِنْ شَاءَ اللهُ بِكُمْ لَاحِقُوْنَ.

Salāmun ʿalaykum bimā ṣabartum fa niʿma ʿuqba 'd-dār(i). Salāmun ʿalaykum dāra qawmim mu'minīn(a), wa innā in shā'a 'Llāhu bikum lāḥiqūn(a).

Peace be upon you all for your patience; what a great final abode! Peace be upon you all, O abode of believing people; and we shall, if Allāh wills, meet with you all.

He should also recite Āyat al-Kursī and Sūrat al-Ikhlāṣ.

It is recommended (*mustaḥabb*) for him to visit Masjid Qubā' on Saturday, as is narrated from him ﷺ, and supplicate as follows:

يَا صَرِيْخَ الْمُسْتَصْرِخِيْنَ، يَا غِيَاثَ الْمُسْتَغِيْثِيْنَ، يَا مُفَرِّجَ كَرْبِ الْمَكْرُوْبِيْنَ، يَا مُجِيْبَ دَعْوَةِ الْمُضْطَرِّيْنَ. صَلِّ عَلٰى سَيِّدِنَا مُحَمَّدٍ وَّآلِهِ، وَاكْشِفْ كَرْبِيْ وَحُزْنِيْ كَمَا كَشَفْتَ عَنْ رَّسُوْلِكَ حُزْنَهُ وَكَرْبَهُ فِيْ هٰذَا الْمَقَامِ. يَا حَنَّانُ يَا مَنَّانُ، يَا كَثِيْرَ الْمَعْرُوْفِ، يَا دَائِمَ الْإِحْسَانِ، يَا أَرْحَمَ الرَّاحِمِيْنَ.

---

715 All markers of the graves in this cemetery, including this dome, are unfortunately no longer there today.

Yā Ṣarīkha 'l-mustaṣrikhīn(a), yā Ghiyātha 'l-mustaghīthīn(a), yā Mufarrija karbi 'l-makrūbīn(a), yā Mujība daʿwati 'l-muḍṭarrīn(a). Ṣalli ʿalā Sayyidinā Muḥammadiw wa ālih(ī), wa 'kshif karbī wa ḥuznī kamā kashafta ʿar rasūlika ḥuznahū wa karbahū fī hādha 'l-maqām(i). Yā Ḥannānu yā Mannān(u), yā Kathīra 'l-maʿrūf(i), yā Dā'ima 'l-iḥsān(i), yā Arḥama 'r-rāḥimīn(a).

O One who is called by those who cry out! O [Bestower of] Succor for those who seek help! O Reliever of the distress of those in difficulties! O One who responds to the call of those in utter need! Send blessings upon our Master Muḥammad and his family, and relieve my distress and grief, just as You gave relief to Your Messenger from his distress and grief in this place. O Compassionate, O Benefactor, O Plentiful in bounty, O Constant in excellence, O Most Merciful of those who show mercy.

Bibliography

ᶜĀbidīn, ᶜAlā' al-Dīn. *Al-Hadiyya al-ᶜAlā'iyya.* Ed. Muḥammad Saᶜīd al-Burhānī. Sixth Edition. Damascus: Maktabat al-Imām al-Awzāᶜī, 1426/2005.

Abū 'l-Ḥājj, Ṣalāḥ. *Al-Jāmiᶜ fī Aḥkām al-Ṣiyām wa 'l-Iᶜtikāf wa 'l-Ḥajj wa 'l-ᶜUmra.* First Edition. Amman: Dār al-Jinān, 1426/2006.

al-Bājūrī, Ibrāhīm ibn Muḥammad ibn Aḥmad, and Ibrāhīm ibn Ḥasan al-Laqqānī. *Tuḥfat al-Murīd ᶜalā Jawharat al-Tawḥīd* [Bājūrī's commentary on Laqqānī's poem]. Ed. ᶜAbd al-Salām ibn ᶜAbd al-Hādī Shannār. First Edition. Damascus: Maktaba Dār al-Bayrūtī, 1423/2002.

Barōtī, Meherbān ᶜAlī, *Imdād al-Awzān.* Harsoli: Kutub Khāna Ḥayāt al-Islām, 1410/1989,

al-Birgivi, Muḥammad Bīr ᶜAlī. *Dhukhr al-Muta'ahhilīn wa 'l-Nisā' fī Taᶜrīf al-Aṭhār wa 'l-Dimā' wa Sharḥuhu.* Ed. Hidaya Hartford and Ashraf Muneeb. First Edition. Damascus: Dār al-Fikr, 1426/2005.

al-Bukhārī, Muḥammad ibn Ismāᶜīl. *Al-Jāmiᶜ al-Musnad al-Ṣaḥīḥ al-Mukhtaṣar min Umūri Rasūlillāh wa Sunanihī wa Ayyāmihī.* Istanbul: Al-Maktaba al-Islāmī, 1399/1979.

Effendī, Abū 'l-Suᶜūd. *Irshād al-ᶜAql al-Salīm ilā Mazāyā 'l-Kitāb al-Karīm* [Tafsīr Abī 'l-Suᶜūd]. 9 vols. Reprint. Beirut: Dār Iḥyā' al-Turāth al-ᶜArabī, 1414/1994.

al-Ghaznawī, Sirāj al-Dīn ᶜUmar ibn Isḥāq. *Sharḥ al-ᶜAqīda al-Ṭaḥāwiyya* [Ghaznawī's commentary on Ṭaḥāwī's *ᶜAqīda*]. Ed. ᶜAbd al-Salām ibn ᶜAbd al-Hādī Shannār. First Edition. Damascus: Maktaba Dār al-Bayrūtī, 1430/2009. [This work was incorrectly ascribed to Bābartī by the publisher.]

al-Ḥalabī, Ibrāhīm ibn Muḥammad ibn Ibrāhīm. *Ghunyat al-Mustamlī Sharḥ Munyat al-Muṣallī* (*Ḥalabī Kabīr*) [Ḥalabī's larger commentary on Kāshgharī's *Munyat al-Muṣallī wa Ghunyat al-Mubtadī*]. Istanbul, n.d. Photocopy.

Ibn ᶜĀbidīn, Muḥammad Amīn ibn ᶜUmar al-Shāmī, Muḥammad ibn ᶜAlī ᶜAlā' al-Dīn al-Ḥaṣkafī, and Muḥammad ibn ᶜAbdillāh al-Tumurtāshī. *Ḥāshiya Radd al-Muḥtār ᶜalā 'l-Durr al-Mukhtār Sharḥ Tanwīr al-Abṣār* [Ibn ᶜĀbidīn's marginal gloss on Ḥaṣkafī's *Al-Durr al-Mukhtār*, an interlineal exegesis of Tumurtāshī's

Tanwīr al-Abṣār]. Bulāq print. 7 vols. 1272/1855. Reprint. Beirut: Dār Iḥyā' al-Turāth al-ʿArabī, n.d.

Ibn al-Humām, Kamāl al-Dīn Muḥammad ibn ʿAbd al-Wāḥid al-Sīwāsī, and Burhān al-Dīn ʿAlī ibn Abī Bakr al-Marghinānī. *Fatḥ al-Qadīr li 'l-ʿĀjiz al-Faqīr Sharḥ al-Hidāya* [Ibn al-Humām's commentary on Marghinānī's *Hidāya*]. 9 vols. 1319/1901. Reprint. Beirut: Dār Iḥyā' al-Turāth al-ʿArabī, n.d.

Ibn Nujaym, Zayn al-Dīn ibn Ibrāhīm ibn Muḥammad, and Abū 'l-Barakāt Ḥāfiẓ al-Dīn ʿAbdullāh ibn Aḥmad al-Nasafī. *Al-Baḥr al-Rā'iq fī Sharḥ Kanz al-Daqā'iq* [Ibn Nujaym's commentary on Nasafī's *Kanz al-Daqā'iq*]. 9 vols. First Edition. Beirut: Dār al-Kutub al-ʿIlmiyya, 1417/1997.

ʿItr, Nūr al-Dīn. *Al-Ḥajj wa 'l-ʿUmra fī 'l-Fiqh al-Islāmī*. Damascus: 1416/1995.

al-Kāsānī, ʿAlā' al-Dīn Abū Bakr ibn Masʿūd. *Badā'iʿ al-Ṣanā'iʿ fī Tartīb al-Sharā'iʿ* [Kāsānī's commentary on ʿAlā' al-Dīn al-Samarqandī's *Tuḥfat al-Fuqahā'*]. Ed. Muḥammad ʿAdnān ibn Yāsīn Darwīsh. 6 vols. Beirut: Dār Iḥyā' al-Turāth al-ʿArabī, 1421/2000.

Khusro, Mullā. *Durar al-Ḥukkām fī Sharḥ Ghurar al-Aḥkām* [Mullā Khusro's interlineal exegesis on his *Ghurar al-Aḥkām*, with Shurunbulālī's marginal gloss *Al-Shurunbulāliyya*]. 2 vols. Istanbul: Fazīlet Nesriyat ve Ticaret, n.d.

al-Lakhnawī, Muḥammad ʿAbd al-Ḥayy. *Al-Fawā'id al-Bahiyya fī Tarājim al-Ḥanafiyya* and *Ṭarab al-Amāthil bi Tarājim al-Afāḍil*. First Edition. Beirut: Dār al-Arqam ibn Abī 'l-Arqam, 1418/1998.

Lane, Edward William. *An Arabic-English Lexicon*. Beirut: Librairie Du Liban, 1968.

al-Maḥbūbī, ʿUbayd Allāh ibn Masʿūd Ṣadr al-Sharīʿa al-Aṣghar. *Sharḥ al-Wiqāya* [Maḥbūbī's commentary on Tāj al-Sharīʿa's *Wiqāya*]. Ed. Dr. Ṣalāḥ Abū 'l-Ḥājj. 2 vols. Amman: Mu'assasat al-Warrāq, 1427/2006.

al-Marghinānī, Burhān al-Dīn ʿAlī ibn Abī Bakr. *Al-Hidāya Sharḥ Bidāyat al-Mubtadī* [Marghinānī's commentary on his *Bidāyat al-Mubtadī*]. 2 vols. Beirut: Dār Iḥyā' al-Turāth al-ʿArabī, n.d.

al-Mawṣilī, ʿAbdullāh ibn Maḥmūd ibn Mawdūd. *Al-Ikhtiyār li Taʿlīl al-Mukhtār* [Mawṣilī's commentary on his *Mukhtār*]. Ed. Bashshār Bakrī ʿArrābī. 2 vols. Damascus: al-Maktaba al-ʿUmariyya, 1425/2004.

al-Maydānī, ʿAbd al-Ghanī al-Ghunaymī. *Al-Lubāb fī Sharḥ al-Kitāb* [Maydānī's interlineal exegesis on Qudūrī's *Mukhtaṣar*]. Ed. Bashshār Bakrī ʿArrābī. Damascus: Dār Qubā', 1423/2003.

———. *Sharḥ al-ʿAqīda al-Ṭaḥāwiyya al-Musammā bi Bayān al-Sunna wa 'l-Jamāʿa* [Maydānī's interlineal exegesis on Ṭaḥāwī's *ʿAqīda*]. Ed. Muḥammad Muṭīʿ al-Ḥāfiẓ and Muḥammad Riyāḍ al-Māliḥ. Fourth Edition. Damascus: Dār al-Fikr and Beirut: Dār al-Fikr al-Muʿāṣir, 1428/2007.

al-Qārī, Mullā ʿAlī ibn Sulṭān Muḥammad. *Fatḥ Bāb al-ʿInāya* [Qārī's commentary on Maḥbūbī's *Nuqāya*]. 4 vols. Beirut: Dār Iḥyā' al-Turāth al-ʿArabī, 1426/2005.

———. *Minaḥ al-Rawḍ al-Azhar* [Qārī's commentary on Abū Ḥanīfa's *Al-Fiqh al-Akbar*]. Ed. Wahbī Sulaymān Ghāwjī al-Albānī. Beirut: Dār al-Bashā'ir al-Islāmiyya. First Edition, 1419/1998.

———. *Mirqāt al-Mafātīḥ* [Qārī's commentary on Tabrīzī's *Mishkāt al-Maṣābīḥ*]. 12 vols. Beirut: Dār al-Kutub al-ᶜIlmiyya. First Edition, 1422/2001.

al-Rāzī, Zayn al-Dīn Muḥammad ibn Bakr ibn ᶜAbd al-Muḥsin. *Tuḥfat al-Mulūk* [Rāzī's primer with marginalia by the editor Dr. Ṣalāh Abū 'l-Ḥājj named *Nafaḥāt al-Sulūk ᶜalā Tuḥfat al-Mulūk*]. First Edition. Amman: Dār al-Fārūq, 1427/2006.

al-Shurunbulālī, Ḥasan ibn ᶜAmmār ibn ᶜAlī. *Imdād al-Fattāḥ Sharḥ Nūr al-Īḍāḥ wa Najāt al-Arwāḥ* [Shurunbulālī's larger commentary on his *Nūr al-Īḍāḥ*]. Ed. Bashshār Bakrī ᶜArrābī. 1 vol. Damascus: 1423/2002.

———. *Marāqī 'l-Falāḥ Sharḥ Nūr al-Īḍāḥ wa Najāt al-Arwāḥ* [Shurunbulālī's summarized commentary on his *Nūr al-Īḍāḥ*, with Aḥmad al-Ṭaḥṭāwī's marginalia *Ḥāshiyat al-Ṭaḥṭāwī* at the bottom of the page]. Ed. ᶜAbd al-Karīm al-ᶜAṭā. 2 vols. Damascus: Maktabat al-ᶜIlm al-Ḥadīth, 1422/2001.

———. *Marāqī 'l-Saᶜādāt*. Ed. Muḥammad Riyāḍ al-Māliḥ. First Edition. Beirut: Dār al-Kutub al-Lubnānī, 1393/1973. [This edition was used as the primary text for the translation of this work.]

Usmani, Muḥammad Rafīᶜ. *Al-Maqālāt al-Fiqhiyya*. Karachi: Maktaba Dār al-ᶜUlūm Karachi, 1426/2005.

al-Yaḥṣubī, al-Qāḍī ᶜIyāḍ ibn Mūsā ibn ᶜIyāḍ, and Muslim ibn al-Ḥajjāj al-Naysābūrī. *Ikmāl al-Muᶜlim bi Fawā'id Muslim* [Qāḍī ᶜIyāḍ's commentary on *Ṣaḥīḥ Muslim*]. 9 vols. Second Edition. Mansura: Dār al-Wafā', 1425/2004.

al-Zaylaᶜī, ᶜUthmān ibn ᶜAlī, and Abū 'l-Barakāt Ḥāfiẓ al-Dīn ᶜAbdullāh ibn Aḥmad al-Nasafī. *Tabyīn al-Ḥaqā'iq Sharḥ Kanz al-Daqā'iq* [Zaylaᶜī's commentary on Nasafī's *Kanz al-Daqā'iq*, along with Shalabī's marginal gloss]. 6 vols. Cairo: Dār al-Kitāb al-Islāmī, 1313/1895.

Zāda, ᶜAbd al-Raḥmān ibn al-Shaykh Muḥammad ibn Sulaymān, and Ibrāhīm ibn Muḥammad ibn Ibrāhīm al- Ḥalabī. *Majmaᶜ al-Anhur fī Sharḥ Multaqā 'l-Abḥur* [Zāda's interlineal exegesis on Ḥalabī's *Multaqā 'l-Abḥur*, along with Muḥammad ibn ᶜAlī ᶜAlā' al-Dīn Ḥaṣkafī's interlineal exegesis *Al-Durr al-Muntaqā fī Sharḥ al-Multaqā* on the same primer in the margin]. 2 vols. Istanbul: Dār al-Ṭibāᶜa al-ᶜĀmira, 1316/1898. Reprint. Beirut: Dār Iḥyā' al-Turāth al-ᶜArabī, n.d.s.

About the Translator

Faraz Ahmed Khan has lived in Amman, Jordan, for several years studying and teaching traditional Islamic sciences, with a focus on Ḥanafī jurisprudence, ḥadīth studies, theology, logic, and Arabic grammar. His teachers include Shaykh Aḥmad al-Jammāl, Dr. Ashraf Muneeb, Dr. Salāḥ Abū 'l-Ḥājj, Shaykh Faraz Rabbani, Shaykh Ḥamza al-Bakrī, and Shaykh Naeem Abdul Wali. They have given him permission and encouragement to teach what he has studied. The texts he covered include: *Marāqī 'l-Falāḥ*, *Al-Lubāb fī Sharḥ al-Kitāb*, *Al-Mukhtār*, *Sharḥ al-Ṣāwī ʿalā Jawharat al-Tawḥīd*, *Bad' al-Amālī*, *Al-Fiqh al-Akbar*, *Al-Bidāya fī Uṣūl al-Dīn*, *Imām Taftāzānī's Sharḥ al-ʿAqā'id*, *Al-Sullam fī 'l-Manṭiq*, *Nuzhat al-Naẓar Sharḥ Nukhbat al-Fikar*, and others. He is a teacher at the Qasid Institute, and is Associate Scholar of the Risala Foundation in Houston, Texas. He currently resides in Amman where he is pursuing advanced Islamic studies.

Also from
White Thread Press

Prayers for Forgiveness

The Path to Perfection

Provisions for the Seekers

Sufism & Good Character

The Differences of the Imāms

Saviours of Islamic Spirit

Ghazālī's The Beginning of Guidance

Reflections of Pearls (Printed Edition)

Fiqh al-Imam: Key Proofs in Hanafi Fiqh

The Islamic Laws of Animal Slaughter

Birth Control and Abortion in Islam

Absolute Essentials of Islam

Ṣalāt & Salām: A Manual of Blessings on Allāh's Beloved

Imām Abū Ḥanīfa's Al-Fiqh al-Akbar Explained

Reflections of Pearls (Audio Book)

Saviours of Islamic Spirit (Audio)

White Thread
PRESS

www.whitethreadpress.com